Also by Judy Kessler
Inside Today: The Battle for the Morning

INSIDE People

THE STORIES BEHIND THE STORIES

Judy Kessler

VILLARD BOOKS

NEW YORK

1994

All rights reserved under International and Pan-American Copyright Conventions. Published in the United States by Villard Books, a division of Random House, Inc., New York, and simultaneously in Canada by Random House of Canada Limited, Toronto.

Villard Books is a registered trademark of Random House, Inc.

Grateful acknowledgment is made to the following for permission to reprint previously published material:

Esquire: Excerpts from a spoof of *People* magazine, from the December 16, 1974, issue. Reprinted courtesy of *Esquire* magazine and The Hearst Corporation.

Library of Congress Cataloging-in-Publication Data

Kessler, Judy.
    Inside people / Judy Kessler.
        p.   cm.
    ISBN 0-679-42186-6
    1. *People* magazine (New York, N.Y.)   I. Title.
PN4900.P46K47   1994
051—dc20   93-47468

Manufactured in the United States of America
9 8 7 6 5 4 3 2
First Edition

For Char & Ackie

AUTHOR'S NOTE

This book deals with outstanding moments, and outstanding people, in the history of one of the world's most influential and widely read magazines. It would be impossible in such a short space to capture everyone who has worked so hard to make *People* magazine what it is. The reader must realize that for every person mentioned in the following pages, there are dozens who have made important contributions—many of whom have been there since the earliest days of the magazine, among them: Christopher P. Anderson, Dick Durrell, Gail Jennes, Ross Drake, Nancy Faber, Holly Holden, Ralph Novak, Otto Fuerbringer, John Loengard, Cheryl McCall, Dick Friedman, Paula Glatzer, Nancy Houghtaling, Martha Smilgis, Bing Bernard, Bob Windeler, Jim Watters, Roger Wolmuth, Sarah Moore-Hall, Nancy Williamson, Cheryl McCall, Bob Ginna, Campbell Geeslin, Elton Robinson, and Linda Witt. And then there are those whose influence has been felt more recently, including Michelle Green, John Saar, and Susan Toepfer. Regardless of their visibility in these pages, *People* magazine would never have become the success it is without each and every one of them.

ACKNOWLEDGMENTS

With special thanks to my friends and colleagues at *People*, without whom this book could not have been written: among them Sam Angeloff, Ron Arias, Lois Armstrong, Susan Baldwin, Harry Benson, Dick Burgheim, Patricia Burstein, Garry Clifford, Brad Darrach, Kent Demaret, John Dominis, Ross Drake, Mary Dunn, Cutler Durkee, Bill Ewald, Beth Filler, Dick Friedman, Maureen Fulton, Jim Gaines, Todd Gold, Karin Grant, Sarah Moore-Hall, Holly Holden, Karen Jacovich, Harry Johnston, Lanny Jones, Steve Kagan, Toby Kahn, Jack Kelley, Beth Knesiak, Jeremy Koch, Louise Lague, Christopher Little, M. C. Marden, Nancy Matsumoto, Kristin McMurran, Robin Micheli, Maddy Miller, Jack Mitchell, Mercedes Mitchell, Ann S. Moore, Ann Morrell, Rachelle Naishtut, Irene Neves, Florence Nishida, Ralph Novak, Jane Podesta, Neal Preston, Sally Proudfit, Susan Reed, Jean Reynolds, Ellen Rubin, Pat Ryan, Marilyn Sahner, Mark Sennet, Jim Seymore, Bill Shaw, David Sheff, Vicki Sheff, Martha Smilgis, Terry Smith, Dick Stolley, Patty Strauss, Stan Tretick, Mary Vespa, Randy Vest, Carol Wallace, Joyce Wansley, Gail Cameron Wescott, Maria Wilhelm, Barbara Wilkins, Nancy Williamson, Hal Wingo, Dale Wittner, and Taro Yamasaki. With thanks, too, to *People* subjects Donna Rice and Carol Ann Demaret.

With deep appreciation to my agent, Esther Newberg, who for good reason is known as the best; to Amanda Beesley, who is a close second; to my editor and publisher, Diane Reverand, who has seen me through two separate incarnations now; to Jane Centofante, who is a superb researcher and more; to Katy Nishida, who almost literally broke her back for me; to the indispensable Maureen McMahon and Melanie Cecka at Villard; to my amazing production editor, Benjamin Dreyer; to Art and Josie Vella of the great Celestino's, who fed me by night, and Judy Samuels and my friends at Savories, who fed me by day; and to my sister Wendy Lesch, who arrived just in time to push me over the finish line.

Most of all, with everlasting love and gratitude beyond words to my parents, Charlette and Harry Kessler, to my aunt, Nina Kessler, and to my sister Leida Sanders, who have held me up and seen me through the best of times, and the worst of times. And to the memory of my husband, Harold Hayes, whose spirit never fades—ever.

CONTENTS

PROLOGUE
Holy Cow!

"Time didn't invent stories about people—the Bible did."

—*HARRY LUCE,*
founder and editor in chief,
Time *magazine*

TWENTY YEARS AGO, on February 25, 1974 (although the issue was dated March 4), while she was married to André Previn, after she had left Frank Sinatra, and before she had ever met Woody Allen, Mia Farrow appeared on the first cover in the history of *People* magazine.

On that same day—the day that more than one million copies of *People* first hit the newsstands—Diana Frances Spencer was a twelve-year-old student at a boarding school called West Heath in Kent, approximately 30 miles from Buckingham Palace, where she would one day reside as Princess Di.

Liz was about to split from Dick, but she would marry him again before *People* was two; John Travolta, a high school dropout, was set to appear in his first Broadway musical; Fergie was a fourteen-year-old tomboy at boarding school who hardly seemed a likely candidate for a royal marriage; and Jacqueline Kennedy had maintained a royal image for the last five years as "Jackie O."

Cher was still attached to Sonny—but only barely; and Farrah was not yet a Charlie's Angel, since the show had not been created yet. Princess Caroline had not even heard of her first husband, Philippe Junot, while fifteen-year-old Michael Jackson was a member of the Jackson Five and bore no resemblance to Diana Ross.

Madonna was two years older than Di, an A student at Adams High School in Rochester, Michigan—and Mylar had not yet been invented.

They did not know it at the time, but all of these people—with the exception of Mia Farrow—would have one thing in common after the next twenty years: They would have appeared on the cover of *People* more than any other people in the world.

In fact, the Mia Farrow cover was not the real beginning—it began with Elizabeth Taylor in the summer of 1973. The idea had already been floating around the Time & Life Building in midtown Manhattan for quite a while— the idea of a magazine based on personalities in the news, like an expanded version of the "People" section of *Time*. Nobody knew exactly whose it was, but everyone said it was theirs—or someone else's.

Some said it was Andrew Heiskell's idea. Heiskell was the chairman of the board of Time Inc. But others, including Mrs. Heiskell, said it came from her. Still others said Clare Boothe Luce, the wife of Harry Luce, the company's founder and editor in chief, claimed the idea was hers. Harry Luce himself once said, "*Time* didn't invent stories about people—the Bible did."

It was in the early spring of that year that Andrew Heiskell decided to do something about it, regardless of whose it was. He discussed the idea for *People* with Otto Fuerbringer, the head of magazine development for the company. They called it *People* partly because that was what the section of *Time* was called. The name seemed to have the right ring to it.

As it turned out, the timing was exactly right, too. The painful era of Vietnam was ending. The germinating "Me Decade" was about to begin. American life had been brimming with anger, and now much of that anger was dissipating. People were turning away from demonstrations, from masses of people, inward toward themselves. They were turning toward other individuals, as well.

Suddenly people were oddly willing to talk about themselves—their sex lives, their families, their religion. At the same time, they were more and more curious about other people and the details of *their* lives. It was a new wave that *People* would catch as it crested. This magazine would do something new. Topical issues would be strictly secondary. They would be dealt with, but only through personalities. Personality journalism was about to be born.

In August 1973, one year after the death of *Life*, a magazine that had become an American institution, the first test issue of *People* was ordered. A former *Life* editor, Phil Kunhardt, was put in charge. Richard B. Stolley, a lifelong journalist and another *Life* staffer, who in fact edited the final issue of *Life*, was working on another new project but was asked to work on the test issue when he could.

There were lessons to be learned from *Life*. Mourned by millions after its demise, the magazine had been a victim of skyrocketing postal rates. *People* would not make the same mistake. If Time Inc. decided to go ahead with it, there would be no subscriptions. Instead, *People* would be sold exclusively on newsstands.

The test issue, dated August 23, 1973, would be tried in eleven cities. It would provide a good indication of the public's response to the magazine.

SHE WAS THE perfect choice for the cover. Not only was Elizabeth Taylor one of the best-known faces in the world, but there was *news*. The Burtons were splitting. Or reconciling. Or splitting. It was hard to be sure.

The cover line read: "The Burton Split-Up." The inside pictures were dark and grainy: Liz and Dick were attempting a reconciliation poolside at Sophia Loren's villa in Rome. The photographs of Loren and her guests looked like they had been taken with telephoto lenses by ruthless paparazzi who must have had to climb trees around Sophia Loren's villa to get the murky shots. In fact they had.

The whole test issue exuded a sleazy, tabloid quality, with its rough photographs and its typewriter type and its police-gazette layouts. There was even a picture of the Chiquita Banana Girl, Barbara Carrera, with her breasts bared, totally topless, except for the shiny beads around her neck. Still, the magazine was crammed with news, if you could call it that—and many did—of *people:* Ali MacGraw and Steve McQueen; Bobby Riggs and Billie Jean King; Ethel Kennedy and "Bobby's" kids; Barbara Walters and Sally Quinn; Led Zeppelin, Joe Namath, Ari Onassis, Faye Dunaway, Jacqueline Susann, and more.

That was the idea. It worked.

THE RESULTS OF the test issue were phenomenal. In some cities the magazine was promoted on television, and in those it sold 85 percent, a dazzling figure for magazine sales. Research showed that half of those who read it had attended college; the estimated median age was thirty-four; and they came from families with incomes over ten thousand dollars. More than half of those who read it were women. The figures could not have been better.

But the test issue, Liz and all, was less than warmly received by its critics—not just *outside* of the Time & Life Building in New York. One high-ranking editor at *Time* wrote that it had "no richness of genius, but rather a poverty of ideas . . . edited to exploit the baseness of the market."

Nevertheless, the sales figures were golden, and Time Inc. was ready to move forward with *People*—the first launching of a national weekly since *Sports Illustrated* had been published twenty years earlier. One essential thing was missing, however: an editor who could make it work. While Phil Kunhardt had presided over the test issue, he had a history of heart trouble and had already suffered one heart attack. The start-up of a weekly magazine is a grueling proposition, often consisting of seven-day work weeks and twenty-four-hour days. It was quickly agreed that Richard B. Stolley would be the perfect choice for the job.

At forty-five, Dick Stolley, who some say resembles Richard Widmark, was an athletic, well-built, adventurous man of boundless energy and insatiable curiosity. In his twenty-seven-year career as a journalist, he had run *Life* magazine bureaus in Atlanta, Washington, Los Angeles, and Paris, before returning to New York to become an assistant managing editor of *Life.*

He had covered everything from the burgeoning civil rights movement in America to the assassination of JFK. He had traveled the world from Israel (where he was nearly killed in an Egyptian mortar attack) to Guam (where he was bitten by a Pacific shrew as he lay sleeping in his bed in an old navy barracks). After undergoing a series of painful rabies shots, he lived—and wrote to tell about it in *Life,* with graphic photographs detailing the dreadful procedure.

But never in *his* life had Dick Stolley done anything that would sap his extraordinary energy as much as his forthcoming editorial role at *People* magazine, in which he would remain for the next eight years.

When he was asked to be *People*'s editor, Dick Stolley had serious reservations about the new endeavor. He thought it was a bold experiment, daringly new and different, with a lot of flaws. The test issue, he later admitted, "looked like a whorehouse magazine." Still, with his uncanny magazine instincts, Stolley understood exactly what was wrong. What he did after that would have a profound effect on personality journalism as we know it today.

Stolley agreed to take the job as editor of *People* on the condition that he could redesign the magazine. Its great potential was obvious to him, but he knew there was a danger in the kind of material it would be dealing with—a new kind of intimate reporting that would be supplying information about celebrities that other magazines were not getting and probably would not publish even if they did.

"We were going to traffic in what back then would prove to be some pretty hair-raising facts," he says. "The reporting would be highly sensitive in terms of intimacy. We'd be asking people about their personal lives, their sex lives, their finances." Stolley knew that if *People* magazine were going to succeed, that is what it had to do, but he also knew something else: It had to be done in a classy way.

He knew that the magazine had to have a conventional look—very cautious, very straightforward. It had to let the material speak for itself, with a layout and design that did not emphasize the salaciousness of the material.

Stolley also knew that he had a lot of freedom. "This was a magazine unlike any other, so we were totally unbound by precedent," he explains. "We could, in effect, do anything we wanted to do."

With the underpinnings of the magazine firmly set in his mind, Stolley went to work on the second issue of *People*, to execute his vision. It was an issue that would never be sold on newsstands—only four thousand copies were printed—but would be shown instead to Madison Avenue and magazine wholesalers who would be crucial to its success, as the prototype for what was to come.

He chose Billie Jean King and her husband, Larry (not the one of CNN fame), for the cover, a choice perfectly consistent with his shrewdly perceived theories. With their shiny skin and their peachy-pink cheeks, Billie Jean and Larry King looked so clean on the cover they could have been advertising Ivory soap. But down in the corner, the cover line read:

BILLIE JEAN AND LARRY KING
"We'd be better off divorced
and living together"

Inside, the story offered "news" about their marriage: They saw each other only four weeks a year, and when they did, they stayed in separate suites—if not in separate hotels; Billie Jean saw more of her doubles partner Rosie Casals than she did of her marriage partner. Here, in the very clean and classy pages of *People*—a Time Inc. publication, no less—the Kings *themselves* were saying that they probably should never have gotten married! "We'd be better off divorced and living together . . . It's not an optimum marriage. We've made an accommodation."

Dick Stolley had been right. People were willing to talk about surprisingly intimate things. Those were the facts, pure and simple. *People* was reporting them in its own, newly inimitable way.

The new look was comfortable, conventional, reportorial, exactly the way he wanted it to be, with a lot of white space and very short text. (Stolley had the words counted to be precise. There were thirteen thousand of them, no more, no less—far fewer than in the text of other periodicals). It conveyed exactly what he wanted it to convey: a look that said quietly, "These are the facts, ma'am, and we're not making any judgments about them."

THE BILLIE JEAN King issue set not only the tone and the look of the magazine but its stalwart philosophy, as well, which remains unchanged to this day: to revisit familiar personalities and tell something about them that was not known before, and to present unfamiliar people in an interesting, provocative way.

"All we were doing," explains Dick Stolley, "was covering human beings, and the goal of this was to enable the reader to understand their public leaders and popular culture stars, because we were convinced that this understanding would be beneficial."

WHO'S APPEARED ON THE COVER MOST*

Princess Diana	55 times
Elizabeth Taylor	26
Fergie	19
John Travolta	19
Madonna	17
Cher	17
Michael Jackson	14
Farrah Fawcett	14
Prince Charles	14
Jackie Onassis	11
Princess Caroline	10
Jane Fonda	9

* Cover appearances, alone, not in inserts; figures according to *People* as of December 1993.

PART I
INSIDE
PEOPLE
the first decade
1974 – 1983

1974

1974 COVERS

Mia Farrow
Martha Mitchell
John Paul Getty
Raquel Welch
Gerry Ford
Ted Kennedy, Jr. & Sr.
Lorne Greene
Tatum O'Neal
Joan Baez
George & Cornelia Wallace
Peter Bogdanovich & Cybill Shepherd
E. Howard Hunt
Pat Nixon
Cicely Tyson
Henry & Nancy Kissinger
Jack Lemmon
Joan Kennedy
Telly Savalas
Suzy & Mark Spitz
Carol Burnett & Rock Hudson
Larry Csonka
Faye Dunaway

Tom & Barbara Eagleton
Barbara Walters & Jim Hartz
Charles Bronson
Betty & Gerald Ford
Catherine Deneuve
John & Mo Dean
Joe Namath
Gloria Steinem
Mary Tyler Moore
Paul Newman
Jackie Onassis
Susan Ford
Burt Reynolds & Dinah Shore
Richard Burton
Prince Charles
Katharine Hepburn & John Wayne
Johnny & Joanna Carson
Hugh Hefner & Barbi Benton
Cloris Leachman
Kathy & Bing Crosby
Dustin Hoffman

YEAR-END DOUBLE ISSUE

Muhammad Ali, Ella Grasso, John Wood,
Gunnar Myrdal, Pat Nixon, Faye Dunaway,
Jimmy Connors, Nelson Rockefeller,
Valerie Harper, Gerald Ford, Stevie Wonder,
Alexander Solzhenitsyn,
Alexander Calder.

Top Films: *The Sting*
The Exorcist
Papillon
Magnum Force
Herbie Rides Again

Oscar: *The Godfather Part II*

Top TV Shows: *All in the Family*
The Waltons
Sanford and Son
M*A*S*H
Hawaii Five-O

Emmys: *M*A*S*H*
Upstairs, Downstairs

Top Songs: "The Way We Were"
—Barbra Streisand
"I Honestly Love You"
—Olivia Newton-John
"You're Having My Baby"—Paul Anka
"Bennie and the Jets"—Elton John
"I Shot the Sheriff"—Eric Clapton
"Feel Like Makin' Love"
—Roberta Flack

Grammys: "I Honestly Love You" (record)
"The Way We Were" (song)

Bestsellers: *Alive*—Piers Paul Read
All the President's Men—Bob Woodward
& Carl Bernstein
Jaws—Peter Benchley

Tonys: *The River Niger*
Raisin

Marriages: Liza Minnelli + Jack Haley
Henry Kissinger + Nancy Maginnes
Faye Dunaway + Peter Wolf

Divorces: Peter Allen & Liza Minnelli
Mickey Rooney & Carolyn Hockett
Jackie Gleason & Beverly McKittrick
Richard Burton & Elizabeth Taylor
Peter Sellers & Miranda Quarry
Gary Lockwood & Stefanie Powers

Deaths: Samuel Goldwyn   Duke Ellington
Agnes Moorehead   Cass Elliot
Chet Huntley   Francisco Franco
Charles Lindbergh   Jack Benny

NEWS

- Patty Hearst kidnapped by the SLA
- Atlanta editor J. Reginald Murphy kidnapped and released
- Connie Francis raped
- Wilbur Mills and Fanne Fox stopped by D.C. police—she jumps into Tidal Basin
- Huey Newton charged with murder of Kathleen Smith
- First murder victim of L.A. "Skid Row Slasher" found
- "Zebra" killings in San Francisco: four black Muslims kill three whites
- Solzhenitsyn expelled from USSR
- Hank Aaron hits 715th home run, beating Babe Ruth's record
- Mikhail Baryshnikov defects to U.S.
- Nixon resigns, Ford becomes president
- Muhammad Ali regains heavyweight title
- Ford grants Nixon a full pardon
- Jimmy Connors and Billie Jean King win U.S. Open
- Betty Ford undergoes breast cancer surgery

CHAPTER ONE
The Second Biggest Bitch in Hollywood

"The big difference between Palm Beach and Hollywood is that Hollywood is a working city. There you can open every door with talent. You can be illegitimate, as Marilyn Monroe was; a former call girl, as I was . . ."

—SHEILAH GRAHAM
in People, March 4, 1974

MARCH 12, 1974. It was nearly 4:00 A.M. and wet snowflakes had begun to fall in the early morning darkness as Dick Stolley, the managing editor of *People*, momentarily put down his editing pencil and peered up wearily from behind his glasses. Somehow, Monday night had managed to spill over into Tuesday morning without warning once again, and he was not close to being finished with the issue of *People* that would go to press that day.

He looked up at the photograph he had chosen for the cover: the wrinkled face of eighty-five-year-old John Paul Getty, the richest man in the world. He was holding a bright yellow daffodil. The picture was shot so close-up, you could see every pore in Getty's bulbous nose. Stolley wondered if he had made a mistake.

A slow wave of exhaustion crept over him—he could feel it pressing hard behind his eyes. He had been working nonstop. That's the way it was in the magazine business. The minute one issue was put to bed, work began on the next.

Hunched over the copy on his desk, Stolley started to fade. Catching himself abruptly, he sprang up and focused on the familiar *New York Times* clipping that was pinned conspicuously to his bulletin board at eye level.

"Who Needs People?" the sarcastic headline blurted in bold black type. A surge of adrenaline shot through him like fire.

It was a column by William Safire that had run on February 28—the week the first issue of *People*, the one with Mia Farrow on the cover, had hit the newsstands. "When the world's most powerful publishing empire launched 'The first national weekly magazine to be started in twenty years,'" Safire had written, "its executives must have asked themselves: What will compel magazine buyers to snatch our new magazine off the newsstands? What subjects are sure-fire audience-grabbers at this point in Time, Incorporated?

"By their choice of topics," he had gone on, "the *Time* people have given us a stop action view of what they think most interests wealthy young people, their prime target audience."

"By their handling of these topics, the editors give us their frank assessment of that audience: A collection of frantic, tasteless fadcats deeply concerned with social climbing and intellectual pretension, panting for a look at celebrities in poses that press agents staged back in the thirties (with wryly detached captions like 'These Playboy Bunnies are, well, hopping mad')."

After describing the contents of the Mia Farrow issue in painfully critical terms, Safire finally concluded, "*People* fails on the tawdry terms it has chosen: The sex is not sexy, the gossip not current, the exploitation not with-it. Great effort is needed to lift it up to superficiality . . ."

Stolley could barely read Safire's column without choking with rage. It worked like a drug. Whenever he got discouraged or tired or dispirited, he would reread the clipping and the instant fury it sparked would invigorate him. He had made a promise to himself the first time he saw it. He decreed that the name of "that son of a bitch," as he quickly came to refer to Safire, would never appear in *People* for any reason under any circumstances—and it would not—in spite of Safire's growing popularity as a columnist, author, and lexicographer.

William Safire was not the only critic to put *People* down. Most of them had been fairly consistent in their condescending attitudes. Some, like Tom Donnelly of *The Washington Post*, were at least more perceptive:

"Could it catch on?" Donnelly had written. "Why not? *People* is gossipy, crisp, shrewdly derivative and smartly edited. It will tax none but the shortest attention spans and it is so undemanding that it can be read while the TV commercials are on (or while 'Hawaii Five-O' is on, for that matter). It is the reading equivalent of those 'convenience foods' that have become so integral a part of the American Way of Life."

Ironically, though, the most hurtful reaction to the magazine had come from within the very walls of its family, from the inner sanctum of the Time

& Life Building itself. In spite of the fact that the budget for the new magazine was extremely lean compared with other Time Inc. publications, that the staff was tiny, and that everyone on it was working virtually around the clock, other Time Inc.-ers, feeling vastly superior, snickered that *People* could be read from cover to cover on the elevator ride from the twenty-ninth floor, where its offices were, down to the lobby. Anyone who deigned to carry a copy hid it under his coat. Some even warned that in no time at all *People* would run out of people to cover. The big joke inside the company was that *People* magazine was going to start by getting into so much trouble that it would never last—that it was going to need a big staff of lawyers and only a small staff of writers because of the potential threat of lawsuits.

"It got quite savage," Dick Stolley said later in an official interview for the Time Inc. Archives. "They thought that for Time Inc. to put out a magazine like this was unseemly. Tacky," he said. "You'd be in the elevator and hear cracks like this all the time. Here we'd be, working 80 and 100 hour weeks, and then to get on the elevator and hear some asshole dump on the magazine—well, it wasn't pleasant." (The official Time Inc. history changed "some asshole" to "someone.")

With the renewed energy fueled by Safire's column, Stolley got up and walked down the hall. One thing he had understood with absolute certainty from the start was the incredible potential of *People* magazine. It was four o'clock in the morning when he ran into one of the staff editors in the men's room. "Oh, you're still here," he said to the editor as he stood beside him at the urinal. "Why don't you go home early tonight?"

With that, he turned around and headed back to his office to edit the story he was working on. He touched up the contents line: "Lucille Ball, at 63, explains, among other things, why she wants to punch Marlon Brando in the nose." The next day, after the Getty issue was closed, he would turn to the next pressing matter at hand. His detractors had been right about one thing: The minute the first issue had hit the newsstand, *People* had been threatened with a lawsuit—by none other than Sheilah Graham.

HAL WINGO, A tall, gentle, devout Texan, who happened to be the son of a Baptist minister, was already deeply immersed in the Graham problem. Stolley had picked Wingo to be his news editor, which meant that he was in charge of all *People* stories emanating outside New York. These were fed, or "filed," to the magazine by an intricate network of part-time correspondents, or "stringers."

It had been *People*'s idea to have Graham write a story for the magazine comparing high society life in Palm Beach (Florida) and L.A., which she had done. She had moved to Palm Beach only a few months earlier and had strong feelings about the sharp contrast between the two places.

Graham had once described herself as "the second biggest bitch in Hollywood," although she had not specified who was the first. For nearly forty years, Sheilah Graham had been one of Hollywood's fiercest and most influential columnists, appearing in more newspapers at the height of her career than either Hedda Hopper or Louella Parsons. She was even better known as F. Scott Fitzgerald's lover during the last three years of his life. She wrote prolifically and sometimes indiscriminately. Her biography of Fitzgerald, *Beloved Infidel*, was critically praised. Her last book, *A State of Heat*, in which she described in graphic detail how she used sex "to get what I wanted out of life," was widely criticized as tasteless.

Graham had happily accepted the Palm Beach assignment from *People*, which fell under Wingo's purview. He arranged for *People*'s Miami correspondent, Jane Rieker, to collect the Graham copy when she was finished with it and transmit it to New York by wire, which she did.

What Graham had written was a first-person observation. At one point in the story, she said, "The big difference between Palm Beach and Hollywood is that Hollywood is a working city. There you can open every door with talent. You can be illegitimate, as Marilyn Monroe was; a former call girl, as I was; have a juvenile delinquency record, as Steve McQueen had; be an ex-lumberjack, like Gable. But you don't have to marry someone rich to make it. Society is the only industry in Palm Beach."

Wingo was astonished when he saw what Graham had written. "I remember when I read that," he recalls, "I thought, Wow, this woman is being very honest. But then, her book, *A State of Heat*, was out at the time."

There was, however, a problem with the text that Graham had turned in—an especially serious problem for a magazine: According to Hal Wingo, Graham's story was almost unreadable as it was written. "It turned out that she could hardly put two words back-to-back," he says. "We had to rewrite the whole column. She was almost illiterate. So we rewrote the column and condensed it and got it into the allotted space."

Wingo knew he had to treat the material carefully. The fact that it was for the first issue of the magazine did not help. The joke floating around the building about *People* needing a big staff of lawyers and only a small staff of writers had not eluded him either. Exercising great caution, he consulted the Time Inc. lawyers, who told him he had to go back to Graham and confirm with her the exact wording of the copy.

This was not easy for Hal Wingo, who had admittedly had his own misgivings about the very nature of *People* when Stolley had asked him to work on it, but his respect and admiration for Stolley had dissipated his fears. Now he embraced his mission with total dedication.

He swallowed hard and dialed Graham's number in Palm Beach. When she answered, he said gently with his soft Southern accent, "Miss Graham, we've got the copy finished now and I need to go over it with you just to make sure everything's clear."

"Fine, fine," she replied.

He breathed deeply and began to read. When he got to the paragraph in question, he stopped and swallowed hard. Then he proceeded to read what she had written back to her: " 'You can be illegitimate, as Marilyn Monroe was,' " he said, hesitating slightly. Then he added, picking up speed, " 'A former call girl, as I was . . .' " He finished the sentence.

"Right, right." Graham confirmed what he had read.

"Whew!" Wingo said to himself, and he continued right on through to the end of the edited piece. When he was finished, he thanked her. They said their good-byes and hung up.

Everything was fine until Graham saw the words she had written in print. "When she saw it she had a heart attack," says Wingo. "She claimed she had said, 'You can be a call girl, as "J" was.' 'J' was the woman who wrote the book *The Sensuous Woman*. That made no sense at all because these other people she mentioned were real people and out of nowhere we got this fictitious character that hasn't got anything to do with Hollywood. But she said she wrote this as 'J' and that Jane Rieker, in picking up the copy, had read it as an 'I' and transmitted it as an 'I.' So the whole thing hung on my word that she had signed off on it after I had read it back to her."

Graham remained steadfast in her position. It was too late to stop publication of the magazine, so she proceeded to hire the best attorney she could find—to sue *People:* Edward Bennett Williams of Washington, D.C.

The handling of this delicate matter continued to fall, for the most part, on Wingo's shoulders. Graham was invited to come to New York with her lawyer for a meeting to try to resolve the matter. The vision of her arrival is still vivid in Wingo's mind. "She came into New York with her wig askew," he recalls, demonstrating the way Graham's wig was sliding off her head when he laid eyes on her for the first time. "We met upstairs in this room and went through this whole thing with her and by that time I think she realized that she didn't really have a case. She wanted us to print a retraction in the next issue."

Stolley took a hard line. He never doubted for a moment that Wingo, of all people, was telling the truth, and he knew he could not cave in. This threatened lawsuit was the first for *People*, but it certainly would not be the last. Now was the time to set a precedent. Refusing to print a retraction, he agreed to run an item in the "Chatter" column, the last page of the magazine. It read: "From Sheilah Graham comes word that the eyebrow-raising phrase in her bylined story on Palm Beach in PEOPLE (March 4) should have read 'former "chorus" girl.' 'As I have written in several of my books,' she says, 'I have always believed in love. I was so busy in this area that I didn't have time to consider the financial aspects.' " Then, to soothe any hurt feelings, Time Inc. paid for Graham's trip to New York and treated her to a fancy weekend on the town, which she gratefully accepted.

People's first potential lawsuit was settled before it got to court.

DICK STOLLEY'S UNSTINTING confidence in *People* soon began to substantiate itself. After only six issues, *People* was receiving 430 letters a week, with praise outnumbering criticism 4 to 1. By May, after less than three months, the print order for the magazine was increased by 10 percent. In spite of the fact that no subscriptions were offered, some five hundred checks for subscriptions were being received every week. It was also clear that the readership of *People* was ideal from an advertising standpoint: young, relatively affluent, and well educated.

It would be a long time before Stolley would have the chance to confront William Safire face-to-face about the devastating critique he had written of *People*. Several years later, when Stolley—calmed by the passage of time and the obvious success of the magazine—finally ran into the columnist at a party, he was able to control himself. He simply told Safire that his column on the first issue of the magazine had dismayed him. Safire looked at him blankly and replied, "Really? I don't remember that. I thought I liked your magazine. I certainly do now."

CHAPTER TWO

Someone's in the Kitchen with Dinah

"She had written me to be on her show, and after three or four
months I finally did go on, saying terrible, unexpected things . . ."

—*BURT REYNOLDS*
in People, *October 28, 1974*

STOLLEY HAD BEEN right to worry about the pores in John Paul
Getty's nose. As it turned out, he should have been just as concerned
about the wrinkles in his face, since they also undoubtedly contributed
to the fact that the Getty cover was one of the worst-selling covers of the year.

Skeptics who had predicted that *People* might run out of people on whom
to do stories, however, had certainly been wrong. In the first year alone—just
for starters—Nixon resigned because of the Watergate controversy, Ford became president, Patty Hearst finally surfaced after being kidnapped by the
Symbionese Liberation Army, Tatum O'Neal won an Oscar at the age of ten for
Paper Moon, Liz and Dick got divorced, Henry Kissinger got married, Chris
Evert and Jimmy Connors got engaged, Sonny and Cher decided to separate,
Prince Charles had failed to find a future queen by the ripe old age of twenty-
six, and "Deep Throat" (Linda Lovelace) had become a household word.

Closer to the Capitol, Teddy Kennedy, Jr., suffered the amputation of his
leg; his mother, Joan, checked into the Silver Hill Foundation; Betty Ford
had a radical mastectomy; Fanne Fox jumped into the tidal basin after being
stopped by D.C. police while riding with an inebriated Congressman Wilbur
Mills; and Margaret Trudeau followed closely on the heels of Joan Kennedy
with a nervous breakdown of her own—another victim of the unrelenting
pressures of political spousehood.

All this provided fodder for Dick Stolley's conclusions about who sold on

People's cover and who did not. Cher sold well on the cover. So did Elizabeth Taylor and Johnny Carson, but people such as Howard Cosell, E. Howard Hunt, and John Paul Getty were disasters. A pattern—not very complex— began to emerge, from which he ultimately extracted a cover formula that has in many respects held up to this day:

> Young is better than old.
> Pretty is better than ugly.
> Rich is better than poor.
> TV is better than music.
> Music is better than movies.
> Movies are better than sports.
> And anything is better than politics.

After John Lennon died in 1980, and the tribute to him on the cover of the magazine in December of that year became the bestselling cover in *People*'s history, an amendment was added to the formula:

> And nothing is better than the celebrity dead.

There were, however, other considerations. "The face had to be recognizable to eighty percent of the American people," Stolley explains. "There had to be a reason for the person being on the cover. There had to be something happening in the person's life the week it was out there. (The cover had to be decided on by Monday in those days—Tuesday at the latest—a week before it arrived on the newsstands.)

"And then there was this X factor," says Stolley. "There had to be something about that person that you wanted to know." The X factor accounted for why Mary Tyler Moore was never a successful cover subject, in spite of the fact that she was the star of one of the most popular shows on television. "There was nothing left of interest about her that people did not already know," he explains. "They loved her, but that wasn't enough for *People*'s cover."

BURT REYNOLDS AND DINAH SHORE were perfect. They fit into nearly every category: They were pretty, not ugly; they were rich, not poor; he was a movie star, she was a well-known singer; as an added bonus, she was also a television star; he was young (thirty-eight), and although she was nineteen years older, she was not exactly old; and most important of all, there was a giant X factor—something about them that people really wanted to know. What people really wanted to know about Burt and Dinah was everything about their relationship—which was in full bloom at the time that *People* set out to do the story.

Before Burt Reynolds's movie career took off, perhaps his biggest claim to fame had been his brazen appearance as *Cosmopolitan* magazine's first centerfold, stripped completely—except for his hairpiece. Now, in the fall of 1974, as the star of the hit movie *The Longest Yard*, he was the number-four-rated male box-office name—behind Paul Newman, Robert Redford, and Steve McQueen. That alone made him a desirable subject for *People* magazine.

That was not all that *People* wanted. There was a larger story—the X factor. It was exponential. As popular as Burt Reynolds was, Burt and Dinah would be much more than twice as valuable as Reynolds alone.

Barbara Wilkins knew that. The former *Time* reporter, outspoken and unrestrained, with her long wild mane of thick white hair, was in charge of the Los Angeles bureau—the hub of many of the magazine's biggest celebrity stories.

Sitting in her office on Roxbury Drive in Beverly Hills, Wilkins dialed David Gershenson, Reynolds's publicist, to request that Burt do a story for *People*. It was a perfect symbiosis—good for Reynolds, good for the magazine. She refrained from specifying that she wanted Reynolds to talk about his relationship with Shore. Gershenson said okay, and they made the arrangements: She would do the interview at Reynolds's Sunset Strip apartment.

When Wilkins phoned New York with the date, *People*'s picture editor, John Dominis, assigned Harry Benson, one of the best and most prolific photographers in the world, to fly to L.A. to shoot the story. On the appointed day, Benson and Wilkins drove up the Sunset Strip and stopped just short of the Playboy Club in front of Reynolds's apartment. They got out and rang the bell.

The second Wilkins walked in the door, she knew it was not going to be easy. The place exuded tackiness. "It was like the Playboy pad," she recalls. "It had red velveteen walls, and instead of a bed there was this raised platform covered with pillows. You could look right out the window and see the Playboy building on Sunset. Burt was involved with Dinah Shore at the time and it was obvious that he was not really living in the house."

Barbara Wilkins sat patiently with Harry Benson, a debonair and charming Scotsman, waiting for Burt to appear. The vision of his arrival is still vivid in her mind. "He stood there with his toupee," she recalls, "and his boots with six-inch heels to make himself taller."

The interview started with a bang. Reynolds scanned the room, turned to Wilkins, and said, "It looks like a whore threw up in here, doesn't it?" It went downhill from there. By the time it was over, Wilkins knew that she had not gotten her story.

David Gershenson knew it, too. A few days later, he called Wilkins to tell her that Burt was staging a fund-raising benefit at his alma mater, Florida State, where he would present the university with a check for fifty thousand dollars. He asked her if she wanted to go. He thought—and undoubtedly hoped—that it might give her story some added dimension.

Of course she would go, Wilkins replied. It was exactly what she needed —a chance for more time with Burt in totally different surroundings. She was to fly to Tallahassee with him on a private jet, a fancy Falcon 880. With luck, the plane ride would give her the opportunity she needed to ask him about Shore, since it would take more than four hours to get there.

On the plane, things started off well. She was seated next to Reynolds, which meant he would be her captive for the ride. Wilkins had been a reporter for a long time and her reportorial instincts were usually on target. After some friendly chitchat high above the clouds, she chose what she thought was the right moment to pounce. Turning to Burt, she smiled and asked, "What about your relationship with Dinah Shore?"

Reynolds looked her straight in the eye. "It's none of your fucking business," he replied.

Marilyn Beck, the gossip columnist, happened to be sitting directly behind Burt. She could not help overhearing Reynolds's words. They seemed to be reverberating in the air, trapped inside the Falcon 880, hanging there thickly, floating ominously above the clouds in the rarefied atmosphere. Beck was, in Wilkins's words, "horrified."

Reynolds knew that he had made a mistake. "He felt so bad," says Wilkins, "that he proceeded to tell me everything about him and Dinah Shore."

They had met three and a half years earlier, after Dinah had asked Burt to be on her show. "After three or four months I finally did go on," Reynolds told Wilkins, "saying terrible, unexpected things. I said, 'I want to talk to you about going to Palm Springs with me for the weekend.' It was hard for her to cope with me," he added. "She was making a stew at the time." (According to Dinah, it had taken "two full hours of taping with Burt to come out with fifteen minutes for use on the air that were not X-rated.")

He told Wilkins how he had fallen "in like" with Dinah, that his relationship with her had become so precious that it was the one thing in his life he could not be facetious about. "It's easy for me to be flippant about my career," he said, "but not about that. There are too many relationships that become public property because people don't take care of them."

He even answered Wilkins's question about marriage: Dinah, he told her, was the one who opposed it. "If we were going to be married, we would be," he said. Wilkins herself added some information about Dinah's feelings on the subject in the piece she wrote: "Hollywood hearsay has it that after two marriages, Dinah has ruled out a third, at least to such a young man. Reynolds has asked frequently, but, as Dinah confided to a friend, 'I don't want to grow old in his arms.' "

After the Tallahassee trip, Wilkins went quickly to work on the story, since it was scheduled to close immediately. "His lifestyle and costuming are studiously vulgar," she wrote. "When a visitor is startled to silence by the overpowering tastelessness of his Sunset Strip pad, Burt agrees cheerily, 'It looks like a whore threw up in here, doesn't it?' " (In the magazine, the word "whore" was changed to "bullfighter" for some reason.)

The cover was a picture of the happy couple. Her head was resting blissfully on his shoulder. The cover line read:

BURT REYNOLDS & DINAH SHORE
The superstar she said "no" to

People had snared the X factor.

IT WAS PRECISELY this calculated *People* style, along with the singular "Peoplese" that was beginning to insinuate itself somewhat wickedly into the English language, that provided perfect material for the lampooning of *People* that took place with increasing frequency as the magazine became more successful and widely read. At the end of the year *Esquire* was unrelenting in its spoof of the magazine, which it called *Peephole*, with cover lines like these:

LIZ TAYLOR
Her heart says I do—
And she does

and:

HENRY KISSINGER
Peeling off the layers of his life,
his loves, his travels, his passport pictures,
his many moods,
what he eats for breakfast,
which pants leg goes on first,
his ups, his downs, his smiles, his frowns,
his views on the gay boys in the State Department,
what he eats for lunch, etc. . . . .

The inside pages featured a piece on—who else? Elizabeth Taylor:

> All Europe is talking about Her and Her search for Him. Who is Her? Don't make us laugh. Her is Her and you know who She is because there's something about Her in every issue of this magazine. This week She's in COUPLES, last week on the COVER, the week before that in BIO, and the week before that, a subtle anagram in the PEEPHOLE PUZZLE . . .

After only ten months, *People*'s guaranteed circulation had risen 25 percent, to 1,250,000. The cover price had increased from thirty-five to forty cents, a change that seemed to make little difference to buyers, who did not hesitate to purchase the first higher-priced issue, which—and not by accident—had Paul Newman on the cover.

After *People*'s first anniversary party, which took place at the trendy nightclub Hippopotamus, Sally Quinn wrote a story about it in the "Style" section of *The Washington Post*, in which she captured the evolving attitude of the media toward the new magazine. "Some of the first issues were tasteless, boring, almost 'blue' journalism," she wrote, "a turnoff to most advertisers and a lot of potential readers. Even today, the magazine's detractors call it fluff, puff, superficial movie magazine, tabloid, trash, not to be taken seriously, a poorman's *Life*, and a lot of other unflattering things. And of course, there is that East Coast media thing of everybody putting something down, especially when it looks like it's going to fail, but even more when it looks like it's going to succeed."

By 1975, it looked as if it was going to succeed. In September, only eighteen months after it was launched, *People* turned its first profit, setting a new record. *Time* had taken three years to become profitable, *Sports Illustrated* had taken ten. The price of a full-page, four-color ad went from $7,750 to $10,415. The cost of a full-page, black-and-white ad rose from $6,085 to $8,180.

On July 21 of *People*'s second year, Paul Newman appeared on the cover again. He had, after all, worked very well when the price increased the first time. This time the cover price rose to fifty cents an issue. Before *People* was two years old, more than 120 million copies would be sold.

TOP 5
CHER & GREGG
ELTON JOHN
ROSE KENNEDY AT 85
JOANNE WOODWARD
SONNY BONO

1975 COVERS

Elvis Presley
Judge John Sirica
Liv Ullmann
Billie Jean King & Chris Evert
Cher
Happy Rockefeller
Olivia Newton-John
Christina Onassis
James Caan & Barbra Streisand
Alan Alda
Ann-Margret
Jackie Onassis
Henry & Peter Fonda
Warren Beatty, Goldie Hawn
   & Julie Christie
Paul & Linda McCartney
Ellen Burstyn
Jimmy Connors
Lauren Hutton
Liz Taylor
Nancy Walker
Clint Eastwood
Mick Jagger
Betty Ford
Jane Fonda & Tom Hayden
Bette Midler

Muhammad Ali
Carroll O'Connor
Paul Newman & Joanne Woodward
Candice Bergen
Peter Sellers
Sonny Bono
Elton John
Roy Scheider & Shark
Grace Kelly
Cher & Gregg Allman
Valerie Harper & Richard Schaal
Rose & Ted Kennedy
Howard Cosell
Nancy & Henry Kissinger
Marlon Brando
Julie & David Eisenhower
Robert Redford
Gene Hackman
Bob Dylan
Bea Arthur
Jennifer O'Neill
Julia Child
Jack Nicholson
Roger Daltrey
Billy Graham

YEAR-END DOUBLE ISSUE:
Cher, Woody Allen, Betty Ford

BOTTOM 5
LIV ULLMANN
JULIA CHILD
JACK NICHOLSON
JUDGE SIRICA
BILLY GRAHAM

Top Films: *Jaws*
The Towering Inferno
Benji
Young Frankenstein
The Godfather Part II

Oscar: *One Flew Over the Cuckoo's Nest*

Top TV Shows: *All in the Family*
Sanford and Son
Chico and the Man
The Jeffersons
M*A*S*H

Emmys: *The Mary Tyler Moore Show*
Upstairs, Downstairs

Top Songs: "Love Will Keep Us Together"
—The Captain and Tennille
"Lucy in the Sky with Diamonds"
—Elton John
"Rhinestone Cowboy"
—Glen Campbell
"Fame"—David Bowie
"Mandy"—Barry Manilow

Grammys: "Love Will Keep Us Together" (record)
"Send in the Clowns" (song)

Bestsellers: *Centennial*—James Michener
Humboldt's Gift—Saul Bellow
Ragtime—E. L. Doctorow
Shōgun—James Clavell

Tonys: *Equus*
The Wiz

Marriages: Christina Onassis
+ Alexandros Andreadis
Elizabeth Taylor + Richard Burton

Divorces: Ann Landers & Jules Lederer

Deaths: Susan Hayward   Ozzie Nelson
George Stevens   Josephine Baker
Sam Giancana   Aristotle Onassis
Chiang Kai-shek

NEWS

- Mobster Sam Giancana murdered
- JFK/Judith Exner/Castro assassination plot linked
- Mitchell, Haldeman & Ehrlichman sentenced to prison
- King Faisal of Saudi Arabia killed by crazed nephew
- Samuel Bronfman II, heir to Seagram's fortune, kidnapped and released
- Jimmy Hoffa disappears
- Patty Hearst found and charged with bank robbery
- Lynette "Squeaky" Fromme arrested for attempted assassination of President Ford
- Fourteen die in bombing of La Guardia Airport
- Saigon surrenders to the Communists
- Chris Evert wins the U.S. Open
- John Lennon wins court battle to avoid deportation
- The *QE2* makes its first trip around the world

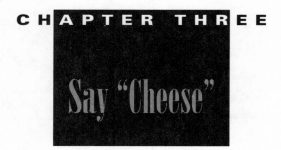

CHAPTER THREE

Say "Cheese"

"Was she wearing her glasses?"
"Wearing her glasses? She wasn't even wearing her clothes!"

—*HARRY BENSON*
*to Dick Stolley after photographing Greta Garbo
for* People *in June 1975*

HARRY BENSON WAS still trembling as he pulled out of Shana Alexander's driveway in Wainscott, Long Island, and headed down the highway toward the beach to pick up his wife and his child. His exhausted dachshund, Lucy, was asleep in the backseat of the car. Harry was not speaking to the sorry animal. He could not believe what she had done.

He should have known, he thought to himself. He *never* took anyone with him to photo shoots, and that included animals. But Shana lived so close to the beach, and it was a hot summer day—much hotter in Manhattan; it had seemed like such a good idea to drop his family at the beach while he went to take the pictures of Shana for the *People* story. God, what a mistake that had been.

The sign at the beach flashed through his mind. If he had known that dogs were not allowed on the Long Island beach, he would have left Lucy at home. Having brought her along, he had no choice but to take her to Shana's.

He had arrived at Shana's house with Lucy in tow. Shana's young daughter, Kathy, was there, and the oversized dachshund—to Lucy's delight—had been invited to join the group. There was plenty of room for her to run around outside.

Alexander had been a columnist for *Life,* and she had become the first woman editor of *McCall's* magazine in fifty years. Now, besides writing a column for *Newsweek* and appearing as a commentator on the television show *60 Minutes,* she had written a new and valuable book, her first: *Shana Alexander's State-by-State Guide to Women's Legal Rights.* She was a perfect subject for a *People* story and Harry Benson was the perfect photographer to shoot it.

First he took a few pictures of Shana and Kathy together, then he got some shots of Shana alone. Right after that, Shana suggested that they all go around to the back of the house so that Kathy could show him her pet bunny rabbits. Harry, who was always thinking of photo opportunities, found the image of Shana, her daughter, and a bunch of cute little bunny rabbits very appealing.

They all made their way to the back of the house, and Shana went inside to get some lettuce to coax the little bunnies out of their cage. When she came back out, she and Kathy got down on their knees with the greens. Shana obviously knew what she was doing—the lettuce worked like a charm. Out came the bunny rabbits—one, two, three, four . . . They just kept coming. Harry was amazed. Six, seven—there must have been at least eight of them.

And then it happened. Harry had totally forgotten about Lucy, who at precisely that moment caught a giant whiff of the bunny rabbits as they toppled out, one by one. Before anyone even knew what was happening, her pure animal instincts propelled her forward toward her prey; she bolted after the bunnies, dashing through the lineup, as Harry would later describe her, "like O. J. Simpson." Lucy the dachshund got every single one of the poor little creatures.

The luscious Long Island afternoon turned into a nightmare. Shana and her daughter were screaming. Within moments they were in hysterics. Harry stood there, mortified, frozen in place, unable to wrest the dog from her uncontrollable frenzy. When he mustered the nerve to look up again, Lucy sat staring back at him with a satisfied smirk on her face. The blood from the bunny rabbits dribbled out of her mouth.

Harry finally managed to grab Lucy. Apologizing profusely to Shana and to Kathy, he dragged the overstuffed dog away. There was nothing more he could do.

"I think the picture taking is finished for the day," he mumbled. Then Harry slunk back into his car with his dog and headed down the road to the beach to pick up his wife and his daughter.

To this day, Harry shudders at the thought of the horrendous scene. He had been totally helpless. "You try stopping a dog in a frenzy," he says. "I couldn't stop her. She would have killed me. It was just awful. There was nothing but blood and dead rabbits."

Harry Benson had photographed thousands of people in his illustrious career—everyone from the Beatles to the Kennedys; Nixon, Ford, Bette Midler, Gilda Radner—an endless list of celebrities, and people from every walk of life. Nothing this bad had ever happened.

He was a genius when it came to getting people to do things you would never think they would do. He shot people in bathtubs and swimming pools and beds. They played for him, kissed for him, stood on their heads. He remembered the time he had had to get pictures of the man in the U.S. Witness Protection Program who had recently had his identity changed. The man, understandably, did not want to take any chances on a picture that would run in a magazine with a circulation of over a million. So Harry had photographed him for *People* with a pair of panty hose pulled over his head.

Sometimes it was easier to keep his distance—to stay away from the people he was shooting, as he had done with Greta Garbo. That had definitely been a highlight of his career, in spite of the fact he had never spoken to the reclusive star. He had fallen into this great coup for *People* by accident.

He had been shooting a boring story for *Town & Country* magazine about a swanky, exclusive, high society club in Palm Beach. Benson had been less than captivated by the scene. "This place was so exclusive," he recalls, "that they didn't even like Nelson Rockefeller. It was really boring."

Harry tried, but his heart was not in it. One of the women from the club, who was pushing the story as hard as she could, kept calling Harry and pestering him at his hotel. What she wanted, she told him, was for him to photograph her at her home on the beach near the club. Harry delicately managed to keep putting her off. His plan was to slip out of town before she knew it. He would just disappear, and that would be the end of it. He had paid his hotel bill and was ready to leave—standing quietly in front of the hotel, waiting for the taxi to pick him up—when he heard someone call his name. "Mr. Benson?" She tapped him on the shoulder. It was the woman with the house on the beach.

Embarrassed that she had caught him in his attempted escape, Harry mumbled something to her about having to leave suddenly—but, he assured her, he would be back. She was insistent. "No, no," she told him vehemently, shaking her head. "Come and see it now, and I'll take you to the airport."

He accepted the fact that he had been foiled. Not wanting to be blatantly rude, he agreed. At least he would get a ride to the airport. The woman from the exclusive club dragged him down to the beach and showed him a few of the club's private cabañas nestled there. Trying to be polite, Harry humored her by shooting a few pictures. "Oh, this is very nice," he told her, doing everything he could to conjure up even an ounce of enthusiasm in his voice.

Suddenly the woman turned to him. "See that beach hut over there?" she said, pointing several feet ahead. "Well, the Trudeaus came two weeks ago and they patched up their marriage there."

Harry's ears perked up. At least things were getting more interesting. He shot a few more pictures. Then she looked at him and said, "And the one next door, see that? On Monday, Greta Garbo is coming."

Harry froze. Greta Garbo? Greta Garbo!, he thought, could it really be? He tried to remain calm, but his mind gathered speed. "Cancel my reservation . . . cancel it!" he said to himself. By then, the woman was ready to take him to the airport. "Well, we had better get going, if you're going to make your plane," she said.

After she dropped him at the airport, Harry waited until she drove off. Then he got right back into a taxi and returned to the hotel from which he had just checked out. He moved quickly, having already devised his plan of action. He thought of his friend—the one who happened to have a chartered boat from nearby Antigua harbor. The friend had a baby. By the time Greta Garbo arrived, Harry, his friend, and the baby were unsuspiciously ensconced within the protective confines of the boat, moored right outside the bungalow that the pesky woman from the club had so generously pointed out to him.

Within half an hour of the elusive Garbo's arrival, like a gift for Harry from heaven, she appeared on the beach. The timing could not have been better. Harry Benson watched in disbelief from the boat as she slowly undressed, taking off every last piece of clothing. Then, completely nude, she jumped into the water and went for a swim as Harry sat photographing her from the boat with his telephoto lens.

He did not feel the least bit guilty when he was done. "She hadn't a clue," he says. "To me, this is real paparazzi, because I didn't disrupt her weekend. I didn't chase her along the beach like Ron Galella would have. When she came back from her holiday and saw the pictures, she wasn't too happy."

If Harry had not been as loyal to *People* magazine as he was—he was in no way legally bound to sell them the Garbo pictures, since they had not been assigned—he could have gotten a lot more for them, he thinks, probably around fifty thousand dollars. But that is not what he did. Instead he called Dick Stolley right away, knowing that *People* could not spend that kind of money, and sold him the pictures for the regular *People* page rate, which was only around two hundred dollars at the time.

When Stolley heard about the Garbo photographs he was beside himself—he was dying to have them. What could possibly be better for *People* than exclusive pictures of one of the *most*-sought-after and *least*-photographed celebrities in the world? True to his character, he maintained his cool.

"Was she wearing her glasses?" he asked Harry Benson nonchalantly. "Wearing her glasses?" Harry replied. "She wasn't even wearing her clothes!"

THE PHOTO DEPARTMENT at *People* had a difficult job. Readers saw the pictures in the magazine—nearly one hundred of them in every issue— but rarely had an idea of what went into planning them, setting them up, and getting them (or not getting them, as was sometimes the case).

Mary Dunn, a petite, pretty blonde, started out as a picture researcher for the magazine and later became the picture editor, replacing the well-respected photographer John Dominis in 1978 when he left the *People* job after four years. Dunn was instrumental in establishing *People*'s distinctive photo style. More than anyone else, she was responsible for encouraging photographers to use their imaginations in producing the pictures that have come to characterize the magazine—in Dick Stolley's words, "a sometimes elaborate setup that was not only refreshing and often funny, but which revealed something of the character and personality of the story subject."

Besides assisting Dominis in selecting pictures from the "takes" that had been assigned, it was Mary Dunn's job to sort through hundreds of pictures daily, choosing existing photographs to supplement assigned stories and tracking down pictures that could not be currently shot. These would come from various places: photo agencies such as Agence France, Sygma, Camera 5, UPI, or Associated Press. Hundreds of pictures were also available from the vast Time Inc. Picture Collection, which contained, among other things, every photograph that had ever been shot for every Time Inc. publication.

Photography was a tricky business. There always seemed to be complications with pictures—especially the kind of candid and unique shots that *People* was after. Dick Swanson, a photographer in Washington, D.C., had nearly gotten killed when he had gone to photograph President Ford in the White House swimming pool. After wearing his swimming trunks to work under his business clothes for days, waiting to receive the required permission to take Ford's picture, the approval had finally come. Knowing that time was precious, Swanson had hustled over to the White House pool and plunged right in next to Ford. Unfortunately, no one had advised the Secret Service men at the pool that Swanson was coming—they had the distinct impression that he was trying to shoot Ford without a camera. Thanks to White House photographer David Kennerly's eleventh-hour intervention, Swanson's life had been spared, but only barely.

It was surprising how many people were willing to cooperate when it came to having their photographic likenesses recorded for posterity. As *People* grew, even politicians began to warm to the magazine's unconventionally captivating ways. In 1975, when *People* did a story on Federal Reserve Chairman Arthur Burns, he agreed to be photographed in his bathroom, which housed a collection of paintings.

Secretary of Agriculture Earl Butz was not such an easy mark. He refused to allow *People* to photograph him in his home. When Washington correspondent Clare Crawford tried to sway Butz by reminding him that Arthur Burns had allowed the magazine to photograph him in his bathroom, Butz replied, "Well, the only thing in mine is a poster of a man and a woman at a urinal. It says, 'Stand up for equality.' "

CHAPTER FOUR

The Beatty Crunch

"My imminent marriage has been announced to every woman
I've seen steadily over the last fifteen years. I have
no intention of getting married. . . ."

—*WARREN BEATTY*
in People, *April 14, 1975*

MARY VESPA SAT at her desk at midnight, trying valiantly to stay
awake, looking longingly at the green-carpeted floor of her office. It
must have been the pork chops. The wine bottles were still open on
the table down the hall in the copy room, where late dinners were catered
every closing night. She fought hard to keep her eyes open—until the sheer
unbridled force of the door slamming next to her office did it for her—almost
knocking her right out of her chair.

J.J. again. He must have just gotten his Cher story back, edited by Dick
Burgheim, Dick Stolley's right-hand man and the Master of the *People* Universe. Every time Burgheim translated Jim Jerome's words to the "Peoplese"
at which he had become so proficient, it drove J.J. into a frenzy. Mary
wondered what Burgheim had written this time.

Well, she thought, as her eyes began to close again. She had to wait for
Stolley to finish editing her piece for that issue, but she would just lie down
on the floor for a few minutes and take a little nap. She threw her coat on top
of herself, curled up on the rug, and went to sleep.

About two hours later, around two-thirty in the morning, she heard the
handle of her door rattling loudly. Waking up, she sat bolt upright, and
scrambled back into her chair as though she had never left it. At least Stolley

had had the courtesy to allow her to redeem herself by rattling the door before he came in.

He apologized for not getting to her sooner, but he had just had a long, rather agonizing call from Kitty Carlisle Hart, who had been sobbing hysterically on the phone. She was begging him, pleading with him not to print her age in the story *People* was doing on her.

"I mean," he said, "she was crying—*sobbing*. She didn't want anybody to know how old she was. She said, 'You'll destroy my political effectiveness. I'm the head of the New York State Commission on the Arts, and if you print my age, my effectiveness in Albany will be seriously damaged. They will not take me seriously if you print my age."

Hart was about sixty-nine at the time. Stolley had understood her point. "In some ways she was on to something," he says, looking back. It was one of those rare moments in which Dick Stolley gave in. "I know when I'm licked," he says. "But I found a way of getting around it, by saying something like, 'She made her stage debut in 1903.' "

Still, a few weeks earlier when Cliff Robertson had come in person to the office after *People* had printed the age of Robertson's wife, Dina Merrill, Stolley had reacted differently. Robertson had not been pleased. He told Stolley that what he had done had been a devastating blow to his wife.

"He's a very solemn man," says Stolley. "He didn't say we got her age wrong, but he said that she had gone to great lengths never to reveal her age and that this would harm her in getting parts. The fact is they were both right. It probably did, but that wasn't our business."

It was a complex issue: the right to privacy vs. the public's right to know. New and important questions had been raised with the evolution of personality journalism that *People* had spawned. Dick Stolley believed that it was important not to be cruel. He also believed it was equally important to uphold basic journalistic principles. He talked about the sensitive options available to *People* on such issues—options distinct from those that would be open to a magazine like *Time*—in a speech he gave shortly after his conversation with Kitty Carlisle Hart.

"It is a complicated question for personality journalism," he said, "because every one of our stories is an invasion of somebody's privacy. Obviously we have a responsibility to the truth—in our case that most fragile of merchandise, the facts about another human being. But truth is sometimes an inadequate guide.

"I could tell you about the popular TV comedian who is a homosexual. The senator who drinks too much. The leading lady who has become a pill addict. This is truth, and we could undoubtedly find enough corroboration to print it and avoid libel or privacy suits. But here truth is cruel and reckless. Part of our responsibility at *People* magazine is to our story subjects themselves—not just to be truthful, but to be careful and tasteful and kind. It is not the sort of problem you have when you are writing about the SALT talks."

WHEN STOLLEY GOT back to his desk after going over Mary Vespa's piece with her, something happened that made him laugh so hard that he felt totally rejuvenated in spite of the fact that the sun was about to come up and he had not been to bed in more than twenty-four hours.

Dick Burgheim, the aforementioned Master of the *People* Universe, was a brilliant Harvard man, a senior editor who not only was indispensable to Dick Stolley, but put his own indelible stamp on the magazine as it developed—editing, rewriting, and remolding virtually every story that fell under the purview of "entertainment" in *People*. It was the first week in April, only a month after *People*'s first birthday, and he had just finished his work on a Warren Beatty story for the upcoming issue. It was a cover with Beatty, Julie Christie, and Goldie Hawn, who were starring together in the new hit movie *Shampoo*.

Stolley sat down at his desk and picked up the edited Beatty copy. Not bad, he thought. Beatty was forthcoming with his adamant feelings about marriage, which were not exactly a secret. He was involved at the time with Michelle Phillips of the Mamas and the Papas, who had previously been involved with Dennis Hopper and Beatty's own pal Jack Nicholson. "My imminent marriage," Beatty told *People*, "has been announced to every woman I've seen steadily over the last fifteen years. I have no intention of getting married. To me, marriage essentially is a contract, and there are so many loopholes in it that Wilbur Mills and the entire Ways and Means Committee at their height couldn't figure it out."

Stolley chuckled when he got to Beatty's line, "Even the promiscuous feel pain." Beatty had been involved with a long list of women, everyone from Joan Collins to Jean Seberg, from Susannah York to Natalie Wood (who had left Robert Wagner after costarring with Beatty in his first film, *Splendor in the Grass*), from Leslie Caron (in whose divorce he was a correspondent) to one of his costars in *Shampoo*, Julie Christie. Not only had Beatty co-authored the smash movie, which looked as though it would gross more than fifty million dollars, but he had produced it and starred in it as well.

The *People* story commented that the theme of the film was "partially Beatty's own film autobiography." The hero, *People* said, "is a Beverly Hills hairdresser who insatiably beds down all of his clients." It was right after reading that enlightening description that Stolley hit what he refers to as the

"Burgheimism" that put him over the edge. When he read it he shouted so loud, you could hear him all the way down the hall. And then he burst into hysterical laughter. "The theme of *Shampoo* is, more or less," Burgheim had written, "the heartbreak of satyriasis . . ."

"It is," says Stolley to this day, "the single best phrase in the history of *People* magazine."

That did not prevent Warren Beatty from being livid about the story *People* had written about him, which involved more than just *Shampoo*. Barbara Wilkins had interviewed Beatty. While the story was being written, an episode had occurred that had nothing to do with the movie, but a lot to do with Warren Beatty, the details of which had made their way into the story, resulting in near chaos.

While she was working on the Beatty story, Wilkins had given a dinner party to which she invited a friend, who was a female photographer, and her boyfriend. During the dinner in Wilkins's Beverly Hills home, the photographer, who was working on the set of Beatty's current film, mentioned that he had been chasing her, calling her at home constantly to ask her to come over—he would not leave her alone. She had told Wilkins that he had even unzipped her pants on the set of the movie, in what Wilkins later described in print as a "playful gesture—that adolescent thing that guys used to do."

After dinner, Barbara filed the details of the photographer's story about Beatty to New York, without mentioning the woman's name. The incident found its way directly into the pages of the Beatty story: "On one of his latest films," *People* reported, "Warren kept trying to seduce the still photographer on the set. When she declined, Beatty had her fired—but only after humiliating her to tears by publicly zipping down her slacks on the set."

When the story ran, all hell broke loose. Warren Beatty called Dick Stolley personally, complaining, insisting that the story about the photographer was not true. It was absolutely false, he screamed at Stolley.

"You are saying," replied Stolley (in spite of the fact that the photographer had not known the story was going to be made public), "that one of the most distinguished photographers in the world is making this story up? That's not possible. That's simply not possible."

Beatty could not be calmed. He ranted and railed. He was furious. "He just went on," says Stolley. "He didn't even try to say that he was fooling around—that it was just a friendly gesture or something like that. I think if he had tried to put that kind of spin on it, then I would have felt a lot worse. But he didn't. He just said it didn't happen. I said, 'I believe it did happen.' It was the heartbreak of satyriasis. Burgheim had gotten it absolutely right."

Beatty was not the only one who was upset. The photographer was beside herself. She was afraid she would be blacklisted in Hollywood. Stolley and Beatty continued to fight.

"Warren and I had screaming arguments," Stolley recalls. "Kind of 'fuck you' arguments, slamming down the phone. The photographer was very upset, too. Everyone was mad at us. Beatty and I had five or six conversations. He demanded a retraction. I said, 'Warren, we can't do that. We will run your letter in the letters' column.' He said, 'That's not enough. You'll hear from my lawyers.' We never did."

Warren Beatty and Dick Stolley did not speak to each other for a long time after that. Several years later, Stolley was at a private club in L.A. when he looked up and spotted Beatty. "I was having a drink," he recalls, "and I looked over and there was Warren sitting all by himself in the corner."

Stolley thought a moment and then said to himself, "Let's do it. Let's try to create peace." He got up from his chair, walked over to the table where Beatty was sitting, and put out his hand.

"I'd like to be friends again," he said. "How about you?"

"Sit down," Beatty replied.

Stolley was pleased. "It was really nice," he says, looking back. "We sat and talked about politics."

THE YEAR OF the Beatty story—1975—was a juicy one for *People*. Among other things, Elvis turned forty; Nelson Rockefeller became vice president; *M*A*S*H* became a smash; Jackie O. became a widow for the second time; Arthur Ashe became the first black man to win at Wimbledon; Bobby Fischer lost his place as chess king to Anatoly Karpov; Liz started dating Henry Wynberg, stopped dating Henry Wynberg, and reconciled with Richard Burton; Lee Salk and Ann Landers split up with their respective spouses; Jimmy Hoffa disappeared; and Martina Navratilova defected.

Then there was Cher. She left Sonny and moved in with David Geffen (admitting in *People* that she was "scared to death"); left David Geffen and married Gregg Allman, filing for divorce after nine days (saying to *People*, "It was all a mistake"); withdrew her petition for divorce and went back to Gregg Allman to give it one more try; and made *People*'s cover three times in the process—two of which were bestsellers.

By the end of the year, Woody Allen and Betty Ford made *People*'s "most intriguing people" list, along with Cher. And Woody Allen said something to Jim Jerome during that year that would become even more intriguing twenty years later: "I'm open-minded about sex. I'm not above reproach; if anything, I'm below reproach. I mean, if I was caught in a love nest with fifteen twelve-year-old girls tomorrow, people would think, yeah, I always knew that about him." [Pause] "Nothing I could come up with would surprise anyone. I admit to it all."

That year was over, and the Bicentennial was on its way. One thing the staff had to contemplate was how to do something creatively new and different to celebrate the nation's two-hundredth birthday in the pages of *People* magazine.

TOP 5
CHER, GREGG, AND BABY
CHARLIE'S ANGELS
THE FONZ
ROSALYNN CARTER
PRINCESS CAROLINE

1976

1976 COVERS

Liza Minnelli
Lee Majors & Farrah Fawcett
Diana Ross & Bob Silberstein
Sophia Loren & Sons
Mary Tyler Moore
Chris Evert & Jack Ford
Nancy & Ronald Reagan
Michael Caine & Shakira
Marisa Berenson
Liz Taylor
Rob Reiner & Penny Marshall
Glen Campbell
The Beatles
Audrey Hepburn
Telly Savalas
Barbra Streisand
Dustin Hoffman & Robert Redford
Truman Capote
Goldie Hawn
Henry Winkler
Frank Sinatra
Paul McCartney
Jerry Brown
Raquel Welch
Rudolf Nureyev
Louise Lasser
Bicentennial: Flip Wilson, Susan Ford,
    Sonny Bono
Amy & Jimmy Carter

Lindsay Wagner
Karen & Richard Carpenter
Peter Falk
Carol Burnett
The Beach Boys
Princess Caroline
David Bowie
Paul Lynde
Phyllis George
Cher & Gregg Allman, Elijah Blue
    & Chastity
Woody Allen
Barbara Walters
The Captain & Tennille
Stevie Wonder
Lee Radziwill
Tony Randall
Rosalynn Carter
Marjorie Wallace
John Travolta
Charlie's Angels (Fawcett/Smith/Jackson)
Robert Wagner & Natalie Wood
Led Zeppelin

YEAR-END DOUBLE ISSUE:
Robert Redford, Farrah Fawcett, Jimmy Carter,
Bert Jones, Nadia Comaneci, King Kong

BOTTOM 5
NANCY REAGAN
MICHAEL CAINE
SOPHIA LOREN
MARY TYLER MOORE
MARISA BERENSON

op Films: One Flew Over the Cuckoo's Nest
All the President's Men
The Omen
The Bad News Bears
Silent Movie

scar: Rocky

op TV Shows: All in the Family
Rich Man, Poor Man
Laverne and Shirley
Maude
The Bionic Woman

mmys: The Mary Tyler Moore Show
Police Story

op Songs: "Tonight's the Night"—Rod Stewart
"Silly Love Songs"—Wings
"Play That Funky Music"—Wild Cherry
"Fifty Ways to Leave Your Lover"
—Paul Simon
"If You Leave Me Now"—Chicago
"DoYou Know Where You're Going To"
—Diana Ross

Grammys: "This Masquerade" (record)
"I Write the Songs" (song)

Bestsellers: The Choirboys—Joseph Wambaugh
Dolores —Jacqueline Susann
Trinity —Leon Uris
Ordinary People —Judith Guest
Roots —Alex Haley
Passages —Gail Sheehy

Tonys: Travesties
A Chorus Line

Marriages: Sidney Poitier + Joanna Shimkus
Natalia Makarova + Edward Karker
Frank Sinatra + Barbara Marx

Deaths: Hugh Auchincloss, Sr.   Richard Daley
Alexander Calder   Benjamin Britten
Agatha Christie   Gregor Piatigorsky
Fritz Lang   Mao Tse-tung
Sal Mineo   Dalton Trumbo
Martha Mitchell   Man Ray
Rosalind Russell   J. Paul Getty
Howard Hughes

NEWS

- Congressman Wayne Hays admits "personal relationship" with Elizabeth Ray, his mistress-secretary
- Arsonist sets fire to New York dance club, killing twenty-five
- Busload of twenty-six children in Chowchilla, California, kidnapped and buried in underground trailer—they are later rescued
- L.A.'s "Hillside Strangler" kills eleven victims
- Anthony "Tony Pro" Provenzano indicted for 1961 Teamster murder
- Skater Dorothy Hamill wins gold at Innsbruck
- Patty Hearst found guilty in bank robbery
- A Chorus Line sweeps Tony awards
- Muhammad Ali retains heavyweight title
- Barbara Walters moves to ABC to co-anchor news with Harry Reasoner in $1 million deal
- Nadia Comaneci and Bruce Jenner dominate Montreal Olympics
- "Legionnaire's" disease strikes convention-goers
- Jimmy Carter elected president

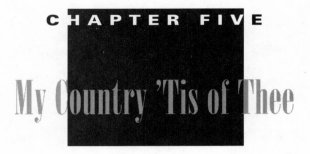

CHAPTER FIVE

My Country 'Tis of Thee

"Why don't you help me? *Help me. HELP ME!* THIS MAN IS
TAKING ME AWAY. I HAVE NO MONEY! CAN'T YOU SEE
WHAT HE'S DONE?"

—*MUHAMMAD ALI*
to onlookers about photographer Harry Benson,
during the shooting of People's Bicentennial issue, 1976

SITTING ACROSS THE long table in Chicago, staring straight into
the unhappy eyes of Muhammad Ali and those of his entire entourage,
by which Ali was flanked like a general, Harry Benson could not help
wondering how he kept getting himself into these messes. Did it have something to do with *People,* or was it just him, these days?

The silly George Washington outfit he had brought from New York—
including the white wig and the opaque stockings, the pedal-pusher-length
pants, and the funny, black, shiny-buckled shoes—were all spread out
around him on the floor.

Ali examined each piece carefully, going over the whole ensemble with
painstaking interest. Finally, he shook his head.

"Nope!" he said emphatically. "I didn't like that man. That man had
slaves. If I was living then, I would be a slave. I would only be a slave."

Well, thought Harry, Ali had a point. When *People* had the brilliant idea
to get celebrities dressed up as historical figures, why had he ever suggested
that Ali dress up as George Washington?

Then Ali turned to Harry and said, "This man had his own niggers and
he treated them bad and he never set them free!"

The Champ's entourage agreed wholeheartedly. "Right on, man, right on!" they cried in unison.

Harry listened calmly. "I'm sitting there," he recalls, "the only white guy in this room. It wasn't pleasant, let me tell you," he says. "Usually with Ali it was pleasant. This was not pleasant."

Ali repeated his concern, this time more emphatically. His voice rose gradually. "If I was living then, I would be a slave," he said.

Harry sat there and pondered the problem. Then suddenly it came to him. "Well, why don't you be a slave?" he asked. "Would you be a slave?"

He could always get someone else to be George Washington, thought Harry. Ali paused. "Yes," he said, "I would be a slave. But you'd have to get a proper slave outfit. I don't want anything stupid, like with britches. It's got to be authentic." Great, thought Harry. Perfect. After discussing it further, they agreed that Ali would be Crispus Attucks, a black man killed in the Boston Massacre who had been a slave before gaining his freedom.

This, however, created another problem. The only time Ali could pose for the photograph was the middle of the following day; he was leaving on a business trip after that. Harry Benson had to find a slave outfit in Chicago, tailored for Muhammad Ali, in less than twenty-four hours.

There were not exactly a lot of slave outfits floating around the Windy City, but one thing that Harry Benson had was unfailing ingenuity. "I went through the yellow pages," he recalls, "and I came across somebody who does theatrical outfits. I went right around to her house, and I went over my desperation of what I needed—the slave outfit—and the height of the person and the width, and what they would wear. She had books on how they dressed back then: burlap and no buttons—toggle things to tie—and she made me a slave outfit, which I picked up at seven o'clock that night."

The next morning, on the way to meet Ali for the shoot, Benson realized he was missing one thing for the desired effect—chains. Lots of them. He managed to find a store that carried metal chains, and he picked up more than he needed.

When he arrived to meet Ali, the fighter had that unhappy look again. Ali carefully examined the slave outfit. Then he slowly began to take off his clothes so that he could try it on. What he liked most about the whole thing, according to Harry, was the chains.

Ali's manager had ordered an extra-long limousine to take them to the location for the photograph. "It was like a big bus," recalls Harry, who climbed in with Ali and immediately began to feel ill at ease. "I'm way at one end and he's at the other and I've got him in chains, and he's not smiling at anything I say to him. He was getting into the character, I guess."

Ali had already known exactly where he wanted the picture to be shot, which as it turned out, increased the mounting pressure even more. As the buslike limo wove its way through the streets of Chicago, it became clear to Harry where they were headed. "It was a place on the south side of Chicago," says Harry, "right in the middle of a really bad neighborhood."

Suddenly the limo pulled to a grinding halt. They all got out. Within seconds, the driver disappeared, along with Ali's manager. "They left us," says Harry. "They left me alone me with him," he recalls, as the scene re-creates itself in his mind.

Harry stood there in the dirt on the perimeter of a park on the south side of Chicago holding the chains—with Ali attached. "I've got him in chains," he says, "and he knows a spot in the park where he wants to go."

The problem was, Ali *was* in chains, and under those circumstances he could not move very fast. "We went step by step by step by step," says Harry, envisioning their slogging movement as he trudged through the park with Muhammad Ali shuffling beside him in chains.

After they had gone about three hundred yards, they rounded the bend and found themselves in a little hollow. There was a sizable group there to greet them. "There must have been about twenty black people, drinking out of bottles, with stockings on their heads," says Harry.

This scene did not surprise Ali, however. He had known exactly what was around the bend. He looked at the crowd facing him and exclaimed, gesturing wildly, as Harry—gripping his chains—stood next to him, "Look at you, you niggers, you do nothing! This man's taken my money, taken my children, taken everything from me, and you niggers, all you do is drink!"

Harry was in an awkward situation. "I'm holding him in chains," he says. "Now they're all looking at me and looking at him, and wondering, *What in the hell?*"

For a few silent moments the crowd looked back and forth at the man they recognized as Muhammad Ali and the white man who was holding him in chains. Harry was mortified. "There is only one person in the world who these people respect," says Harry dismally, "and I am holding him in chains."

Things did not improve. Ali started screaming, his voice rising steadily. "Why don't you help me?" he cried. "*Help me. HELP ME!* THIS MAN IS TAKING ME AWAY. I HAVE NO MONEY! CAN'T YOU SEE WHAT HE'S DONE?"

"Please, for Christ's sake, stop!" Harry said to Ali. He still could not believe what was happening.

"He's all in this shit outfit and he's all poor looking," he recalls, "and they're all aghast—they're aghast. And he's yelling, 'Stop! Stop this white man. This white man is taking this nigger away!' It was awful."

He pleaded with Ali. "I didn't know whether to run or what," Harry says.

Finally, Ali stopped and smiled. "It's only for a photograph, it's only a joke," he told the bestockinged crowd, as they began dancing jubilantly around him.

At last, Harry photographed Ali. He got the pictures he wanted, but they had not come without a cost. "For a few moments it really wasn't funny," says Harry, shaking his head. "It really was not."

Once Harry had gotten Muhammad Ali in chains, everything became a lot easier for the Bicentennial issue. It was usually that way in the celebrity business. If you got *one* heavyweight—and Muhammad Ali certainly was that—it became much easier to get the rest. Having been a member of the *People* staff for over two years by the time the Bicentennial issue was being assembled, I had learned that lesson myself.

When Dick Stolley had put his fledgling staff together in the winter of 1974, he had hired mostly young people with little experience for a variety of reasons. He had wanted people with open minds, with few preconceptions about what the magazine should be—something he would not have gotten if he hired only his former colleagues from *Life*. He also knew that it was going to be hard, and he had figured that young people had more stamina.

I had been one of those he chose—I had filled the bill: little experience, a lot of stamina. Having just arrived in New York from L.A., where I had worked briefly for *The Washington Post*, I had few preconceptions about what *People* should be and had been delighted to have the chance to find out. As open-minded as I might have been, however, never would I have imagined that it would one day fall to me to convince one of the country's most respected newsmen, and one of my personal favorites, to dress up in a wig and tights.

After Harry Benson survived the Crispus Attucks shoot, it had somehow fallen to me to ask John Chancellor, the anchor of *NBC Nightly News*, if he might be willing to participate in our historical tribute to the Bicentennial. I asked him if there was some historical figure he might like to be. Yes, he said: the father of our Constitution, Thomas Jefferson.

Of course, I told him. I proceeded to obtain a Jefferson costume and arranged to pick up Chancellor at his house on the Upper East Side of Manhattan for the ride to the historically authentic Jumel Mansion in Harlem, where Mary Dunn had arranged for us to shoot the picture.

There was, unfortunately, one major hitch. The day of the shoot turned out to be one of the hottest days of the year—a stifling, steaming hot day in New York. It was apparent to me, as I looked at the Jefferson outfit I had picked up, that it was not geared for this kind of weather: thick tights; short, heavy wool pants to the knee; a ruffled blouse; and patent-leather shoes with gold buckles.

I was inspired by Harry Benson's ingenuity. My biggest fear was that the Jumel Mansion had not one iota of air-conditioning, so for the trip up the East River Drive, I rented an air-conditioned limousine. Then I bought a silver ice bucket at Tiffany's and filled it with ice and a bottle of the best champagne I could find.

Chancellor alit from his house with a smile, which got even wider when he saw my ice bucket. We sipped the champagne on the ride to the Jumel Mansion. As it turned out, I had nothing to worry about, although I had been right about the air-conditioning at the Jumel Mansion—it was nonexistent. But John Chancellor was, after all, a *newsman*—he had obviously faced more trying times than these in his twenty-nine-year career. He actually seemed to be enjoying himself!

Content, perhaps more from the champagne than from the prospect of dressing up as Thomas Jefferson on one of the hottest days of the year, he cheerfully wriggled into his tights in the dripping heat, looking, except for his glasses, astonishingly like Thomas Jefferson. The remarkably patient newsman sat there for hours, sweating only moderately, as he wadded up copy after copy of the Bill of Rights to create the right mood for the Jefferson picture. Thanks to John Chancellor, it came out fine.

People magazine was still in dire need of a George Washington, however. Harry Benson had shot football great Joe Namath a number of times in the past, and it occurred to him that he might just be able to convince Namath to do it. He would have to be delicate, though. "Most people would have loved to do it, fussed to do it," says Harry. "Having people like Chancellor and Ali helped." But he could not tell Joe Namath that Muhammed Ali had already been asked to be George Washington and turned it down.

At the time, Namath was in Tuscaloosa, Alabama, where he owned a bar called Broadway Joe's. To get him to do what he wanted, Harry's tactic was to convince Joe Namath of the underlying merits of being George Washington for *People:* It would be the number-one spread (it would open the sequence); Washington was the number-one president of our country, Namath was the number-one football player.

Harry flew down to Tuscaloosa to work his magic, carrying the Washington suit with him again. It was the middle of June 1976, the peak of Joe Namath's football career. Namath's knees had begun to give him trouble by then. The challenge facing Harry this time was not going to be easy. He had to be patient. "He was surrounded by all these guys," recalls Harry. "All these redneck guys from his University of Alabama days. They were all kind of suspicious of it, to say the least. It took me three days to get the George Washington suit on him."

As always, Harry was persistent. "One day he would say he would do it at two o'clock, and you'd go to his place and he was drinking with his friends or eating a big cake," says Harry. He finally managed, however, to get Namath into the George Washington outfit—silly hat, white wig, and all.

Finally, with his long, white curls, his knee-length pants, and his jacket with epaulets, Namath turned to Harry and said, "You go into Broadway Joe's like this tonight, and you're in trouble!"

Harry proceeded to get his pictures. "I did one with Namath trying to throw the ball across [what was meant to be] the Potomac," recalls Harry. "But that didn't work."

He ended up shooting Namath standing shakily in a wooden boat floating in the river. "I never could figure out why he stood up in the boat," Namath said of Washington as Harry shot away. "It's not easy, you know." He was happy with the headline for his picture as George Washington, which opened the spread, as promised: "Washington Is a Stand-Up Guy."

Similar scenes occurred throughout the country as *People* reporters and photographers put the Bicentennial issue together. We managed to get Diane Von Furstenberg to dress up as Betsy Ross; the columnist Art Buchwald peered around a tree for us, clutching a sword in his hand and a cigar in his mouth, portraying Benedict Arnold. Attorney F. Lee Bailey donned a white wig—among other things—and dressed up as his alter ego of two hundred years past, John Adams.

We even got the eighty-one-year-old conductor of the Boston Pops, Arthur Fiedler, to ride a horse in the shadows of Boston's Old North Church, imitating Paul Revere. Comedian Flip Wilson happily bounded along the California landscape for us in historical garb, flying a kite à la Benjamin Franklin; and Sonny Bono, regretting—along with Nathan Hale—that he had only one life to lose for his country (or, in his case, only one photograph to take for *People*), posed with a noose around his neck.

When the Bicentennial issue was done, the cover featured Flip Wilson with his kite, Sonny Bono with his noose, and a white-wigged Susan Ford, who had been talked into dressing as Martha Washington.

The cover line read:

CELEBS OF '76
Thirteen famous citizens dress up
as Bicentennial Bigwigs

People was alive and well for America's two-hundredth birthday.

CHAPTER SIX

Answered Prayers

"I could write a book about my book which would be amusing.
People call and ask me, 'Truman, am I in your book?' 'Not yet,' I
say, 'but we're saving space for you—like we say at Forest Lawn.
We'll fit you all in, coffins to measure.' Ho, ho, ho."

—*TRUMAN CAPOTE*
in People, *May 10, 1976*

AT ABOUT THE time that the boat containing Joe Namath and his
weak knees was on the verge of capsizing in Tuscaloosa, Truman
Capote entered the lobby of the Holiday Inn in Lexington, Virginia,
with Patricia Burstein, a *People* reporter. He was in Virginia for a speaking
engagement at Washington and Lee University and Burstein had accompanied the author after he agreed to an interview with her for the magazine.

It was only days after excerpts from his unfinished book, *Answered
Prayers,* had been published in *Esquire* magazine. Capote had already been
publicly vilified for the biting revelations in the work about the personalities
who populated the fast lanes of the high society in which he himself traveled,
some of whom, until then, had considered themselves his friends. "The Tiny
Terror," as he was often called, was already suffering deeply from the backlash.

The Holiday Inn in Virginia proved to be a respite of sorts. It was one of
the few times that the elflike Capote—a fixture on the talk-show circuit and
recognizable even to those who had never read a word he had written,
bedecked in his trademark tinted glasses and Panama hat—managed to
remain anonymous.

"I like Holiday Inns," he informed Burstein when he entered the lobby with her. "They're fundamentally, deeply mediocre," he explained. "You get a bed, an air conditioner, bad service and anonymity. Everybody who works for them is sooo dumb . . . I mean, they wouldn't recognize Chiang Kai-shek if he walked in the door."

Within moments, as if on cue, the motel clerk looked up at him and asked, "Mr. Capote, what firm are you with?"

Patricia Burstein was a tough and aggressive yet highly sensitive reporter, with excellent connections that often provided her with exclusive access to stories. She had gotten to Capote through an acquaintance of hers, one of Capote's café-society friends, Betty Spiegel, the widow of the late film producer Sam Spiegel. When Spiegel first put her in touch with Capote, she gave her some valuable advice, which Burstein heeded: "Betty warned me at the outset *never* to tell Truman anything I didn't want the whole world to know," she recalls. "Despite the fact he was known as 'Tru,' almost nothing he ever said was."

Her first story about him would turn out to be the beginning of a long relationship between the two. In the course of reporting it, Burstein spent a lot of time with the enigmatic author. She had always loved his work and was intrigued by him. She wanted the piece for *People* to capture the essence of the man and the author—not just to dwell on the erupting brouhaha caused by the publication of the long-awaited *Answered Prayers*. She was a thoughtful, solid reporter, and she had already worked things out with Dick Stolley, who had agreed that, instead of focusing only on Capote's wicked tongue and the apparently violent reaction it was causing once again, the body of the *People* article would deal mainly with his life and his writing. Of course, the newsy "peg" for the story could not be ignored, so Burstein had suggested that they run a separate sidebar to deal with that aspect of the story, which *People* did. When the piece on Capote appeared, next to the article was a page filled with small head shots of each celebrity in question, along with examples of what *People* dubbed Truman Capote's "celebrity skewering":

> **Liz Taylor:** "She has an extraordinary inferiority complex, and it's difficult to get through."
> **Princess Margaret:** "She's a very high-strung girl who wants to be royalty on one hand and on the other a hippie."
> **Sammy Davis, Jr:** "When I saw him kissing Nixon, I thought he was the new Checkers."
> **Candice Bergen:** "She's a really pretty girl with appalling taste in men. There's something spinsterish about her."
> **Nelson Rockefeller:** "He's like a good brand of cereal—nothing is wrong, but nothing is particularly appetizing."

Bob Dylan: "That big phony—he's as urbanized as a graduate of Bronx High."

Capote had been pleased with Burstein's piece. The day it came out he called her repeatedly at work until he finally reached her with a "collect" call from a pay phone on the street. He was genuinely grateful for what she had done. "Thank you," he had said to her, "for being kind."

In the aftermath of the *Esquire* publication, Capote continued his spiraling descent into drugs and alcohol. He finally checked into the Smithers Institute in New York City—a substance-abuse rehabilitation center—in a desperate attempt to pull himself back up. That in itself would have been a compelling story for *People*, but Burstein had carefully refrained from bothering Capote when she realized what bad shape he was in. They had gotten to know each other pretty well over the last few months. "At heart, he was really a dutiful little schoolboy who had outbursts of naughtiness—pendulum swings between the two behaviors," she says. "He had to hit rock bottom or near there in order to quit the self-destructiveness."

Ironically, Burstein had spoken with Capote to ask him for another interview the night before he had checked into Smithers. "He was so devastated that he could barely speak," she recalls. "I called him for an interview and he started weeping, saying how everyone was making a fool of him."

She could not bring herself to pressure him, in spite of the fact that she knew such tactics would probably get her the story, given his vulnerability. Instead, she went out and bought him a stuffed animal, a teddy bear, which she dropped off at his apartment building a few hours later.

When Capote got out of Smithers, he did not forget how kind Burstein had been. He rewarded her for leaving him alone. She had heard that, in his new, healthier incarnation, as part of his self-improvement regime he was going to the gym daily to work out on the Nautilus machines. She thought that would make a nice story and Capote agreed. "When I called him to play the part of Jack LaLanne for the magazine," she says, "and in the process give me and my photographer sister, Jessica, an exclusive story, he said, 'Certainly, my dear.'"

Burstein was aware of the fact that he was still very fragile, so she and her sister planned the story delicately. They arranged to meet for lunch at La Petite Marmite, an elegant Manhattan restaurant, before going over to the gym where Patricia's sister would take the pictures for the story.

They all arrived at the restaurant on time, happy to see each other. Truman appeared a bit fragile, for Truman, but Patricia thought he looked okay under the circumstances. The waiter came over to take their order shortly after they were seated at their table. Without batting an eyelash,

Capote ordered two vodkas with orange juice. He had either fallen off the wagon already or he had never really been on it.

"When I inquired about this," says Burstein, "he did a pirouette with his fingers, as if waving away the question. So I dropped this line of questioning and decided to focus instead on getting through the lunch with minimal damage to his liver in order for him to arrive at the gym in as sober a state as possible."

They made it through lunch, Patricia paid the bill, and they finally headed for the gym. When they arrived there, however, Capote encountered some serious problems with the exercise equipment—namely, he could not stay on it. "He might as well have been drunk," says Burstein, "the way he was falling off the exercise equipment, even the rowing machine. Maybe," she kindly surmises, "it was because he was wearing moccasins and a terry-cloth robe."

This did not make it easy for Patricia's sister to carry out her assignment. Patricia subtly suggested that perhaps a sweat suit and some sneakers might help. The owners of the gym, happily responding to the possibility of publicity in *People*, quickly provided the necessary clothes (which were clearly marked with the name of the gym). With the help of the footwear's rubber soles, the sisters were finally able to get the pictures they needed and enough material for the accompanying captions.

Afterward, while Truman went to the locker room to change, Patricia asked one of the instructors how the author was doing with his exercise program. "Oh," the instructor replied, "he's here every day—for a massage."

She refrained from writing the details of Capote's fictitious exercise regime, which she had inadvertently uncovered. "In retrospect, maybe I should have written that story," she says. "But Truman was still so distraught and possibly suicidal. Weeks before, he had collapsed on stage at a college auditorium while on a speaking tour. After that, while appearing on Stanley Siegel's show, he embarrassed everyone by being totally incoherent. I figured I'd give him a break. After all, he *did* go to a gym."

1977

1977 COVERS

Barbra Streisand & Kris Kristofferson
Ringo Starr
Claudine Longet
Jessica Lange
George C. Scott & Trish Van Devere
Elizabeth Taylor & John Warner
Rod Stewart & Britt Ekland
Ralph Nader
Bjorn Borg & Mariana Simione
Julie Andrews
David Carradine
Faye Dunaway
Dolly Parton
Bruce Jenner & Chrystie
Jacqueline Onassis
Sally Field
Bianca Jagger
Alex Haley
Jane Fonda
David Frost
Cindy Williams
Fleetwood Mac
John Travolta
Halston, Liz, Liza
Peter Frampton
Linda Blair

Farrah Fawcett & Lee Majors
Star Wars—C-3PO
Tom & Nancy Seaver
Jacqueline Bisset
Barry Manilow
David Doyle, Jaclyn Smith, Cheryl Ladd,
    Kate Jackson
Sissy Spacek
Marty Feldman & Ann-Margret
Dan Rather
Susan Saint James
Robert Blake
Cheryl Ladd
Tony Orlando
Remembering Elvis
O. J. Simpson
Linda Ronstadt
Donny & Marie Osmond
Suzanne Somers, Joyce DeWitt, John Ritter
Michelle Phillips
Mick Jagger & Keith Richards
Al Pacino & Marthe Keller
Gilda Radner
Crosby, Stills & Nash
Marlo Thomas

YEAR-END DOUBLE ISSUE:
Shaun Cassidy, Diane Keaton, Jacqueline
Onassis, Anwar Sadat, Reggie Jackson,
Princess Caroline & Philippe Junot, R2D2

Top Films: *Star Wars*

Rocky
Smokey and the Bandit
A Star Is Born
King Kong

Oscar: *Annie Hall*

Top TV Shows: *Happy Days*

Laverne and Shirley
ABC Monday Night Movie
*M*A*S*H*
Charlie's Angels

Emmys: *The Mary Tyler Moore Show*
Upstairs, Downstairs

Top Songs: "You Light Up My Life"—Debby Boone
"Best of My Love"—Emotions
"How Deep Is Your Love"—Bee Gees
"Don't Leave Me This Way"
   —Thelma Houston
"Torn Between Two Lovers"
   —Mary MacGregor
"Hotel California"—Eagles

Grammys: "Hotel California" (record)
"Evergreen" (song)

Bestsellers: *The Thorn Birds*

   —Colleen McCullough
Beggarman, Thief—Irwin Shaw
All Things Wise and Wonderful
   —James Herriot
Falconer—John Cheever
Your Erroneous Zones—Wayne Dyer

Tonys: *The Shadow Box*

Annie

Marriages: William Friedkin + Jeanne Moreau

Deaths: Charlie Chaplin | Bing Crosby
Howard Hawks | Zero Mostel
Freddie Prinze | Maria Callas
Guy Lombardo | Peter Finch
Ethel Waters | Andy Devine
Joan Crawford | Elvis
Groucho Marx | Anaïs Nin
Roberto Rossellini
Natalie "Dolly" Sinatra

NEWS

- Roman Polanski in sex scandal with thirteen-year-old girl
- *Hustler* editor Larry Flynt sentenced for engaging in organized crime
- Gary Gilmore executed in Utah
- *Roots* draws eighty million viewers
- Queen Elizabeth celebrates Silver Jubilee
- Son of Sam caught after killing six people
- Jackie Onassis negotiates $20 million settlement with Onassis estate

CHAPTER SEVEN

Maggie and the Rolling Stones

"I pray that people will not judge Pierre by my wanting to be a woman, but I am a free spirit that must survive in a free world. I am not a weirdo, a wacko or an eccentric for wanting to do good, honest work on a day-to-day basis. I just want to find my individuality. I've had enough of being public property."

—MARGARET TRUDEAU
to Robin Leach in People, March 28, 1977

TRUMAN CAPOTE WAS not the only one with problems. By 1977, as her sixth wedding anniversary approached, Margaret Trudeau had plenty of problems of her own. For one thing, she was tired—tired of being the prime minister's wife, tired of trying to be someone she was not. She was, after all, a child of the sixties. She liked wearing miniskirts and skin-tight jeans. She missed being able to say what she felt.

From the moment she had first run into him at Club Med when she was only twenty, she had liked Pierre Trudeau, but that was all. For him, it had been love at first sight, but Margaret, who was a student at Simon Fraser University near Vancouver, had gone home and gone back to school. It was not until she took a job as a social worker in Ottawa two years later that they began dating secretly. After a year they were married. In spite of their twenty-nine-year age difference, she had fallen in love with him, with his flashy mod clothes and his playboy image, even if he was the Canadian prime minister.

She had never been fond of politics. As the daughter of James Sinclair, a member of Parliament and fisheries minister, she had been exposed to as much as she ever wanted to know about the exigencies of the field. But she tried to be a dutiful wife to her politician husband. While she was still nursing their second son, only three years after their marriage, she had taken to the road to campaign for her husband when it looked as if he was in trouble.

That was in 1974. He had won and she had lost. Within months, Margaret Trudeau had checked into a hospital for psychiatric help. The life of a political wife had taken its toll, as it had done with Betty Ford and Joan Kennedy. "I felt used, exploited, trapped," Margaret said later. "The label 'wife of the prime minister' is like a giant signboard pointing at my head from a Monty Python sketch. But I am not Mrs. Prime Minister. I'm a human being."

Margaret adored her children, but she knew that if she were going to survive, she had to have a life of her own. Ever since King Hussein of Jordan had given her the cameras she had come to treasure, she had taken pictures that even Pierre had admitted were "fantastic." She wanted to try her hand at something that was hers. Photography became her passion.

She made up her mind to leave. Anniversaries meant nothing to her. The fact that she chose to depart on March 5, six years to the day after they had been married, really had no significance to her at all.

Her departure would soon acquire a great deal of significance: She spent most of her first week of freedom with the Rolling Stones band on her way to New York. Suddenly she found that she was deeply embroiled in a scandal she herself had created.

It began the first night she left home, which she spent in a Toronto hotel after being Mick Jagger's guest at a Rolling Stones concert. It was Dick Stolley's impression that Trudeau was traveling with the band by the time she got to Manhattan.

Trudeau was extremely upset when she heard the rampant rumors that she was sleeping with all the Rolling Stones and vehemently denied the gossip. She tried to explain she had wanted only to take pictures of Jagger, that her interest in him was purely photographic. Bombarded by the press, she fled to the Manhattan apartment of a friend, Princess Yasmin Khan.

It was at that point that a photographer who had done some work for *People*, a man by the name of Oscar Abolafia who had occasionally partnered on stories with an aggressive tabloid reporter called Robin Leach, was contacted by a British newspaper and told the news: Margaret Trudeau, the young, beautiful wife of the Canadian prime minister, was in New York. It was rumored that she had arrived at the Plaza Hotel in the company of the Rolling Stones band. Would Oscar go over and try to get some pictures for them?

Oscar Abolafia knew a good story when he glommed on to one, and he set out directly for the Plaza Hotel, where he quickly learned that although Mick Jagger was there, Margaret Trudeau was not. Since he was already in the neighborhood, Abolafia decided to take advantage of the fact that the City Center Ballet was nearby. As it happened, Mikhail Baryshnikov was dancing that night.

It was there that Oscar Abolafia spotted a friend, the Princess Yasmin Khan. Sitting next to her was none other than the stunning first lady of Canada, Margaret Trudeau. He made his way over to them and said hello. His mind churned through the first half of the ballet. By the time intermission came, word of Trudeau's presence had spread, and the throng of photographers who had gotten wind of her presence quickly swelled.

Abolafia did not need a crystal ball to see what was coming. Instead of waiting through the second half of the ballet, he made his way up to Baryshnikov's dressing room, gambling that Yasmin Khan and Trudeau would wind up there themselves when the ballet was over.

His hunch paid off. He was able to shoot a few pictures and chat with Trudeau as the other photographers pressing to get near the hottest developing story in town were locked out of the dressing room. In the short visit that Abolafia had with Trudeau, he learned two crucial things: Margaret Trudeau loved photography, and she was staying at the apartment of Yasmin Khan.

Abolafia's confidence began to build, and he called Mary Dunn at *People*. He was quite sure, he told Mary, that he could get an exclusive interview with Margaret Trudeau. He would like to bring a writer onto the story, and the writer he had in mind was his sometime partner, Robin Leach.

Dunn, too, knew the story was a big one. "Do whatever you have to," she told Oscar, who immediately put in a call to Robin. Then Dunn called Dick Stolley and told him the news.

Leach appeared at the princess's place almost instantly. It was quite apparent to him that the minidrama vérité unraveling before his eyes was one of the biggest celebrity stories of all time—as he later described it, "akin to an abdication." He was not about to let it slip from his grasp.

Like Abolafia, Leach was well acquainted with the princess. Once he knew that Margaret Trudeau was with Yasmin Khan, his path was cleared. "There was an advantage for me," he recalls, "and that is that I knew Margaret was with Yasmin and Yasmin was an old friend of mine, socially, in New York. She's a quiet lady, more than a jet-setter, but our paths had crossed a number of times."

With Abolafia, Leach carefully began to calculate a plan. If they played their cards right, they could get to Yasmin. "I knew that at some point, with Margaret hidden in the house, Yas would have to leave," he recalls. "So Yas literally became the key to Margaret. For me to get access, I had to get to Yas." And that is exactly what Robin Leach managed to do.

Leach and Abolafia patiently parked themselves outside of the princess's elegant apartment building across from Central Park and waited—along with hundreds of other members of the world's press who were camped there in twelve-hour shifts. Leach became the point man for his team. He knew that eventually the princess would have to leave her apartment and he was right. Just as he predicted, she eventually sallied forth. Leach and Abolafia were awaiting Yasmin Khan when she decided to go shopping.

The minute Robin saw the princess emerge from her apartment, he grabbed her and hustled her down a side street and into a small grocery store, where he delivered to her his well-prepared, heart-to-heart talk. "Yas," he told her with concern in his voice, "you're gonna have—and Margaret is gonna have—this nightmare for a long, long time to come." He moved closer to emphasize his point. "In the end she's going to have to speak to somebody," he said, "and in the end she might as well speak to somebody who is sort of a sympathetic ear. At least we'll get it out and get it over with, and whatever she needs we'll accommodate her."

The princess listened carefully to what Robin Leach said. The real need, he reiterated, was to get Margaret Trudeau back to Canada without talking—to anyone but him.

That night, Leach returned to Yasmin Khan's apartment with Abolafia, where they rejoined the crowd of reporters desperately clamoring for the Trudeau story. Leach pulled a note from his pocket and effectively "convinced" the doorman to deliver it to Trudeau. "I will get you out of here and back to your husband safely," it said, "and you will give me an exclusive story." Leach was offering to be Trudeau's bodyguard—to help her defend herself against the army of press flanking her mercilessly on all sides—and shepherd her back home.

Then he stood among the crowd and waited. When the doorman finally reappeared, he motioned Leach and Abolafia to come with him. "He said, 'Please come upstairs,' " Abolafia recalls, "and everybody's faces dropped to the ground as we went." That evening they spent several hours interviewing and photographing the captivating Trudeau.

Trudeau talked openly and showed them some photographs that she herself had done. By the time they were finished, another idea occurred to Abolafia. "Listen, Margaret," he said to her, "why don't we do this? Why don't I get in touch with *People* and why don't we work out something where you can do some shooting?"

He proceeded to call Mary Dunn with the idea. "We're going to try to get her out of the apartment and bring her down to Greenwich Village for her to do some photographs," he told Dunn. "Let's do a combination shoot. I will take some pictures of her doing some things, and she will do some pictures."

Dunn liked the idea. *People* was happy to oblige, and Trudeau was given a couple of assignments to take photographs for the magazine. "We gave her an assignment to go out around New York and take pictures," recalls Mary Dunn. "Washington Square Park. Just people. Things that you see in the most amateur photographs."

As it turned out, getting Margaret Trudeau out to complete her *People* assignment was not easy. When Leach and Abolafia returned to get her the next day, they could barely get through the crowd of press themselves. That is when they devised their plan: Leach, who had a flair for the dramatic, arranged to have not one, but five chauffeur-driven limousines lining the street in front of Yasmin Khan's apartment. The minute the limousines arrived, an endless string of cabs filled with reporters lined up behind them. When Abolafia got in the first one and it pulled away, the line of taxis followed him—right back to his own apartment—while Trudeau and Leach snuck out the service entrance on the side street.

"With all the limos lining the street, nobody watched the cleaning lady leave the side door," Leach explains. The cleaning lady happened to be Margaret Trudeau, who walked undisturbed from Yasmin Khan's apartment to Robin Leach's car, two blocks away. "By that time nobody nabbed her," he says. "They all followed the fake limos." Leach and Abolafia had arranged to meet in Greenwich Village, where Trudeau would take her photographs. They did.

When her assignment was completed, Robin Leach squired his charge up to the twenty-ninth floor of the Time & Life Building, directly into the offices of *People* magazine. Dick Stolley remembers the day well. "He brought her up," he says. "She was very shy, really beautiful. Everybody just kind of went nuts around her. I remember sitting down and talking with her for a while."

Trudeau seemed young, vulnerable, and fragile. "She was not at all defiant that she had left," says Stolley. "She was very anxious that her husband not be politically hurt by this. She was so naïve . . . 'Thanks a lot, Maggie.' I mean, she went on the road with the Rolling Stones. 'Come on, Maggie, you don't think there's going to be any political fallout?' "

Stolley himself had been a great admirer of Pierre Trudeau. He was under the impression that Margaret had left Pierre several times before— after all, Harry Benson had been told by the woman at the fancy club in Palm Beach that they had patched up their marriage there once at the cabaña at the beach. And Margaret Trudeau's problems had been well documented—in *People,* among other places.

Mary Dunn remembers the pictures Trudeau took in Greenwich Village as "just terrible." Dick Stolley remembers them as "not bad." That did not deter the wife of the Canadian prime minister from her new goal to pursue a career in photography. But she still had to return to Canada, and Robin Leach had promised to help her. The plan to get the wife of the Canadian prime minister back to the Canadian White House was set in motion.

Since ravenous reporters remained everywhere, Leach had to find a way to avoid them. He contacted Air Canada, the airline that would fly Trudeau to Ottawa, and explained who their passenger was. The airline agreed to allow Trudeau to board the plane directly from the tarmac instead of stopping to check in at the terminal, and Leach and Abolafia, along with Yoke (Abolafia's wife), accompanied Trudeau on her journey home.

Everything proceeded smoothly after the plane took off for Toronto with one exception: Reporters from the *National Enquirer* had managed to get on the plane with them. They were not in first class with the foursome—they were in the back, but that did not stop them from going after Margaret. "They did try to talk to her," Leach recalls, "but she didn't say anything." It was enough to make Leach nervous, however, and he was anxious to get rid of them. The fact that they were airborne did not stop him. "The only way to avoid the nightmare and to save us being trapped with the *Enquirer* on board was to get the pilot to stop in mid-runway in Toronto," he explains, "and transfer her to the connection to Ottawa in the middle of the runway." Once again, they boarded their flight from the tarmac.

With Margaret Trudeau now free of the *Enquirer* reporters, as they neared Ottawa, their final destination, Robin Leach was not about to let up. When the plane was ready to land in Ottawa, the home of the prime minister, he made another phone call. "We called the Canadian White House to say she was on the plane," he says, "and we had the plane stop in the middle of the runway in Ottawa. 'Canada One,' which was Prime Minister Trudeau's car, came onto the runway to get her. She looked at me and said, 'You'll come with me.' "

Margaret Trudeau was understandably apprehensive about seeing her husband again. "She was very concerned about the reception she was going to get upon returning home," says Leach. As it turned out she had reason to be. When they arrived at the Canadian White House, Margaret Trudeau went upstairs to her bedroom and invited Robin Leach and the Abolafias to wait for her downstairs. They were there when Margaret descended to face Pierre Trudeau for the first time since her return.

The prime minister was predictably unhappy with his wife. "To say that he went ballistic would be an understatement," says Leach. "He ripped right into her. A bottle of Scotch and a letter opener went flying between them, and then there was huge screaming, and then it was, 'Well, I'm leaving,' and off she stomped."

Shortly thereafter, Margaret Trudeau left the Canadian White House once again, accompanied by Robin Leach and the Abolafias. The next day, according to Oscar, the Canadian newspapers reported that Canada's mounted police had gone to New York to bring Margaret Trudeau back to Ottawa at the request of the prime minister, and that she had arrived escorted by two plainclothes policemen (Oscar Abolafia and Robin Leach) and a big, blond nurse (Oscar's wife, Yoke).

When Margaret Trudeau arrived back in the United States, Robin Leach continued to serve as Trudeau's "bodyguard." The market for Trudeau stories had by no means been exhausted. "We brought her back to my home in Connecticut," says Leach. "She stayed there for a week. By all accounts she had vanished. The truth was that she had not really vanished, but nobody knew where to look for her." During that week, Robin Leach spent many more hours interviewing Margaret Trudeau. "She poured her soul out to a tape recorder," he says. "She was literally without accommodation away from Canada, and she decided she wanted to start a new life in New York." What did she do? What *could* she do? She could take photographs.

"I know it will blow minds," Margaret Trudeau told Robin Leach that week, "but I plan on finding an apartment in New York. I'll commute to Ottawa, so I can still be Pierre Trudeau's wife and the mother of our three children—but I also want to be a working photographer."

Not long after the story about Margaret Trudeau ran in *People*, accompanied by several of her photographs, the Trudeaus officially decided to separate.

Pierre and Margaret Trudeau were divorced seven years later, in 1984. Margaret gave up her career in photography after a short time to pursue a career in acting. She got married again one week after her divorce was final.

"It was a time in her life, not unlike what has happened to Princess Diana today," observes Robin Leach. "She became a prisoner of the Canadian White House, and a rebellion took place in terms of her wanting to strike out on her own and be her own woman and find herself. I think the photography helped her do that to the point where she was capable of earning dollars for herself. She got whatever that was out of her system and went back to life as Mrs. Anonymous. But she has her place in history, and with history you can never be anonymous. She'll always be Margaret Trudeau."

CHAPTER EIGHT

Elvis: Gone but Not Forgotten

"He was dead for three hours before anybody found him. People should have been checking on him. Where was everybody when he needed them?"

—*LINDA THOMPSON*
in People, *September 5, 1977*

IN THE SPRING of 1977, around the time that Margaret Trudeau was off on assignment for *People*, Dick Burgheim called me into his office and told me that he had an assignment for me. It was to be a guarded secret: Tony Orlando, the popular singer who performed with the backup group Dawn, wanted to talk to *People* about his nervous breakdown.

For some reason, Burgheim thought I would be the right one to report the story of Tony and his wife, Elaine. It would prove to be a another perfect example of Stolley's theory about the X factor.

Tony Orlando had started his career as a talented young man who sang composers' demonstration recordings because he was too fat to appear in public. He gradually made his way into music publishing and was working for CBS Records when the chance came in 1970 for him to record a song called "Candida" with two Motown backup singers, Telma Hopkins and Joyce Wilson. That had been the beginning of Tony Orlando and Dawn. Tony managed to drop nearly one hundred pounds, and his career took off. Soon the group, with their hit songs "Knock Three Times" and "Tie a Yellow Ribbon," were on the top of the charts. By 1974 they even had a hit prime-time television show.

But Orlando's career took the twists and turns and experienced the highs and lows so familiar in the entertainment business. After a meteoric rise, the popularity of the group diminished, the CBS television show was canceled, the pressures in his life increased, and he turned to cocaine to boost his flagging energy.

The 1975 death of his sister Rhonda, who was retarded, added to the singer's angst. And then two years later, his good friend Freddie Prinze, who looked uncannily like Orlando, shot himself in the head. Orlando had cradled Prinze in his arms as he died at the UCLA Medical Center. It was more than he could take. Tony Orlando had a nervous breakdown.

His publicist, a kind and gentle man named Frank H. Lieberman, thought that going public with the story would be good for Tony both personally and professionally. Ironically, the publicity in *People* about his nervous breakdown—a perfect example of what Dick Stolley referred to as the crucial X factor—would recharge public interest in him; not only would the story become the best-selling cover of the year for *People*, it would remain one of the most successful in the twenty-year history of the magazine.

The success of the Tony Orlando issue taught *People* another valuable lesson: The public was powerfully attracted to the combination of celebrity and tragedy. Maybe the reason was that the tragic provided a common denominator for everyone—celebrity as well as pauper—or maybe it was simply prurient interest on the part of *People*'s readers. Whatever the cause for their popularity, such revelations of disaster by the famous would continue to be among the most successful and widely read stories in the magazine in the years to come.

Tony, Elaine, and I started meeting on a regular basis. He was kind and obviously still very fragile, still deeply enmeshed in the process of recovering from what he had been through. She was supportive, loving, and attentive. Through hours of heart-wrenching conversations, we grew to like each other genuinely, and we established a close and trusting relationship. They were surprisingly candid about the intimate details of their lives—another call that Stolley had made correctly: the curious willingness of people to talk about profoundly personal things.

The Orlandos talked of the problems that had surfaced in their marriage. Tony admitted that he had been unfaithful to his wife. He had announced that fact publicly to a stunned audience as he had teetered on the brink of his nervous breakdown at a performance onstage in Cohasset, Massachusetts: "Now my wife will be able to trust me again," he had said, after breaking into tears. Then he had announced to the unsuspecting crowd that he was quitting show business.

Orlando had taken time after that to sort through the onslaught of overpowering emotions he felt were crushing him, and now Tony and Elaine Orlando were talking openly about events like Prinze's suicide. "Freddie would come over early in the morning while Tony was still in bed," Elaine said to me, "and Tony would stroke his hair. It was definitely a big-brother thing, and one day in our own backyard, he told Tony he might kill himself. Tony said that was no way to approach life, but Freddie saw it as a way of becoming immortal—you know, getting your face on the front page of every newspaper. He planned it."

Tony was clearly struggling with the guilt that he was feeling: "As much as I loved Freddie and hated what he did," he said, "there wasn't anything I or anybody else could do about it."

What soon became apparent from the relationship that was established among Lieberman, the Orlandos, and myself was the unanticipated professional value of such bonds. Although my story on Tony did not run until October, the secure trust among us had already been established when Elvis Presley died on August 16, 1977.

THE SUN WAS coming up on Tuesday morning as Dick Stolley put the finishing touches on the cover story for the week: Marty Feldman and Ann-Margret were starring in the movie *The Last Remake of Beau Geste*. What a funny contrast, he thought, looking at the cover picture of the two of them. Feldman's bug-eyed face cheek to cheek with the beautiful Ann-Margret, who just happened to be a close friend of Dick Stolley's.

The news hit as he was halfway through the cover line. Elvis Presley had just been found dead at his Memphis home, Graceland. These things always seem to happen on Tuesday, the day the magazine was supposed to close. It was very difficult, if not impossible, to make any changes then—especially when it came to something major, like the cover.

Damn, he thought. Elvis Presley was dead. On Tuesday. Wouldn't you know it. The information made its way through the circuits of Stolley's weary mind. He considered the possibilities. Still sitting at his desk, he thought for a moment. Then he got up, opened his door, and charged down the hallway to the office of M. C. Marden, a picture researcher who was by that hour the only member of the photo department left in the office.

She could hear him coming a mile away. He flew down the hall so fast that he reminded M.C. of the way a dog looks when it sticks its head out of the window of a car that is speeding. "It was typical Stolley," she says. "When something big happened, you would hear Stolley's door open like a powerful wind. There was a unique electricity. That's what it was like when Dick really wanted something to happen."

He burst into her office. "Listen," he said to M.C., who had already heard the news about the King, "I'm gonna put Elvis in 'Star Tracks.' Do we have any pictures of him?"

M.C. said she would take care of the pictures, and she set out immediately to round up what was available from inside the building, at the Time Inc. Picture Collection and elsewhere—at the Associated Press and other picture agencies. She quickly got what she needed and assembled the prints in the office to show Stolley. He chose the most recent one. Then he pulled out one of the "Star Tracks" that had been scheduled to run and replaced it with the picture of Elvis—"The late Elvis Presley," as the contents line read. It was, in M.C.'s words, a picture of fat Elvis performing. "That is what we did for the King," she says.

To this day, Stolley has not forgiven himself for that decision, which he now sees as one of the grave miscalculations of his *People* career. "I probably should have been fired for not putting him on the cover back then," admits Stolley. "But it was a Tuesday. We got the news on a Tuesday morning and we closed on Tuesday evening. We just didn't think we had that kind of flexibility."

He understands what he was thinking at the time. The constrictions of the magazine's schedule were pressing. "The magazine actually was meant to close on Monday night," explains Stolley, "and we had this saying, 'Tuesday is for tinkering.' Well, then we kept pushing and pushing against the deadline, and my instincts weren't honed enough . . . Surprisingly nobody came in pounding on my desk, saying, 'This has got to be a cover.'"

The value of "dead celebrities" was a lesson for *People* that had not yet been learned. "I don't know," Stolley shrugs, thinking back. "We missed it. Our antennae weren't up enough. And at that point we didn't realize that dead celebrities were going to be that hot."

The ability to deal with dead celebrities on the cover of *People* would ironically become one of the advantages it held over other Time Inc. publications. *Time* had a policy of never putting dead people on the cover. Even after the assassination of John F. Kennedy, *Time* refrained from putting him on the cover, although *Life* broke their policy when Kennedy died and did put him on the cover. "You didn't spend a lot of time covering dead people back then," says Stolley, "unless they were world figures, presidents and the rest, and even then probably not on the cover. So we just missed it, that's all. God knows," he adds, "we made up for it with Elvis afterward. We did about five covers. Every time they brought out another toy or belt buckle, we put him on the cover."

THE LACK OF an Elvis cover that week made the call I received from Frank H. Lieberman at my home, late at night shortly following Elvis's death, even more important than it would otherwise have been. Tony Orlando and Elvis had been close friends—so close, in fact, that Frank and Elaine, Tony's wife, were both worried about the negative effect Elvis's death might have on the progress Tony was making in sorting out his life.

Lieberman's call took me completely by surprise. I had not even been aware that Tony and Elvis were friends.

"Judy," he said to me over the phone, "I can get you Linda Thompson."

I was not an avid Elvis fan and was embarrassed to admit to Frank that I did not know who he was talking about. On top of that, it was after midnight and I had been sound asleep. Still, I managed to refrain from the obvious question: "Who is Linda Thompson, Frank?" Instead, I said, with what little enthusiasm I could muster, "Gee, that's *great*, Frank."

"You know she lived with Elvis for the last five years, until just a few months ago," he kindly informed me.

"Sure, Frank," I said with certainty.

At least I was smart enough to know that Linda Thompson was an important story for *People.* I trusted Frank; he gave me her number and told me to call her right away, so I did.

Thompson was gracious and sweet and she clearly wanted to talk. It was apparent to me that she was anxious to establish herself as the most impor- tant person in Elvis's life since Priscilla—in spite of the fact that at the time it was rumored he was about to marry a new, younger love by the name of Ginger Alden.

When I hung up the phone, I booked a flight to Memphis. The next morning Dick Stolley was thrilled to hear the news. Within hours, I was standing face-to-face with Elvis's pretty, blond former "live-in lover," as *People* would soon refer to her, at the home that Elvis had bought for her near Graceland.

I was surprised to find that I liked Linda Thompson a lot. She was completely candid with me and—as Stolley had predicted—much more forth- coming than one would ever have expected. We spent the next two days together, talking about her life with Elvis. By the time I left, I had an intimate portrait of Elvis's life up to a few months before he died, when Linda Thompson had left Graceland. The story ran the week following Elvis's death, and although Thompson's face was not sufficiently well known for the cover, the timeliness of the inside story on Elvis Presley's intimate life made up—to a degree, at least—for the lack of an Elvis cover the previous week.

That was only the beginning of the Elvis saga. A month later *People* ran a cover, "Remembering Elvis," about the billion-dollar industry launched by the hoards of "imitators, fans, and rip-off artists" who were exploiting the late King. The six-page story enumerated every hustler who had popped up in the few weeks since Elvis had died and the "goods" for sale: a man in Ohio who had accumulated $60,000 worth of bubblegum cards, buttons, and 45s (Presley record sales had tripled to $4,500 a week since his death); vendors on Memphis streets who were selling copies of Elvis's will for $4; the parts of a Cadillac Elvis had once owned melted down into pendants that were selling for $4.95; a tacky line of watches, chains, and tchotchkes licensed by the Presley estate itself; a list of books; an endless line of Elvis impersonators; Harry Lee Geissler and his son, who managed to swing a deal with Colonel Tom Parker and Vernon Presley for exclusive rights to the King's name and face, figuring to garner around $10 million, some of which would obviously go to the Presley estate.

In August, for the first anniversary of Elvis's death, I was sent to Memphis for yet another cover:

THE ELVIS LEGEND,
One Year Later:
What's happened to the family,
the hangers-on, the loves—
and the money

Trudging through Memphis in the wet summer heat, I pursued everyone I could find who had ever had anything to do with the King.

Soon thereafter, the big story came. Priscilla was ready to talk, a piece of surprisingly welcome news imparted to me by none other than Frank H. Lieberman.

I was getting to like Lieberman's phone calls. He had already convinced Priscilla that she could trust me. She had not given an interview in years. She had virtually disappeared—publicly at least—since Elvis's death. Now she had decided to pursue a career in acting and would make her television debut on a Tony Orlando special. That is where Lieberman had come in.

He gave me Priscilla's number. Again, he told me to call her right away. I did not need to be convinced this time. Even *I* knew who Priscilla Presley was. I was about to meet Elvis's former wife, the mother of his only child.

I called her at her home in Los Angeles and we set up the details of the interview: It would be a cover. It would be exclusive. She did not have to talk about Elvis. (She ended up talking about Elvis.) It would be done in California. I flew there the following week.

Priscilla's well-secured house sat on the hill of a canyon in Beverly Hills. At 4:00 P.M. I arrived in my rented car. When I pressed the buzzer that was staring out at me from its little box at the top of her driveway, the gates swung open. I drove through and saw Priscilla standing there to greet me.

I was astonished at how beautiful she was. Her pale skin was flawless, her blue eyes were almost transparent, and her straight, honey-colored hair bore little resemblance to any picture I had ever seen of her—so soft and shiny it was impossible to imagine that it had ever been piled into what had once appeared to be a geodesic dome on the top of her head.

This was a new Priscilla, new at least to me. She was soft-spoken, gracious, and polite. We walked into the house and suddenly it occurred to me that, although the soft, warm, seductive California air was over seventy degrees outside, I was still wearing my New York clothes: heavy coat, wool muffler around my neck, and winter boots—hardly a match for Priscilla, who looked as if she belonged on the cover of *Vogue,* not *People.*

She offered me a glass of champagne, which I gratefully accepted. When she brought it to me, a fresh ripe strawberry floated in it, delicately forcing the rising bubbles in the fine crystal glass to encircle it. Something about the strawberry in the champagne symbolized everything to me about California— and Priscilla—at that moment.

Since I was going to spend as many days as I needed in Los Angeles to get my story, we sat there and sipped our champagne and talked. There was no need to do anything more. She introduced me to her current love, Michael Edwards, a model and actor who lived with her. She seemed to be extremely dependent on him. After the few initial minutes we had alone together, Edwards would be present constantly for the rest of the trip. It became a challenge to get a picture of Priscilla without him in it. And who but Frank H. Lieberman himself had gotten the assignment to take the photographs (which he had requested as part of the deal) for the Priscilla Presley story?

The true shock of the week I spent there was the moment I first saw Lisa Marie. It was like seeing Elvis as a child, his hooded eyes, his pouty lips— she *was* Elvis, with Priscilla's coloring. I got my story, but I was exhausted by the time I did —and saturated with everything Presley. My mission was accomplished.

When the pictures came into New York, Mary Dunn looked at the cover photos and knew that she had a winner. The photographer, Tony Korody, had captured every nuance of Priscilla's striking beauty. Dunn turned out to be right. The Priscilla Presley cover, which ran on December 4, 1978, would be the second-biggest-selling cover of the year. To this day it remains on *People*'s list of bestselling covers of all time.

How ironic, thought Mary. It was December, and until the Priscilla cover had run, twelve-year-old Brooke Shields, who had appeared on *People*'s cover for her starring role in the film *Pretty Baby*, had been the best-selling cover of the year. Yet three years before, in 1975, when Mary had received a call from Teri Shields, the then-unknown little actress's mother, she had turned down pictures of Brooke and felt deep concern for the young child.

Now, thinking back, she remembered the poignant moment clearly. Mary had been sitting amid mountains of transparencies and photographs in her office when her phone had rung. The woman on the line told Mary that she had some pictures of her young daughter, who she said was becoming a well-known model. She wanted to show the photos to the magazine. The woman was quite insistent, and Dunn, a perfect picture herself of a Southern belle, with her delicate features and genteel accent, had a young daughter of her own. She agreed to look at the pictures.

Teri Shields sent them over to Mary's office. When Mary opened the large manila envelope that contained them, she was surprised. The child was nine or ten years old at the time, yet she was wearing pearls and a big fox fur. Mary had stared at the pictures and thought, How can anyone do this to a child?

"It was so inappropriate," she says. She pondered the matter. "I thought, there is nothing we can do with these pictures. There is no story here. The child was not working. She was not a 'Lookout' [*People*'s guide to the up-and-coming]. There was no other reason I could see to use the pictures for the magazine."

It was obvious to Mary that Teri Shields would be disappointed, but she called her and told her that she did not think that *People* could use the pictures. Several hours later, she was stunned when she looked up from her desk and saw the beautiful young child standing in the doorway of her office alone. "So you didn't like the pictures?" Brooke had said sweetly to Mary. Her mother had sent her to pick them up.

"I will never forget that little child—that beautiful little child standing in the office all alone," Mary says. "It was awful. I remember asking myself how anyone could put a child in that position—to be the recipient of such disappointment. It later became clear just how complicated that mother-daughter relationship was." In spite of the complexity, little Brooke appeared on *People*'s cover nine times between 1978 and 1983.

1978 COVERS

John Travolta & Karen Gorney
Elton John
Helen Reddy
Penny Marshall, Mike McKean, David
    Lander, Cindy Williams
The Bee Gees
Clint Eastwood & Sondra Locke
Henry Winkler
VP & Mrs. Mondale
Goldie Hawn
Richard Pryor
Genevieve Bujold
All in the Family Cast: Carroll O'Connor,
    Jean Stapleton, Rob Reiner,
    Sally Struthers
Best Actress Nominees: Diane Keaton,
    Anne Bancroft, Shirley MacLaine,
    Jane Fonda, Marsha Mason
Cher (Inset, Gene Simmons)
Pat & Debby Boone
Linda Lavin
Steve Martin
Sly Stallone
Shaun Cassidy
John Ritter
Brooke Shields
Loretta Lynn & Crystal Gayle
Ron Howard
Cheryl Tiegs
Jane Fonda & Jon Voight

Princess Caroline & Philippe Junot
Ed Asner
Carly Simon
Ali MacGraw & Kris Kristofferson
Olivia Newton-John
Joan Kennedy
Carrie Fisher & Darth Vader
Elvis Legend
Ann-Margret
Margaret Trudeau
Michael Landon, Melissa Gilbert,
    Melissa Sue Anderson
Cheryl Ladd
Joe Namath
Battlestar Galactica Cast: Lorne Greene,
    Richard Hatch, Dirk Benedict
Jaclyn Smith
Chicago
Liz Taylor & John Warner
Robin Williams & Pam Dawber
Patty Hearst & Bernard Shaw
Jackie Onassis
Kristy & Jimmy McNichol
Angie Dickinson
Priscilla Presley
Suzanne Somers, John Ritter, Joyce DeWitt
Ann-Margret

Top Films:
Grease
Close Encounters of the Third Kind
National Lampoon's Animal House
Jaws 2
Heaven Can Wait

Oscar: *The Deer Hunter*

Top TV Shows: *Laverne and Shirley*
Happy Days
Three's Company
60 Minutes
Charlie's Angels

Emmys: *All in the Family*
The Rockford Files

Top Songs:
"Night Fever"—The Bee Gees
"Baby Come Back"—Player
"Three Times a Lady"—The Commodores
"You Don't Bring Me Flowers"
   —Barbra Streisand & Neil Diamond
"Grease"—Frankie Valli
"Miss You"—The Rolling Stones

Grammys: "Just the Way You Are" (record)
"Just the Way You Are" (song)

Bestsellers: *Chesapeake*—James Michener
Eye of the Needle—Ken Follett
The Women's Room—Marilyn French
Mommie Dearest—Christina Crawford
My Mother/My Self—Nancy Friday
Scruples—Judith Krantz

Tonys:
Da
Ain't Misbehavin'
Dracula

Marriages: Olga Korbut + Leonid Bortkevich
Princess Caroline + Philippe Junot
King Hussein + Elizabeth Halaby
Prince Michael of Kent + Baroness Marie-
   Christine von Reibnitz
James Earl Ray + Anna Sandhu
Christina Onassis + Sergei Kauzov

Divorces Governor George & Cornelia Wallace
Jack Haley & Liza Minnelli
Lord Snowdon & Princess Margaret
John & Jeanne Ehrlichman

Deaths: Edgar Bergen   Charles Boyer
Bob Crane   Will Geer
Robert Shaw   Pope Paul VI
Pope John Paul I   Henry Moore
Barbara (Babe) Paley   Norman Rockwell
Jack Warner   Gig Young
Dan Dailey   James Daly
Totie Fields   Margaret Mead
Hubert Humphrey   Golda Meir
Aldo Moro   Morris the cat
Gene Tunney

NEWS

- Roman Polanski flees U.S.
- Sid Vicious kills his girlfriend
- Bob Crane found slain in Arizona
- Gig Young kills himself and new bride
- San Francisco Mayor George Moscone and Supervisor Harvey Milk assassinated
- Larry Flynt shot
- Calvin Klein pays ransom for kidnapped daughter
- Betty Ford has plastic surgery at sixty
- First test-tube baby born in London
- Pope John Paul II elected first non-Italian pope in 455 years
- 909 die in Jonestown mass suicide
- Anwar Sadat and Menachem Begin share Nobel Peace Prize

CHAPTER NINE

The Unforgiven: Dick vs. Clint and Sondra and Merv

"Everybody would love for us to say, 'It's all true, we're madly in love.' But people will believe whatever they want to believe. Even if it were true—which it isn't—I certainly wouldn't talk about it."

—SONDRA LOCKE
(about her relationship with Clint Eastwood),
in People,
February 13, 1978

DICK STOLLEY SAT in the makeup chair down the hall from the greenroom at *The Merv Griffin Show* in Hollywood as the hairdresser brushed back the strand of graying blond hair that had fallen onto his forehead. He was beginning to get used to this. With all the publicity *People* was getting, he had acquired a degree of stardom himself, but this was the first time he had appeared on *The Merv Griffin Show*.

His nose powdered for the cameras, he got up from the chair and walked back to the greenroom. He felt good about the way things were going. Circulation was up to nearly two million, with a "pass-along" readership of more than eighteen million people a week. *People* was being called the most successful new magazine in modern publishing history: In just three years it had gone from zero to ninth among all magazines in number of advertising pages.

Within moments, the production assistant showed up in the greenroom to take Stolley into the studio. It did not feel the least bit foreign to him. The stage manager came up, attached the tiny microphone to his lapel, and dropped the cord inside his jacket, just as Merv's other guests—*Esquire* editor Clay Felker, *Newsweek* editor Ed Kosner, and *Ms.* editor Gloria

Steinem—joined him on the set. They all knew each other, and he was happy to see them.

They sat there chatting until Merv came in and greeted each of them personally. When he shook Stolley's hand, he said jovially, "Hi, Fred," confusing him with tennis player Fred Stolle.

Griffin talked with his guests for a while before the taping began, to warm everyone up, make them feel more comfortable—it was customary on television talk shows. Then the camera's little red light went on, indicating the show was on the air. Merv introduced his guests, and during the first segment of the show everything went well as they chatted amiably about magazines.

During the commercial break, Clay Felker leaned over to Merv, who had continued to call Dick Stolley "Fred," pointed at Stolley, and whispered discreetly, "Merv, his name is *Dick*."

Merv turned to Stolley. "Fred," he said, "I'd like to ask you a few questions."

"Of course, Marv," Stolley replied, to retaliate for the mistake.

The minute the commercial break ended, Griffin pounced. "Fred," he said to Stolley, "that was just a reprehensible story you did on Clint Eastwood and Sondra Locke." The blood rushed into Merv's round face, as the color of his cheeks took on a purplish hue. It was plain that he could hardly control himself. His voice rose as he pointed at Stolley and added accusingly, "It was absolutely untrue. I don't know where you got it."

Stolley was totally unprepared for the attack. There had not been even an inkling of impending hostility during the first segment of the show. He had had no warning, no idea at all that Merv was upset about the story *People* had done a few weeks earlier on the relationship between actress Sondra Locke and Clint Eastwood, who were costars in the film *The Gauntlet*, which had grossed fifty million dollars by the time the story ran.

He had been aware that Eastwood was a close friend and also a neighbor of Griffin's in the northern California town of Carmel, but that had not made any difference to him. Now Merv's attack was beginning to make sense.

"It was very tough. It was really ugly," Stolley says, describing what happened on Griffin's set. He had no qualms whatsoever about the Eastwood-Locke story, which had been reported by one of *People*'s best reporters, Lois Armstrong. She was a highly reputable journalist, a former *Time* correspondent who had written extensively—often, as it happened, for the "Religion" section of *Time*.

When Lois did the *People* story on Eastwood and Locke at the beginning of 1978, rumors were rampant in Hollywood that the costars, who were both married—and not to each other—were deeply involved romantically. Lois, who had by then taken over the job as Los Angeles bureau chief from Barbara

Wilkins, called Eastwood's publicist and requested an interview with Clint and Sondra. Eastwood had agreed. He wanted to publicize *The Gauntlet,* but he said he would do the interview only on the condition that the story would deny the rumors about his relationship with Locke, which he insisted were not true. Dick Burgheim had agreed to Eastwood's request. If he wanted *People* to print the truth and he was willing to talk about it, why not?

Armstrong was invited to Locke's house for the first part of the interview. "I went to see her at her home, where she was living with her husband," she recalls. "They had been high school sweethearts. It was obvious that they were presenting a phony front. They met in high school—I think she must have been very naïve—but she invited me there so I would see how she was this happily married woman."

Locke spoke with Armstrong about her marriage, explaining that she and her husband were together "a lot" except when their schedules did not coincide. "We are very independent and have a strong direction of our own," she said. "He's very committed to his interests and his work, and so am I. To me, the basis of any relationship [is] a strong friendship."

The language sounded oddly familiar. Eastwood's assessment of his twenty-four-year marriage to onetime model Maggie Johnson had been almost identical: "Everybody talks about love in marriage," he had said, "but it's just as important to be friends."

Armstrong was open-minded, but she was not overly impressed with the attempts on either side to prove how strong their respective marriages were—especially after she and Sondra boarded a plane and flew to nearby Monterey, California, where Clint met them at the airport.

From that instant, Lois could hardly believe her eyes, considering the fact that the story was being done on the condition that it deny a romantic relationship between Eastwood and Locke. "My God, the sexual electricity was unbelievable," says Lois. "I couldn't ignore it."

She and the photographer assigned to the story climbed into their car and followed the couple, who went on ahead of them in their truck. "You could see that they could barely keep their hands off each other," says Lois. "And then, during the photo shoot, he had his arms around her, and you could plainly see it in their eyes—it was just unbelievable. And he kept making it last longer and longer. It was really great as far as he was concerned."

It was difficult enough for Lois to ponder how she was going to deny the rumors. Little tidbits like this emanating from Locke did not help at all: "Nobody's going to complain about playing opposite Clint as a romantic lover on screen."

How on earth could Lois ignore what was so blatantly obvious? "We had a good time, and we spent the entire day," she recalls. "But even the pictures clearly showed that they were so in love. And then we wrote the story in which Clint Eastwood attempted to deny the rumors . . ."

After Armstrong filed her story to New York, the staff writer there who was assigned to write it called her and asked if she had any ideas for the cover billing. She thought for a moment and then she replied, "Yes, how about, 'Clint Eastwood and Sondra Locke run a gauntlet of rumors'?"

When the story ran, she felt confident that she had kept her part of the bargain. "We ran it that way," she says. "I thought, 'That doesn't give anything away. It denies the rumors, too.' So we thought we had really done a good job of satisfying him and satisfying our own needs. We couldn't close our eyes to this relationship," she says, "which incidentally lasted for another thirteen years, for crying out loud. He shared a house with her. We did what I consider to be good reporting."

Clint strongly disagreed. He wrote a letter to the editor condemning *People* for "having ignored a very talented actress in favor of her personal life." After Stolley ran the letter in the "Mail" column, he assumed that the entire episode of hard feelings was over. But on the set of *The Merv Griffin Show*, it became obvious to Dick Stolley that he had thought wrong.

Luckily, he got some help when it came to defending the magazine. Clay Felker went first: "I don't know the particulars of this story," he said to Merv, "but I will tell you that *People* magazine is a Time Inc. publication . . . I worked at *Life* magazine and I do know the fact-checking that goes on at that magazine in that company is unlike anywhere else. And they would not have printed that story, I can assure you, if they did not have absolute strong evidence that it was true."

Stolley sat there listening, still taken aback by what had just occurred. When Felker finished, it was Steinem's turn. She herself had had some negative moments with the magazine, she admitted, but she insisted that she supported *People*, and Dick Stolley, in spite of that. "I have to say that what Clay said is true," she told Merv. "*People* did a cover story on me. I was very upset when I found out they were doing this story. I didn't want it done." She explained that it had been done at a time when she had publicly announced that she wanted to start a new, low profile. "I tried to talk them out of it," she went on, "but when the story came out, it was right. They didn't get anything wrong. I might not have liked it, but it was true."

By the end of the show, Stolley felt vindicated. Afterward, the booker who had put him on the show ran up to him and said, "I shouldn't be telling you this, but I apologize for what happened out there. I hope that other people from your magazine will come back on this show."

1979

1979 COVERS

Superman
Diana Ross
Neil Diamond
Waltons' Women
Rod Stewart
Pam Dawber & Robin Williams
Barbra Streisand & Jon Peters
John & Annie Denver
5th Anniversary Issue
Loretta Swit
Billy Joel
Betty Ford
Voight, Beatty, and De Niro
Donna Pescow
Michael Douglas & Jane Fonda
Burt Reynolds
Linda Ronstadt & Jerry Brown
Live-in Lovers
Three's Company Cast
Johnny Carson
Rather, Safer, Reasoner, Wallace
Kate Jackson
Mariel Hemingway
Carl and Rob Reiner
Paul Newman
Edward Kennedy

Olivia Newton-John
Stockard Channing
Sly Stallone & Talia Shire
Stan Dragoti & Cheryl Tiegs
The Bee Gees
Moonraker Cast
Farrah Fawcett-Majors
Phil Donahue
Miss Piggy
The Music Industry
Margot Kidder (*The Amityville Horror*)
Shelley Hack
Carol Burnett and Carrie
Nick Nolte
Suzanne Somers
Cher
Robin Williams
Jill Clayburgh
Loni Anderson & Howard Hesseman
Vitas Gerulaitis, Erik Estrada, Andy Gibb
Fleetwood Mac
Dick Van Patten & *Eight Is Enough* Cast
Kenny & Marianne Rogers
Dallas

YEAR-END DOUBLE ISSUE:
Johnny Carson, Willie Stargell, Rosalynn Carter,
Bo Derek, Pope John Paul II, Deborah Harry,
Sylvester Stallone

BOTTOM 5

FLEETWOOD MAC
ROBIN WILLIAMS
JILL CLAYBURGH
TV'S *EIGHT IS ENOUGH*
INSIDE TV'S *60 MINUTES*

Top Films: *Superman*

Every Which Way But Loose
Rocky II
Alien
The Amityville Horror

Oscar: *Kramer vs. Kramer*

Top TV Shows: *Laverne and Shirley*

Three's Company
Mork & Mindy
Happy Days
Angie

Emmys: *Taxi*
Lou Grant

Top Songs: "My Sharona"—The Knack

"Bad Girls"—Donna Summer
"Do Ya Think I'm Sexy"—Rod Stewart
"I Will Survive"—Gloria Gaynor
"YMCA"—Village People
"We Are Family"—Sister Sledge

Grammys: "What a Fool Believes" (record)
"What a Fool Believes" (song)

Bestsellers: *Chesapeake*—James Michener

The Dead Zone—Stephen King
Dress Gray—Lucian Truscott

The Far Pavilions—M. M. Kaye
Sophie's Choice—William Styron
War and Remembrance—Herman Wouk

Tonys: *The Elephant Man*

Sweeney Todd

Marriages: Joseph Kennedy II + Sheila Rauch
Susan Ford + Charles Vance
Patricia Hearst + Bernard Shaw
Chris Evert + John Lloyd
Eric Sevareid + Suzanne St. Pierre
Anatoly Karpov + Irina Kuimove

Divorces O. J. & Marguerite Simpson
André Previn & Mia Farrow
Patrick & Luci Johnson Nugent
Mick & Bianca Jagger

Deaths: Joan Blondell / Mamie Eisenhower
Peggy Guggenheim / Arthur Fiedler
Jack Haley, Sr. / Conrad Hilton
Barbara Hutton / Emmett Kelly
Zeppo Marx / Jean Seberg
Merle Oberon / Mary Pickford
Jean Renoir / Nelson Rockefeller
Vivian Vance / Sid Vicious
John Wayne / Michael Wilding
Darryl Zanuck / Richard Rodgers

NEWS

- Nelson Rockefeller dies of heart attack
- "Hillside Strangler" pleads guilty to killings
- Jeffrey MacDonald convicted of killing his family
- Billy Carter goes on the wagon
- Shah of Iran forced to leave country; Ayatollah Khomeini assumes power
- President Carter commutes Patty Hearst's sentence
- Lee Marvin sued for palimony by Michelle Triola Marvin
- Three Mile Island nuclear accident in Pennsylvania
- Karen Silkwood estate awarded $10.5 million in damages from Kerr-McGee
- Muhammad Ali announces retirement
- Iran seizes U.S. embassy in Tehran and takes hostages
- Mother Teresa wins Nobel Peace Prize
- Margaret Thatcher elected first female prime minister of Great Britain

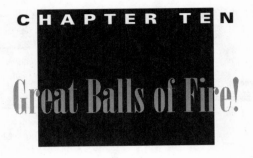

CHAPTER TEN

Great Balls of Fire!

"Have you heard? This place is ready to blow. You've got to get out
of here. We're leaving immediately . . ."

—*One* People *reporter to another while covering
the nuclear disaster at Three Mile Island, April 1979*

BY *PEOPLE'S FIFTH* anniversary, on March 4, 1979 (the
same year that Barbra Streisand fell in love with Jon Peters, Robin
Williams became famous in *Mork and Mindy*, Fidel Castro invited
Billy Joel to Cuba, Burt Reynolds invited Sally Field home to the family in
Florida, and Michelle Triola sued Lee Marvin for palimony), it was clear that
the magazine was a huge success. Its circulation was almost three million
copies a week. The price of a full-page, black-and-white ad rose from $19,000
to $20,900, and a full-page, four-color ad went from $24,300 to $26,800.

Still, the schedule for the staff had not improved at all. The grueling
nights were longer than ever, and for Dick Stolley, who by now had developed
the invaluable ability to go to sleep on the couch in his office for a few
minutes at the drop of an eyelid and wake up completely refreshed—a ritual
familiar to everyone on the staff who knew enough to tiptoe quietly around
him during these interludes—they were often never-ending.

It was on such a night during *People*'s sixth year that Dick Stolley,
exhausted and still laboring over a batch of copy in the wee hours of the
morning, felt himself fading and decided to take one of his restorative cat-
naps. He reclined on the nubby beige couch in his office adjacent to the
layout room and immediately passed out completely, slipping into one of his
fleeting but profound sleeps, when a new copy clerk, unfamiliar with the

managing editor's idiosyncratic habits, entered his office for the first time in his fledgling career to deliver some copy for top editing. He took one look at Dick Stolley in his horizontal state and froze in terror. Then he turned around frantically and ran back down the hall to the copy room screaming at the top of his lungs, "Mr. Stolley is dead! Mr. Stolley is dead!"

Dick Stolley was not dead, but the case could be made that for the most part, the *People* staff was. Dead tired, that is, from working late nights and often through the weekends. There came a distinct turning point in the willingness of the staff to give of themselves relentlessly when, only a few weeks after *People*'s fifth birthday, the worst nuclear accident in the history of the United States occurred at the Three Mile Island nuclear generating plant in Pennsylvania.

Although the initial event at Three Mile Island occurred at 4:00 A.M. on Wednesday, March 28, word about the disaster was not released until late that afternoon—a delay that would in time be called into question by the American public—just as most members of *People*'s worn-out staff were beginning to fantasize about their weekend plans and figure out a way to escape any reason to have to work over the weekend. Not until Thursday was it obvious that the story was indeed a major one. Stolley flew down the hall with his hair streaming back as he always did at these crucial moments, looking for reporters he could send to cover the story.

He was shocked at the response. Nobody wanted to risk his life. The first reporter he asked looked at Stolley as though he were crazy and replied that he had no intention of "frying his balls," as he put it.

"He was afraid he'd go down there and become sterile," recalls Stolley. And in a way Dick Stolley understood. "Cows were dropping dead," he admits. On the other hand, Stolley himself was the kind of reporter, and had been throughout his life, who would have seized the opportunity to be a part of such a big story even if it did mean risking his life, or any part of his anatomy. It was the way he had been brought up in journalism, as Hal Wingo later tried to explain.

"Nobody would go," recalls Wingo. "That's the maddest I've ever seen Dick Stolley. Everybody was afraid, of course, that they were going to get radiated. Stolley didn't push it. He couldn't make anybody go, but he was really frustrated by it."

It was Stolley's nature, Wingo explained, trying to grapple with the rather violent reaction of *People*'s relatively young staff. "Stolley would have stepped into the lion's den if that's what it took to get a story," says Wingo. "There was a generation that maybe thought that way about their responsibilities. I felt that way when I went to work for *Life*. There was a time when I was going to have to jump out of an airplane and land on a tiny little southern atoll island in the Pacific because a ship had gone aground there. We were trying to get there to do a story on all these people who were living with the natives. The only way to get there was to fly a plane down there and the guy said, 'There's no runway there, so you'll just have to parachute out over the island.' I thought, that's what you do. You work for *Life* magazine, you jump out. I was so dumb, I thought you jump out if they tell you to jump out."

It was not that way on the afternoon of March 29 in the offices of *People* magazine, though. The unified voice of the staff rang out: "We're not going to stick *our* necks out for radiation."

"Maybe they were right," Wingo muses. "They probably were. But Stolley said to me, 'I wish I could go. I'd be right down there. I'd go myself.' "

As it turned out, however, not everyone responded the same way the exhausted full-time staff of *People* did. When no one from the staff would agree to go to Three Mile Island, freelancers were called in. Rich Rein, a former *Time* reporter who lived in Princeton, New Jersey, and was then freelancing for *People*, did not think twice when Jim Gaines, the editor of the "Up Front" section, which deals with current news stories, called him and asked if he would go. The magazine usually called upon him for stories that required working on the weekend. As a freelancer, Rein refers to such assignments as his "money time"; unlike full-time staff members, freelancers get paid for only the stories they actually do. "I was an eager freelancer and I was ready to work," he explains. "The story would have been like three hundred dollars to me."

That had been Rich Rein's main concern. "Maybe the thought of danger flitted through my mind," he recalls. "It wasn't a big concern. I figured I was getting the job not because anybody was afraid, I simply thought it was a weekend assignment and that's the way it worked and I would go. The reports coming out said there had been some leakage but I wasn't concerned. I thought, considering the number of people converging on that town, that if it was a real safety danger, we'd be stopped at a point faraway."

The thirty-one-year-old Rein was working on a piece about little Ricky Schroder, who was starring with Faye Dunaway in the movie *The Champ*. When he got the call from Gaines, he left his forwarding number with Faye Dunaway's publicist, since he was awaiting a call from her to discuss Ricky Schroder. Then he set out immediately for Three Mile Island.

The minute Rein arrived on the scene, he checked in with the press office that had been hurriedly set up there and was given a dosimeter, a device to measure radiation intake. This also helped to allay his fears. He proceeded to his hotel, the Holiday Inn in Harrisburg, Pennsylvania, where he was soon met by the photographer who had been assigned to work with him on the story, Michael Abramson.

They immediately tried to size up the situation. Unlike the rest of the press—the network news shows, the nation's newspapers, and other publications covering the events as they unraveled—the *People* team needed human-interest stories, not just details of the technology that had gone awry, causing the disaster.

As it turned out, these stories were not difficult to find. Right away Rein learned that there were a few "hot spots." People had left Harrisburg, for instance, and gone to shelters that had been set up in Hershey, Pennsylvania. "They were staying in this arena in Hershey," says Rein. "We went over there and interviewed some families. When we really stopped and analyzed it, they had gone to a shelter that was actually closer to Three Mile Island than where they lived. That was the sort of concern that was affecting some residents in the area. They just had to go to a shelter, and so they ended up in one that was miles closer to the place than where they had actually left."

Rein figured the shelter was the obvious place to start. On the way there, checking his dosimeter all the while, registering the fact that so far he had received virtually no radiation, he spotted a sight that floored him and became a picture that ran on the lead page of the *People* article the following week. There on the street in front of him was a tourist with a camera, taking a picture of his wife with the imperiled Three Mile Island cooling towers in the background. "Michael," Rein whispered to the photographer as he watched, mesmerized, "take that."

The man, James Brown, a chemistry teacher from Corning, New York, was driving through, had heard about the disaster, and had driven *to* it in order to take the picture of his wife in front of the potentially lethal towers. "I thought this would be a good way to show my students it wasn't as dangerous as people said," Brown told Rein. As *People* observed, "The very invisibility of the threat seemed to prove it was benign." Whether, in fact, it had deceived Mr. Brown had yet to be known.

Not long after Rein and Abramson had immersed themselves in the multitude of potential angles for *People* stories, to their surprise, a second reporter-photographer team arrived on the scene—two more freelancers sent by *People*, both women. Reporter Andrea Pawlyna was from Baltimore; photographer Judy Gurovitz from New York. Taken aback at the appearance of an added team and feeling slightly competitive and insecure, Rein remembers thinking to himself, "They're sending in the real guns to cover this thing because they don't think we can do it." Thereafter he began to refer to the two women as "The A Team." In reality, that was not the case at all. The editors in New York, aware of the fact that there was so much to cover and delighted that they had found another team willing to go, had complete confidence in all of them. They later admitted they were worried about them, too.

The next few days were like a roller coaster. When Pawlyna and Gurovitz arrived, things seemed to be under control, with little potential of a meltdown, the worst-case scenario. Radioactivity continued to leak from the plant, with low levels of radiation detected in the atmosphere as far as twenty miles away, but the reactor had cooled enough to allow technicians to turn off the emergency core cooling system. Officials believed the situation was manageable. President Jimmy Carter was scheduled to make a visit.

The two teams went their separate ways to pursue various stories for *People.* The women found a couple, Ron and Mary Miller, who disagreed about whether or not they should evacuate their house. Although Mary wanted to take her two children and flee, Ron refused to leave his house to the possibility of looters. They stayed.

Next, Andrea and Judy found a widow and her son, who was helping her pack so that they could get out as fast as possible. "I'm young yet," Jeff, the boy, explained to them. "I've got a life ahead of me. I've got to have kids yet. I don't want to die." His mother, Romaine, had been to see the just-released film *The China Syndrome,* which was about a nuclear disaster. It had been the first public warning about the potential dangers posed by nuclear power plants, and the poignant message had struck a chord with the American public—ironically right on the cusp of the *real* thing, Three Mile Island. Still, the movie was only fiction. The true impact of the latent dangers of nuclear power had yet to be realized.

For another angle, Rich Rein and Michael Abramson found volunteers who were checking for radioactivity along the residential streets of the area; they also went to a home for the elderly in Middletown, Pennsylvania, which had had to move its 240 residents because not enough staff members had shown up at work to care for them. In addition, they found a mother who took one of her three children with her to the shelter that had been set up in Hershey—so she could be close enough to continue her waitressing job, since she desperately needed the money—and sent her other two children farther away to stay with her parents.

Rein found something else significant in the course of covering the story for *People.* There was a prevailing sense of surprise that *this* magazine was covering a story like Three Mile Island. Although a large percentage of the magazine dealt with noncelebrity stories, it was only five years old and that perception had not yet sunk in. "So many people were surprised to hear that I was there on behalf of *People* magazine," says Rein. "There was real surprise. Every time I introduced myself, people would do a double take. Somebody joked, 'What are you going to do? Have some sort of a raft bringing celebrities down the Susquehanna River?' Sarcastic jokes like that from other journalists."

Looking back, Rein remembers thinking at the time that Three Mile Island was an event making a statement to the world and to the American people, specifically about the safety of nuclear power plants. "Like anything else, it really did have a personality about it," says Rein. "It became an event to cover and it had those characteristics of any kind of a person—for that matter, any kind of celebrity."

When Rein and Abramson got back to the hotel, the reporter found to his surprise that he had a greeting party awaiting him. Faye Dunaway had returned his call to talk about Ricky Schroder and *The Champ;* the entire staff at the Holiday Inn in Harrisburg was agog that the well-known actress had called there. "They were all in a titter," Rein recalls. He went to his room, returned the call, and got Dunaway on the phone right away. She was clearly more eager to talk about Three Mile Island than about Ricky Schroder.

"This is a really dangerous thing, don't you think?" Dunaway said to Rein. "We're watching it here in California. How do you feel? Are you scared? What's really happening?"

"I'm really not scared," said Rein. "Everybody here doesn't seem to be scared."

"Are people getting ready to evacuate?" she asked. "Is it dangerous?" It was a long time before they got around to Ricky Schroder.

Later Rein reacted to their conversation. "It made me stop and think about how scared I should be," he said. "She was sitting back in L.A., watching it on TV and getting a different impression entirely. She wondered what I was doing there. What was going on there. She actually was the first person that gave me some inkling that the outside world was thinking that this was a really super-dangerous situation."

After he hung up Rein and Abramson went down to dinner at the restaurant in the Holiday Inn. There he found his golden opportunity. Harold Denton, the director of reactor regulation at the Nuclear Regulatory Commission, who had left his office in Washington to take charge of the chaos in Harrisburg and was fast becoming a national celebrity, was sitting right next to him. Rein did not hesitate. He went up to Denton and said apologetically, since he was interrupting his dinner, "We'd really like to spend a half hour with you. We know you're crazy—busy and everything else—but we would really like to interview you for *People.*"

"There's no problem," Denton replied. "I'd be happy to meet you first thing tomorrow morning at seven-fifteen and we'll have breakfast together. Sit with me then. If that's okay with you, it'll be all right with me."

"That's wonderful," said Rein. "That's all we need." After all, he thought to himself, we don't want to stop this guy from doing his job. It was about eight-thirty at night and they made the appointment for breakfast. Wow, Rein marveled. This is a pretty good day. He had nailed the big guy for an interview and would be able to get a picture of him tomorrow morning at seven-thirty.

While Rein was in the process of arranging the interview with Denton, a report had gone out on a Harrisburg TV station announcing that Three Mile Island was about to blow up. The report recommended that the area be evacuated immediately. Although the station quickly learned that it had broadcast an erroneous report and retracted it immediately, "The A Team" had already heard it on TV and panicked. They were not alone. The rumors were flying wildly.

Just as Rein and Abramson were leaving the restaurant at the Holiday Inn, high from their conversation with Denton, "The A Team" ran up to them, looking terrified. "Have you heard?" asked Pawlyna, her eyes filled with fear. "This place is ready to blow. You've got to get out of here. We're leaving immediately."

"No," said Rein, having just finished talking with the head of the whole mess, "I don't think you're quite right there. We just talked to Harold Denton and we made an appointment to have breakfast with him tomorrow morning."

"I don't care who you just talked to," Pawlyna replied sharply. "This place is blowing. You gotta get out of here. We're leaving *now*!"

Rein was confused. Geez, he thought, what's going on? He checked the TV, he asked around in the bar where there was constant updating, and he could find no intimation of pending disaster, the kind that had occurred in *The China Syndrome*. So Rein and Abramson stayed.

"I figured that if that was about to happen," Rein later said, "that guy Harold Denton wouldn't have been sitting there eating dinner, relaxing and making plans to have breakfast with us, of all people. I know *People* is a powerful medium and all that, but not that powerful."

Rein got the Denton story for the magazine. Fourteen years after Three Mile Island he seems to be having no ill effects from the experience. There was, however, some controversy over whether *Time* correspondent Peter Stoler, who covered the nuclear disaster for his magazine and died of cancer nine years later, had been a victim of the radiation leak at Three Mile Island. Stoler strongly believed that he had.

As it turned out, ironically, that same week *People* had a cover on *The*

China Syndrome with Michael Douglas and Jane Fonda shot and ready to go.

It was a perfect cover for the issue containing the story on the nuclear accident. The week after the Three Mile Island disaster occurred, the magazine was out on the newsstands with excellent coverage, thanks to the nonstaff reporters who had been willing to "stick their necks out for radiation." With an inset of the cooling towers overlapping a picture of Fonda and Douglas, the cover line read:

A DISASTER MOVIE COMES TRUE

In spite of the magnitude of the Three Mile Island story, there were, in 1979, other stories of far less global import that still had a significant impact on the evolution of the magazine's standard operating procedure. It seemed that the lessons to be learned were infinite. Before the year was over, *People* made a giant mistake that it would never repeat. The magazine had learned that Lee Radziwill was about to marry San Francisco hotel owner Newton Cope. Because of *People*'s tight schedule, it had to close the story on the wedding before it actually took place. The details of the affair were meticulously reported in advance by staff members who gleaned every detail that could be gotten from everyone who would have anything to do with the wedding—relatives and caterers, bakers and dressmakers. The headline read:

SMITTEN AT FIRST GLANCE
by Lee Radziwill, Newton Cope
Took Her Home to Meet His Hotel

The story had distinctly enumerated who was at the ceremony and who was not:

> The simple ceremony last week at the Telegraph Hill home of socialite rancher Whitney Warren was attended by five friends, Lee's big sister [Jackie O.] not among them.

As it turned out, Lee Radziwill did not marry Newton Cope at the home of Whitney Warren or anyone else. She decided not to marry him at all. But since *People* had written the story before the event was to occur, readers would not have known that the wedding had been canceled.

Deadline or not, *People* would never again close a story saying something had happened until it really had.

1980

1980 COVERS

Bette Midler
Lee Majors
Steve Martin
Elvis Presley
John & Chris Evert Lloyd
Bo & John Derek
Robert Redford
Goldie Hawn
Lindsay Wagner
Britt Ekland
Mackenzie Phillips, Valerie Bertinelli, Bonnie Franklin
Readers' Poll
Tatum O'Neal & Kristy McNichol
Richard Gere
Larry Hagman
Andy Gibb & Olivia Newton-John
Penny Marshall
Jacqueline Bisset & Paul Newman
The Who
Jodie Foster
Mac Davis
Valerie Harper
Yoda
Soap Opera Stars
John Travolta

Glen Campbell & Tanya Tucker
Harrison Ford, Billy Dee Williams, Carrie Fisher & Mark Hamill
Larry Hagman
Ronald & Nancy Reagan
Jack Nicholson
Dan Aykroyd & John Belushi
Brooke Shields & Chris Atkins in *Blue Lagoon*
Kiss
John Davidson
Willie Nelson & Family
The Cast of *Airplane!—The Movie*
Angie Dickinson
Richard Chamberlain
Best- & Worst-Dressed People in the World
Carly Simon
Cathy Lee Crosby of *That's Incredible!*
Elizabeth Taylor & John Warner
Soap Opera Teens: Genie Francis, Kristen Vigard & Kelli Maroney
Paul Simon
Linda Gray of *Dallas*
Mary Tyler Moore & the Cast of *Ordinary People*
John Lennon: A Tribute

YEAR-END DOUBLE ISSUE:
Ronald & Nancy Reagan, Brooke Shields,
Robert Redford, Goldie Hawn,
Sugar Ray Leonard, Larry Hagman

Top Films:
The Empire Strikes Back
Kramer vs. Kramer
The Jerk
Airplane!
Smokey and the Bandit II

Oscar: *Ordinary People*

Top TV Shows: *60 Minutes*
Three's Company
That's Incredible!
Alice
*M*A*S*H*

Emmys: *Taxi*
Lou Grant

Top Songs: "Lady"—Kenny Rogers
"Call Me"—Blondie
"Starting Over"—John Lennon
"Another One Bites the Dust"
—Queen
"It's Still Rock and Roll to Me"
—Billy Joel
"Sailing"—Christopher Cross

Grammys: "Sailing" (record)
"Sailing" (song)

Bestsellers: *The Bourne Identity*—Robert Ludlum
The Covenant—James Michener
The Executioner's Song—Norman Mailer
Princess Daisy—Judith Krantz
Smiley's People—John le Carré
Anatomy of an Illness—Norman Cousins
Thy Neighbor's Wife—Gay Talese

Tonys: *Children of a Lesser God*
Evita
Morning's at Seven

Marriages: Angela Davis + Hilton Braithwaite
Raquel Welch + Andre Weinfeld
Candice Bergen + Louis Malle
Ronald Reagan, Jr. + Doria Palmieri

Divorces Bob Green & Anita Bryant
Harry & Kathleen Reasoner
Philippe Junot & Princess Caroline
Jerry & Patti Lewis

Deaths: Jimmy Durante   Alfred Hitchcock
John Lennon   Steve McQueen
Henry Miller   Jean-Paul Sartre
Erich Fromm   Peter Sellers
Marshall McLuhan   George Meany
George Raft   Mae West

NEWS

- David Kennedy arrested for drunk driving
- Robert Evans arrested for cocaine possession
- Sophia Loren sentenced for tax evasion
- John Lennon murdered
- Paul McCartney deported from Japan
- Richard Pryor sets himself on fire in freebasing accident
- Abbie Hoffman surrenders after six years in hiding
- Playmate Dorothy Stratten slain by husband
- Dr. Herman Tarnower killed by Jean Harris
- Mary Cunningham quits job at Bendix amid rumors of romance with chairman William Agee
- Failed rescue attempt of U.S. hostages in Iran
- Families evacuate Love Canal area in New York near abandoned chemical dump
- Mount Saint Helens volcano erupts
- Johnny Carson signs new three-year deal with NBC
- Shah of Iran dies in Egyptian exile
- U.S. boycotts Moscow Olympics
- Lech Walesa leads Polish Solidarity movement
- Toxic shock syndrome linked to tampons
- Ali loses title fight to Larry Holmes
- Ronald Reagan elected fortieth president

CHAPTER ELEVEN

Sex, Drugs, and Rock & Roll

"The first thing you gotta know is, I don't snort cocaine
anymore . . ."

—SLY STONE
to David Sheff in an interview for People, January 1980

IF STOLLEY'S COVER theory was correct, TV did better than music,
but music did pretty well. The problem was that so many music stories
seemed to be fraught with layers of complexity—uniquely thorny aspects
that other stories did not have. Maybe rock stars were just more difficult
because of their inherent lifestyles.

Still, by 1980, Cher had already appeared on *People*'s cover six times:
alone and scared without Sonny; with her new love, Gregg Allman; with
Allman and her kids, Elijah Blue and Chastity; as one of *People*'s most
intriguing people of 1975; with another new love, Gene Simmons; and without Gene Simmons but *about* Gene Simmons.

On the other hand, Michael Jackson, who would have appeared on the
cover more than a dozen times by *People*'s twentieth birthday, did not emerge
as a music star worthy of a *People* cover until 1983.

There were also those music stories that were not covers but were no less
difficult for the reporters who did them. Take Sly of Sly and the Family Stone,
for instance, a story assigned at the beginning of 1980 to a young freelancer
living in Los Angeles by the name of David Sheff, who was developing a
proficiency, albeit a nascent one, in stories of the rock-and-roll variety.

Sheff was thrilled when Jim Jerome, the editor and reporter on the New
York staff who did many of the music stories and oversaw most of those he
did not do, called to assign him the Sly Stone interview. Sheff admitted he

was a complete Sly Stone fan. He accepted the assignment and was elated when, in arranging the interview, he was invited to meet Sly Stone at the home of his manager in Mandeville Canyon, near the ocean in L.A.

On the appointed day, Sheff arrived at Stone's manager's house, which turned out to be typical of a certain L.A. style—a sprawling home that seemed to go on forever with a swimming pool, and bungalow after bungalow lining the pool. He was summoned into one of the bungalows, where he encountered not Sly Stone himself, but a large array of people reminiscent of an entourage befitting the likes of Muhammad Ali, all of whom were related in some way, directly or indirectly, to the singer. When he entered the room, the entire group was seated around a table, silent. No one spoke, and as Sheff sat there he began to wonder whether Sly Stone was going to show up at all.

Eventually he did. Like a bolt of lightning he burst forth into the room, emitting megavolts of energy, flashing a giant smile with gleaming white teeth. Before Sheff could even say hello or introduce himself, Stone slapped him on the back heartily, plopped himself down, and blurted confessionally, "The first thing you gotta know is I don't snort cocaine anymore."

Sheff smiled politely at him, quickly calculating the meaning of that statement, thinking to himself that he was about to get into a story about Sly Stone's recovery from drugs. Then Stone's face lit up with his big smile again, and he added, "I smoke it."

It was no secret to anyone in the room that David Sheff was taping the interview. His tape recorder was set squarely in front of Sly Stone on the table, capturing every word that was said. No one seemed to mind. But as the interview progressed, even Sheff was surprised that no one seemed to mind. He was aware of the fact that most of what was being said was not making any sense at all.

Finally he decided to try a different tactic, so he suggested that they go out to eat something. Stone agreed, and Sheff, having cautiously sized up the situation, offered to drive, in spite of the fact that his car was a tiny four-door Fiat. Stone was not a small man, and although it was not easy, he managed to squeeze himself into the front seat of the Fiat. Two members of his "entourage" miraculously stuffed themselves into the backseat of the car, which was beginning to sag under the weight that was so obviously exceeding the car's capacity. Then Sheff released the emergency brake and headed for the freeway that would take them to the West Side restaurant where they had decided to go to eat.

It was rather an odd sight, the four of them packed like sardines into the tiny Fiat, sputtering down the L.A. Freeway with Sheff at the wheel. It became even odder when Sheff looked over and noticed that Sly Stone had pulled a blowtorch out of the briefcase he was carrying and began to light up a smoke of cocaine. Petrified, Sheff could not believe his eyes, which he did not dare take off the road for even a second. His car may have been sputtering, but his mind was racing. He just prayed they did not get stopped by the police.

They did not. At the restaurant the two "friends" proceeded to order gigantic meals, obviously aware of the fact that *People* was footing the bill. To Sheff's chagrin, the only thing that Sly Stone ordered was a triple piña colada. The minute he finished it, he got up and disappeared, never to return. The interview, what there had been of it, was over.

It was not, however, as over as Sly Stone would have liked it to have been when he came to his senses later that night. David Sheff was at home, sound asleep, with his wife, Vicki, curled next to him, when his ringing telephone jolted him out of his peaceful slumber. It was Sly Stone. He wanted the tape of the interview back.

Dazed, Sheff muttered something; then, as he tried to gather his thoughts, he told Stone to call him the next day. "The story is done," he said. "I can't give you the tape. That's not the way it works."

Stone was not amused. "He very, very subtly threatened me," says Sheff. "He said that 'his guy' was going to come by and get the tape." When he hung up, Sheff began to realize how worried he was about the conversation that had just transpired. The "guy" did not show up that night, but the shaken writer called Jim Jerome in New York early the next morning and told him what had happened. "I don't know if he knew this already or if he looked in the file," recalls Sheff, "but somehow he found out that the same guy who Sly was going to send over to me had very recently been let out of jail. He had been accused of murdering somebody, but he beat the rap because Sly was in the next room and he said he didn't hear anything, so there was no evidence. It was," he adds in an impressive understatement, "a fairly terrifying few days." To Sheff's relief, the guy was never heard from after that.

As the months passed, David Sheff continued to add music stories to his accumulating experience as a reporter, and in August he was assigned a piece that he could not wait to sink his teeth into: The Blues Brothers, John Belushi and Dan Aykroyd—stars of the hip television show *Saturday Night Live*, epitomizing the very cutting edge of entertainment—were also starring in a soon-to-be-released movie, one of the most expensive films ever made, which had generated a greatly anticipated sound-track album.

With experiences like the one he had had with Sly Stone, a good deal of Sheff's naïveté was wearing off, and although he had never met either Belushi or Aykroyd, he had read enough about them in preparing for the interview to know that they were not going to make it easy for him. He was right.

Universal Studios had invested a fortune in the film. There would be a massive opening that involved a press junket, which had been scheduled to take place at the Plaza Hotel in New York. There, Belushi and Aykroyd, along with director John Landis, as well as some of the soul singers who appeared in the film—Aretha Franklin, Ray Charles, and James Brown— would be made available to the press in a sort of assembly-line fashion.

With the rest of the press, Sheff attended the junket at the Plaza, where he was able to spend some time talking to each of the stars and some time just observing the junket as it unfolded. The little time he got with Belushi and Aykroyd was not very productive for him, at least from the standpoint of the kind of reporting that *People* was always looking for. "Trying to get them to tell a story that was not specifically related to the movie was as if you had asked them to tell a dirty secret about their mother molesting them when they were a child or something," says Sheff.

In spite of that, over the few days he spent hanging out at the Plaza Hotel he was able to establish some kind of a rapport with them. That *People* was planning a cover also gave him some added cachet. "They were getting a lot of pressure that this was a *People* cover and there was so much at stake in this movie that they had to be nice to me, basically," says Sheff. Which is what, he believes, led Belushi to come up to him a few days into the junket, escort him off to a corner, making sure that nobody else was standing too close, and say, "If you promise to keep it a secret, I'll invite you to a Blues Brothers rehearsal tonight, but it will have to be 'off the record.'"

Sheff did not hesitate to say yes, hoping as most reporters usually do that one thing could lead to another and with any luck he might at some point ask if he could use some of what he got "on the record." It was not until midnight that he was to show up at the Manhattan warehouse where the Blues Brothers album was being recorded, and when the time came, he invited his wife to go along. "We showed up at this warehouse that was completely hidden," recalls Sheff. "It was like the Blues Brothers movie, where we had to climb up five flights of unlit stairs and there was this big guy, a security guard, at the door. I told them that John had invited me, so he let me in."

Sheff stood watching the rehearsal with his wife, mesmerized. The stage was lit up and the Blues Brothers were on it, practicing the song "Soul Man." In the middle of the song, Belushi left the stage and walked up to Sheff. The two shook hands, Belushi looked straight at Vicki, and Sheff said, "John, I'd like you to meet my wife." Belushi looked at Vicki, turned around, and returned to the stage to finish the song.

The minute it was over, Belushi hurried back over to where Sheff was standing with his wife. He lurched forward and grabbed Sheff's arm, clenching it in a viselike grip, and then he proceeded to drag the reporter roughly across the room. He pushed him out the door and threw him into the stairwell, slamming the door violently behind him, and then John Belushi stood there ferociously glaring at David Sheff, barely in control of himself. "I told you this was off the record." The words spewed angrily out of his mouth.

Sheff was stunned. "I know this is off the record," he said, wondering what the hell was going on.

"Then what are you doing bringing someone from *Life* magazine?" Belushi growled.

"What are you talking about?" Sheff asked tremulously.

"You just told me that girl was with *Life*," said Belushi.

"No, I didn't," said Sheff. "I said that she was my *wife!*"

Belushi was mortified. "He completely melted," says Sheff. "He felt so stupid, he just transformed, and all the sort of veil and pretense and façade of tough and unavailable instantly melted away, and the rest of the interview was completely the opposite. He came back out and gave Vicki a big hug. He was pretty embarrassed about it."

In the days that followed, Sheff got to know the Blues Brothers in a way few members of the press did, due mostly to the faux pas John Belushi had committed. He never stopped trying to make up for it. Sheff was allowed access that no other journalist got; Belushi let his guard down.

Sheff spent a lot of time with them after that in New York. He was invited to the Blues Brothers' Bar, which Dan Aykroyd had opened so the players would have a place to hang out after *Saturday Night Live.* "All the windows were boarded up," says Sheff. "It was like Las Vegas. You never knew when it was daytime. So they would show up there after *Saturday Night Live,* and the party would begin, and it would end usually sometime on Sunday afternoon. When I went there with them it was really like a wild roller-coaster adventure, just like the movie."

He followed Belushi and Aykroyd to Chicago, where they went to prepare for the Blues Brothers tour, and he got to know the two personalities who were, according to Sheff, like night and day: Belushi, the open, easy teddy bear; Aykroyd, the aloof, tough-to-talk-to guy with an attitude. Years later, long after John Belushi's death, when Sheff interviewed Aykroyd for *Playboy* magazine, he would learn the more accurate picture behind the Blues Brothers façade. "What appeared to be the way they dealt with the world was fairly accurate," says Sheff today. "But it was the complete opposite of what was going on inside. Whereas Aykroyd was much more at peace and much more in control, Belushi, for all his outward appearances of being an open, nice, gentle guy without any guard up, had so much going on inside of him that was just torturing him. Ultimately, it had a lot to do with his death."

Sheff knew, like most others in close proximity, that Belushi was involved with drugs, but he was unaware at the time of that first interview how deep Belushi's turmoil was. Nor was he aware of the severity of his problem with drugs. To this day, Sheff says, Aykroyd feels guilty about it. "Not that he's responsible in any real way," says Sheff, "but when you love somebody and you see them going down the path that is going to kill them, I think there's a feeling of responsibility that's always there, and there is a feeling that there must have been more that you could do."

Aykroyd later admitted to Sheff that they thought about trying to help Belushi out with his drug problem. "They did try to do stuff," says Sheff. "I mean they talked to Belushi about it. But they didn't do other things they thought about. He [Aykroyd] said at one point that the only thing that might have worked was one of those AA-type confrontational meetings. He said Belushi would have said they were all full of shit and walked out of the room. And that is probably true, but still, I think Aykroyd feels some responsibility. Because he [Aykroyd] certainly drank his share, but I don't think he was ever out of control with drugs. As we now know, everyone knew that Belushi was. It wasn't out of control to the point that I could see him sitting in the corner doing drugs and crawling around on his hands and knees. I mean, he was Jake Blue, sort of running the show and having a blast."

After Sheff's *People* story ran he got a call from the Blues Brothers about it. They thanked him and told him it was a great story, but he knew they were not leveling with him. "I knew for sure they didn't like it that much," he says. "They thought it was okay, but they didn't love it. I wrote as much as I could about their personal lives. I remember Belushi going on and on about it. But I could tell they were in someone's office, probably Bernie Brillstein, who was their manager and publicist, who was telling them to call me up, sort of making them say thanks, with the idea of, Who knows when we'll need *People* magazine again?"

The Blues Brothers were not the only couple to confound David Sheff that year. Glen Campbell and Tanya Tucker were right behind them. The relationship between *People* and its subjects has always been a tenuous one— sometimes symbiotic, when there is something in it for everyone; often adversarial, when the issue of privacy is called into question. Yet it is ironic how often subjects express their dissatisfaction with a story and repeatedly come back for more. Glen Campbell and Tanya Tucker were a perfect example.

In 1980, Glen Campbell and Tanya Tucker fell madly, passionately in love with each other. It was clearly something neither had a desire to hide. Sheff was assigned to do a *People* story on the two; according to the reporter, there was no way they could have hidden their mutual desire, had they wanted to. It was reminiscent of the situation the magazine had encountered two years earlier with Clint Eastwood and Sondra Locke. "These two people couldn't keep their hands off each other," says Sheff. "They loved each other so much it was completely obsessive and wild. We photographed them and I think we could barely keep Tanya's hands off him. She wrapped her whole body around him." However, as the *People* story reported, Glen Campbell was still married to someone else at the time.

The cover line read:

GLEN & TANYA
The wildest love affair in showbiz today:
Campbell, 44, and Tucker, 21

In the story, Campbell was quoted as saying, "I gave God a prayer and He gave me Tanya Tucker." Sarah, his wife at the time, was quoted as saying, "Well, I gave God a prayer, too, and he let Glen find Tanya Tucker."

The whole thing made David Sheff uncomfortable. Like many *People* reporters, he often found it difficult to deal with such personal matters. In this case, however, he did not even have to ask for the intimate details. "They were feeding them to us on silver trays in a way that was just so embarrassing," he says. "Then the stories would come out from their press people that they were really upset about them. Then six months or nine months later they would come back and do it again. Every time. You know, 'Hit me again.' "

It happened often, and not just with Glen and Tanya. *People* did two more stories on Glen and Tanya, and finally, less than a year after the first one, another cover:

TANYA vs. GLEN
It's kaput for the Rhinestone Couple,
and a spurned Tucker tells why

Why certain people have a desire to air such personal issues publicly is an intriguing question. *People* magazine is living, thriving proof that people—especially celebrities—often do, confirming Dick Stolley's original instincts when *People* was still in its formative stages. Who would have guessed how quickly it would spawn an infinite number of other forums from print to radio to television talk shows to satisfy the seemingly essential and unfulfilled need people had to confess even the most intimate things publicly?

Still, some reporters had a difficult time on the receiving end of these revelations, and Sheff was one of them. The culmination of his reluctance to delve into such private matters came when he was asked to contribute to a piece about the actress Loni Anderson that was well in the works at the time. The Los Angeles bureau of *People* had done an interview with Anderson; several last-minute questions needed to be answered to complete the story, and Sheff was given a list of those questions, drawn up by the editors who were putting the story together. "They asked me to ask her ten questions," says Sheff, "and the first nine were normal: tell us how you feel about the movie, stuff like that. The last question was: Is it true that you have had your breasts reduced? I thought that I just wasn't going to do it. There is a line of that stuff that is just too personal. Maybe they just asked the wrong person to do it. Maybe someone else would have said it isn't that big a deal."

To Sheff, however, it was a big deal. "I just drew the line," he says. He asked the first nine questions and filed Anderson's replies to New York. "I don't remember if I said I didn't ask the tenth question or if I said she didn't want to talk about that," he admits. He did not hear more about it. The story closed and it was out on the stands when he got a call from an editor in New York three days later, telling him to turn on *The Mike Douglas Show*. Puzzled, Sheff switched his TV set on, and there was Loni Anderson talking effusively about her recent breast reduction.

"I had been trying to save her from these ghoulish people," says Sheff. "I guess I should have known better."

CHAPTER TWELVE

Help!

"It's not that I don't like people. I enjoy them. It's that it gets
wearing. People don't realize they aren't the only ones who want
something. The postman wants an autograph. The cabdriver wants a
picture. The waitress wants a handshake. Everyone wants a piece of
you. It's never-ending."

—*JOHN LENNON*
to reporter David Sheff several months before
his death on December 8, 1980

NOT ONLY DID Mount Saint Helens erupt in 1980, hurling a cubic
mile of earth and ash into the unsuspecting atmosphere, the United
States boycotted the Olympic Games, Muhammad Ali ended his boxing
career at the age of thirty-eight after being beaten in Nevada on October 2 by
thirty-year-old Larry Holmes, and Ronald Reagan was the first movie star to
become president of the United States. On top of that, as the year's television
season ended, nobody had the slightest idea who shot J. R. Ewing of *Dallas*.

Unfortunately, there was no doubt about who shot John Lennon, on the
cold dark night of December 8, 1980, as he returned home to his apartment
at the Dakota on Central Park West in Manhattan after a night of recording
with his wife Yoko Ono. A heavyset man had stepped out of the shadows and
fired four bullets into Lennon's back. When the police arrived, they found the
man, an unemployed amateur guitarist, patiently waiting to be arrested. His
name was Mark David Chapman. While he waited for the police, he thumbed
through a copy of J. D. Salinger's *The Catcher in the Rye*. As word of the
shooting spread, hundreds of mourners gathered by candlelight outside the
Dakota. "All you need is love. Love is all you need." That is what they sang.

Across town and down twenty blocks, in the offices of *People* magazine on the twenty-ninth floor of the Time & Life Building, the staff was trying to close the week's issue. It was Monday night, relatively early in terms of a closing night—around 11:00 P.M.—when word of Lennon's death hit. First Hal Wingo tried to reach Mary Dunn, but she had not arrived home from the office yet, so he called M. C. Marden at home to tell her what happened.

"Hi, Hal!" M.C. said, wondering why he was calling.

"John Lennon's been shot," she heard him say next.

"Oh, who's the photographer?" replied M.C., assuming Wingo could only be referring to pictures.

"No, M.C.," said Wingo, "he's been shot with a gun. Can you come in?"

M.C. was stunned. She hung up the phone and stared out her window onto Seventy-eighth Street, not far from where John Lennon had just been shot. God, I can't believe this, she thought, he's been killed.

She had, as she later recalled, about two minutes to really feel how horrible it was. Then she got in a cab to go to the office. Since she lived only a few blocks from the Dakota, the cab went down Central Park West, passing Lennon's cavernous apartment building, where the crowd was beginning to gather. Choking back her emotions, needing to tell *somebody* what had happened, she said to the cabdriver, "John Lennon's been killed." The cabdriver did not understand what she was saying. He spoke little English and he did not know who John Lennon was. "I couldn't even share it with him," she recalls.

When she arrived at the *People* offices, the mood changed drastically. There was work to be done, a cover to close. Somehow the urgency always pulled you out of the despair, or the chance to think about the meaning of the tragedy. The minute M.C. got out of the elevator, Dick Stolley grabbed her. He was shouting: "How can we get pictures of John and Yoko! Where can we go? Where can we go? We've got to do this!" An overwhelming sense of urgency prevailed. "We've got to have something for the cover," he told M.C.

In addition to the current issue for that week, which was to have "Charlie's Newest Angel," Tanya Roberts, on the cover, *People* was preparing to close its annual year-end issue, the double issue that named the magazine's choice of the twenty-five most intriguing people of the year. Ironically, John and Yoko Lennon, who were making a comeback with a new album, *Double Fantasy*, after virtually dropping out for five years, had already been included. Thanks to Maddy Miller, a freelancer in the picture department who was working exclusively on the year-end issue at the time, the magazine had just gotten ahold of a stunning take of pictures of John and Yoko by the photographer Jack Mitchell. M.C. flashed on that immediately. They had already selected the photograph for the double issue. "Why don't we take the picture off of the year-end and make that the cover?" she said.

The rest, in terms of pictures, was fairly easy, given the circumstances. The staff pulled together solidly, as it always did during a crisis, and rose to the occasion. Everyone in the picture department disbursed to collect every Lennon picture they could get their hands on—pictures that would end up filling eleven pages of the magazine. Many were gleaned from the impressive and invaluable Time Inc. Picture Collection. In spite of the fact that it was late at night, M.C. had a key to that collection. It was contained in an enormous room in the subbasement of the Time & Life Building, filled with file cabinets that held thousands and thousands of pictures: every picture, for instance, that has ever run in *Life* magazine, from the first assignment in the history of *Life* through the last; every picture acquired by Time Inc. for any of its magazines from the multitude of picture agencies in the world, like AP and UPI. Endless photographs, filed by the person's name and by subject.

M. C. Marden knew precisely how to use the picture collection, where to go to get what she needed. The photo department staff assembled an amazing array of pictures of John Lennon: a recent portrait; a picture with ex-wife Cynthia Twist; a picture of John with his mother, Julia; Beatles pictures, including the famous one of a pillow fight taken by Harry Benson at the Hotel George V in Paris in 1964 at the height of their career; Yoko and John, naked, as they posed for the jacket of their first LP, *Two Virgins*, in 1968, the year before they were married; an ironic drawing for a book, *The Beatles Illustrated Lyrics*, in which artist Michael Leonard envisioned what John, Paul, Ringo, and George might look like at age sixty-four; a picture of John in front of the Statue of Liberty upon winning a long battle for permanent American resident status (after he was ordered deported by the Justice Department for smoking marijuana). More than enough to fill the pages that would become the tribute to John Lennon.

Still, there had to be words to go with the pictures—that was a separate problem. What would the story be? The magazine had to close the next day, with only the details of the murder that would be available by then. For once, the timing was lucky. This time the big story had happened conveniently on a Monday. They would not be beaten by anyone.

The minute he heard about John Lennon's murder, something occurred to Stolley in a flash. He remembered the lengthy *Playboy* interview with Lennon, the first that Lennon had done in years, which had come out on the newsstand that very day—Monday, December 8, the same day that Lennon was shot. Stolley had received an advance copy of the magazine the previous

Friday. The in-depth interview, which was quite impressive, had been done several months earlier—*Playboy* had approximately a three-month "lead" time. The piece had been written by none other than David Sheff, one of his most reliable freelancers.

In the midst of the frenzy following the news of Lennon's death, Stolley asked Hal Wingo to call Sheff in L.A. and get him to New York instantly to write the Lennon article that had to close the next day, Tuesday. He then got on the phone to Sheff's editor at *Playboy* to convince him to allow Sheff to do a Lennon piece for *People*. After all, the information Sheff had gotten about Lennon had been paid for, essentially, by *Playboy*, and the magazine was on the stands at that very moment.

There was a lot of negotiating back and forth, and finally Stolley was able to work out a deal: He agreed to print in the opening paragraphs of the *People* story the fact that Lennon had granted the most extensive interview of his career to David Sheff and that the interview appeared in the current issue of *Playboy*.

While Stolley and M. C. Marden scurried around, collecting and choosing pictures and putting the rest of the issue together—there was more to the issue than just the Lennon story—Wingo got on the phone to Sheff in L.A.

Moments before his phone rang, David Sheff had been sitting on the couch at home with his wife, watching *Monday Night Football*. When the shrill ringing of the telephone pierced the air, he was still in shock from what he had just heard in the middle of the football broadcast, when Howard Cosell had interrupted the game to convey the tragic news that had just come over the wire. It had fallen to him to inform the millions of football fans engrossed in the game that Monday night that John Lennon had been shot and killed. David Sheff could not believe it.

He had become so close to John Lennon—and Yoko, too. And their little five-year-old son, Sean. The time he had spent with them doing the interview for *Playboy* only a few months before was one of the most extraordinary experiences of his life. He was only twenty-four years old, and although he had already done quite a few pieces for *People*, it was the first interview he had done for *Playboy*. The fact that he had gotten the assignment had been something of a fluke. He had actually been in the *Playboy* offices pitching them a story on the Blues Brothers, after he had done it for *People*. As he was leaving the office, just as he was about to shut the door behind him, the editor stopped him and asked him if he had any connections to John Lennon. Sheff had told the editor he did not, but savoring the possibility of doing a story on John Lennon, he made up his mind to try damn hard to find one.

He checked around with his music contacts, did everything he could, then he composed a letter that he sent to Lennon. John and Yoko were finishing up their album, coming out of hiding after five years of hibernation. John had felt burned out, he needed to regenerate his creative side. *Double Fantasy* was almost finished and they had just decided that they would do only two magazine pieces to promote it: one for a weekly (they selected *Newsweek*); and one for a monthly (they chose *Playboy*).

It was at precisely the moment they had made that decision that Sheff's letter had arrived in the mail. Shortly after that, Sheff had received a call from Yoko's assistant, asking him, of all things, when he was born and where. After Yoko did his numbers and his astrological chart, she decided that he should be the one to do the piece.

That is how it had begun, one of the most poignant and memorable experiences of David Sheff's life. He had flown to New York and checked into a hotel, where he stayed for three weeks while he spent the time he needed with John and Yoko Lennon for his *Playboy* interview. Every morning he met them at the Dakota. Sheff would go up to the seventh floor in what became his daily ritual: John or one of the housekeepers opened the door, and after a few moments he and John slipped out and walked over to La Fortuna, a little coffee shop at Seventy-first near Columbus, where they ate breakfast and talked. They would sit and sip coffee, often for two or three hours. Then Yoko picked them up in their limousine, and they would head for the recording studio, where they spent the next twelve hours or so.

John and Yoko were still in the process of making *Double Fantasy*. David Sheff got to sit in the studio and watch them, to see a couple very different from the way they had been perceived and portrayed by the world. "What I saw," recalls Sheff, "were these two people, almost like teenagers, the way they were so involved with each other and so totally obsessed with each other. If one of them wasn't in the room, the other was aware of where they were, always watching and looking over their shoulder. They'd just be checking on each other constantly. John would be behind the console, being the engineer, turning buttons and stuff while musicians would be playing. And Yoko would be there lying on the couch, knitting or taking a nap. Or vice versa: She'd be in the control room and he would be just taking a nap. I just watched. Sometimes John would be there playing a new song, like 'Starting Over,' or something like that, behind the glass, and he'd have his guitar and then the engineers would be fixing the tape and doing the technical work. John would be just messing around, and all of a sudden he'd play the most soulful, haunting version of 'Help' that one could ever hear. It was just an astounding thing."

When the long day in the studio was done, at eight or nine or ten o'clock,

Sheff returned to the apartment at the Dakota with the Lennons, where they had an easy dinner—usually something like sushi. Then, sometimes they told him that was it for the day. Sometimes they dropped him back at the hotel. Sometimes he took a cab home. But there were those rare and wonderful nights for David Sheff when John Lennon was just too wound up to stop talking, when he would ask Sheff to stay and they talked long into the night.

What Sheff remembers most was John Lennon, the father, with his son Sean. "Sean would run into the kitchen and jump on his lap," recalls Sheff. "You saw this guy who had had it all, according to so many people's measures, in terms of the creative abilities to express himself in so many different ways and who certainly made a lot of money and had been more famous as a Beatle than anybody could ever be—you just saw that the only thing that he cared about, the thing that was really defining and shaping his life was his relationship with his son."

Those moments were so powerful for David Sheff that they would affect his own life profoundly. "There was something about the magic I saw there," he admits, "that influenced me when I came back after that experience. The fact that I came home and Vicki and I decided to have a baby had a lot to do with being inspired by seeing John Lennon with Sean."

Sheff also got a lasting picture of John Lennon, the man and his words. "He spoke like a poet who could turn a phrase at the end of some impassioned speech and make it funny and ironic at the same time," he recalls. "A thought would begin and then he would go off on some tangent and then return to the same point in a way that was remarkable."

Although the time he had spent with the Lennons had begun in August and ended in September, the story did not come out in the magazine until December because of the "lead time." People who got their issues in the mail received the *Playboy* in which Sheff's Lennon story was published on Friday, December 5. The following Sunday, Yoko had called Sheff to tell him that she and John had gotten an early copy of the magazine from *Playboy*. "They had read the piece," says David, "and they were really pretty excited about it." The next day John Lennon was dead.

So when Hal Wingo called David Sheff on the phone that Monday night, Sheff was understandably shaken. Yet even before the reality had a chance to sink in, before he could begin to absorb what had happened, Sheff found himself doing something he would later regret to a degree, since it denied him the chance to deal with his own emotions at the time: Within seconds, he was on the phone finding the only way it was possible for him, given the time of night, to fly to New York and arrive there by morning.

Since there were no direct flights from L.A. to New York at the time

Wingo called, David and his wife spent the entire night on a circuitous route in order to get to their destination. They went through Pittsburgh and then Atlanta, they flew and they drove, but somehow they made it in time for Sheff to put in an appearance on the *Today* show at NBC, across the street from the Time & Life Building, before arriving at *People* magazine. But not before he called Yoko, left a message with his condolences, and sent her a beautiful bouquet of flowers.

By the time Sheff, half dazed, left 30 Rockefeller Plaza, where the *Today* studio was and walked over to the Time & Life Building, across the street, he was thoroughly exhausted, not only emotionally but physically—as completely exhausted as Dick Stolley and Jim Gaines were anxious for him to arrive at *People*, sit down at the typewriter, and divest himself of the story about John Lennon they were praying that he had percolating inside him.

When Sheff stepped out of the elevator on the twenty-ninth floor early on the morning of Tuesday, December 9, the day the magazine had to close, Stolley was there to greet him. He quickly hustled Sheff down the hall to the office they had ready and waiting for him, stuck him in it, and said simply, "Write." Sheff remembers what went through his head, as tired as he was. Write what? he thought to himself.

Stolley left the office to which they had consigned Sheff and quietly shut the door behind him. About a half hour later, he returned. He stood very quietly outside the door, straining to hear the tapping of the typewriter keys that were, with any luck at all, spewing forth David Sheff's Lennon story. He listened. Nothing. He moved closer, finally pressing his ear to the door of the office. Still he heard no sound at all. What was going on with David Sheff, he wondered.

David was on overload. He sat and stared at the typewriter, running through his mind the time he had spent with John and Yoko and Sean, trying to recapture the intensity of what he had felt when he was with them, the details of the weeks he had shared with them doing the *Playboy* piece. He was exhausted, mentally and physically drained, and it was a difficult assignment. The minutes were ticking away. Finally he began to type.

As the deadline got closer and closer, Jim Gaines walked into David Sheff's office. He knew that Sheff had all the ammunition, and he began to try to help him extract it. He started asking him questions, every question he could think of about John and Yoko Lennon and David's experience with them. Jim and David worked late into the day on Tuesday and late into the night. Finally, the John Lennon story was complete. As it turned out, the closing was the latest in the history of the magazine. They did not wrap up all the details for the final close until Wednesday at noon, which was unheard of at the time.

The cover line of the John Lennon issue said simply:

**JOHN LENNON
1940–1980
A TRIBUTE**

Not only was it the first time that *People* had ever put a dead person on the cover, it became the bestselling issue in the history of the magazine, selling 2,644,000 copies, breaking the magazine's record for newsstand sales of a regular issue. The "Tribute to John Lennon" issue of *People* remains the top-selling cover to this day.

TOP 5
THE ROYAL WEDDING
LIZ & LUKE & LAURA
LADY DI: A SNEAK PREVIEW
BROOKE SHIELDS (*ENDLESS LOVE*)
BO DEREK IN *TARZAN*

1981

1981 COVERS

Yoko Ono

Jane Fonda, Dolly Parton
& Lily Tomlin (*9 to 5*)

Charlene Tilton of *Dallas*

Frank Sinatra

Tanya Roberts

Ringo Starr & Barbara Bach

Sally Struthers & Daughter Samantha

John Phillips & Daughter Mackenzie

Soap Opera Actors: Christopher Bernau
& Michael Corbett

Deborah Harry

Jacqueline Onassis

Victoria Principal of *Dallas*

Catherine Bach

Ronald Reagan

Jodie Foster

Danielle Brisebois & Carroll O'Connor

Tanya Tucker & Glen Campbell

Farrah Fawcett & Ryan O'Neal

Readers' Poll

Larry & Billie Jean King

Phyllis George & Son Lincoln

Lauren Bacall

Alan Alda

Lady Diana Spencer

Richard Pryor

Christopher Reeve

Morgan Fairchild

Harrison Ford & Karen Allen

Bo Derek with Miles O'Keefe in *Tarzan,
the Ape Man*

Prince Charles & Lady Diana

Brooke Shields

John Travolta & Nancy Allen

Margot Kidder

Mark Hamill

Kris Kristofferson & Daughter Casey

Dudley Moore & Susan Anton

Best- and Worst-Dressed People

Pat Benatar

Faye Dunaway

Sandra Day O'Connor

Jaclyn Smith

Lindsay Wagner

Richard Simmons

Valerie Bertinelli

Elizabeth Taylor, Genie Francis
& Anthony Geary

Princess Diana

John & Caroline Kennedy

Johnny Carson

Priscilla Barnes, John Ritter
& Joyce DeWitt

Larry Hagman

YEAR-END DOUBLE ISSUE:
Elizabeth Taylor, President Ronald Reagan,
Princess Diana, Mick Jagger, Tom Selleck,
John McEnroe, Barbara Mandrell

BOTTOM 5
SANDRA DAY O'CONNOR
DANIELLE BRISEBOIS
LINDSAY WAGNER
MARK HAMILL
DUDLEY MOORE

Films: *Raiders of the Lost Ark*
Superman II
Stir Crazy
9 to 5
Stripes

...ar: *Chariots of Fire*

...TV Shows: *Dallas*
The Dukes of Hazzard
60 Minutes
*M*A*S*H*
The Love Boat

...mys: *Taxi*
Hill Street Blues

...Songs: "Physical"—Olivia Newton-John
"Bette Davis Eyes"—Kim Carnes
"Endless Love"—Diana Ross
& Lionel Richie
"Kiss On My List"—Daryl Hall
& John Oates
"Slow Hand"—The Pointer Sisters
"Jessie's Girl"—Rick Springfield

...ammys: "Bette Davis Eyes" (record)
"Bette Davis Eyes" (song)

...stsellers: *Brain*—Robin Cook
Gorky Park—Martin Cruz Smith
The Hotel New Hampshire—John Irving

Loon Lake—E. L. Doctorow
Noble House—James Clavell
The Cinderella Complex—Colette Dowling
Pathfinders—Gail Sheehy

Tonys: *Amadeus*
42nd Street
The Pirates of Penzance

Marriages: Georgia Rosenbloom + Dominic Frontiere
Bruce Jenner + Linda Thompson
Cary Grant + Barbara Harris
Maureen Reagan + Dennis Revell
Ringo Starr + Barbara Bach
Cheryl Tiegs + Peter Beard
Prince Charles + Lady Diana Spencer
George Wallace + Lisa Taylor

Divorces Grant Tinker & Mary Tyler Moore
Jeff Wald & Helen Reddy

Deaths: Jack Albertson   Richard Boone
Omar Bradley   Paddy Chayefsky
Moshe Dayan   Ariel Durant
Will Durant   William Holden
Hoagy Carmichael   Bob Marley
Robert Montgomery   Anwar Sadat
William Saroyan   Vera-Ellen
Natalie Wood   William Wyler
Harry Chapin

NEWS

- Billie Jean King sued for palimony by lover Marilyn Barnett
- Anwar Sadat assassinated
- JFK airport bombing kills one
- John Hinckley, Jr., crazed Jodie Foster fan, tries to kill President Reagan
- Norman Mailer protégé Jack Henry Abbott arrested for New York murder
- Porno star John Holmes arrested for four L.A. murders
- Carol Burnett wins $1.6 million libel case against the *National Enquirer*
- Iran releases 52 American hostages
- First space shuttle, *Columbia*, launched
- Pope John Paul II wounded in assassination attempt in Saint Peter's Square
- Prince Charles and Lady Di wed
- Sandra Day O'Connor named first woman to Supreme Court
- Walkway collapses in Kansas City Hyatt Regency hotel killing 111 people
- Simon and Garfunkel reunion in Central Park
- AIDS virus identified

CHAPTER THIRTEEN

To Di For
(The Fairy-Tale Years)

"I'm amazed that she's brave enough to take me on."
—*PRINCE CHARLES*,
as quoted in People's *first story about Diana Spencer,
his bride-to-be, March 9, 1981*

FROM DAY ONE, Dick Burgheim had been Dick Stolley's right-hand man. If anyone worked as hard or was as loyal or gave as much around the clock, day in, day out, as Stolley did, it was this sweet, bright, shy, munchkinesque man, the Harvard grad who had such an amazing facility with the written word, but an equally difficult time communicating out loud. When you walked into Dick Burgheim's office late at night or around the time the sun was coming up, the picture was always the same: Burgheim sitting there at his desk with his red-rimmed, bloodshot, tired eyes, never more than a few inches from a can of diet Coke, usually having had a brandy or two to stimulate his mind and keep him awake, with the familiar, slightly crooked half-smile on his face, slaving over a piece of copy, employing his unique aptitude to form the mutant words that comprised the distinctive new language that had come to epitomize *People* magazine. He explained it himself once, saying, "Compression is the art. The readers are in a hurry and we want to amuse them but not confuse them." Dick Burgheim was the wizard of compression.

By 1981 there was, for instance, tacked to the walls of numerous *People* offices a list of 220 synonyms for "says," which included: "palavers," "pants," "pipes," "prattles," "sasses," "snits," "sneers," "squelches," "tattles," "twinkles," and "beams." *People* had by then coined such words as "megabucks," "glitterati," "altar-shy," and "bicoastal." But the true genius of the Peoplesque twist, aside from what Stolley had referred to as the best "Burgheimism" in the history of the magazine (about Warren Beatty and the "heartbreak of satyriasis"), was exemplified by an item in a "Chatter" column about a posh but drug-laden Hollywood picnic. The headline read: "Lunch on the Grass." The point, as Stolley once put it, was "to say what we have to say as quickly as possible and get on to something else."

Perhaps the best moment in this regard came for Dick Stolley when— seven years after his scathing column bashing the first issue of *People*— William Safire actually praised a subhead in the magazine in his own *New York Times* column. "Subheads are the last refuge of the inside joke," he wrote, referring to the *People* subhead 'Lumpen Proletariat,' which was written for another "Chatter" item about Congresswoman Millicent Fenwick, who frequently carried a box of spaghetti in her bag. "The sophisticated subhead writer," wrote Safire, "was playing on Mrs. Fenwick's lumpy bag and the rags worn by working women—a neat, bilingual pun."

This very style was what made *People* such a perfect target for parody, and the *Harvard Lampoon* seized the opportunity that same year, with *People*'s blessing. The *Lampoon*—even better than *Esquire* had done several years earlier—managed to capture that singular *People* style: with a cover billing that read "TV's Fabulous Sluts"; a picture of actress Morgan ("Pothead") Fairchild wearing a tin can on her head; a profile of "Boxing Nun Sister Mary Stigmata" accompanied by a headline that read, "Pow! In the Boxing Ring, Sister Mary Stigmata Is Clearly Second to Nun"; and an interview with "Agent Orange." Nobody at *People* complained.

There were, of course, those who took exception to *People*'s distinctive use of the English language. But there was no one who could legitimately criticize the extraordinary effort the magazine made to check the hundreds of facts in each story, to do everything that was humanly possible to assure that every printed word, concept, fact, and description, right down to the exact color of a person's pet goldfish (and the spelling of the fish's name) was correct.

Even *The Wall Street Journal* was impressed enough to do a long, front-page feature story about the fact-checking process, which in itself was a turning point for the magazine. The fact that *The Wall Street Journal* devoted a front-page piece to the accuracy of *People* impressed potential advertisers mightily. *People* was spending eight hundred thousand a year on its fact-checking department by that time to assure that the answers to the questions about birth dates, sex lives, eating habits, and other intimate details of its subjects' lives that were so prevalent in the magazine's pages were correct. Things like: How old is Victoria Principal, *really*? Does Walter Cronkite eat meat? Does Saul Bellow stand on his head?

Seven years after it was launched, it seemed that everywhere you turned, *People* was getting attention. According to the W. R. Simmons research firm, 11.8 million women and 8.6 million men were reading the magazine by 1981. The year would be rich in news stories, too: The hostages in Iran were freed; President Ronald Reagan was shot; Sandra Day O'Connor became the first woman in history to be named to the Supreme Court; Dan Rather replaced Walter Cronkite (who *did* eat meat); Billie Jean King was sued by a woman who claimed to be her former lover; Elizabeth Taylor showed up at Luke and Laura's wedding on the popular soap *General Hospital;* IBM introduced the personal computer; and AIDS was actually identified for the first time.

Something else happened in 1981 that would have a greater effect on *People* magazine than all of those things combined—an effect that would permanently alter the course of the magazine, not to mention the English monarchy: Prince Charles finally found his royal bride. Luckily for *People,* she was Lady Diana Spencer, who would, by the end of the magazine's first twenty years, not only appear on its cover more than any other person in the world but also would be singularly responsible for an estimated seven million dollars in profits over the next twelve years—profits that undoubtedly would not otherwise have been earned, according to Jeremy Koch, the magazine's associate publisher—from the first time she appeared in *People*'s pages in 1981 until the end of the magazine's second decade of life in March 1994.

People had always paid proper attention to royalty, but until "Shy Di" showed up, the subject had not commanded that much interest. Along with all of Great Britain, *People* magazine had been worrying about Charles for some time. In November 1974, a womanless Prince Charles appeared on the cover in his riding clothes, solo, with this cover line:

PRINCE CHARLES
He's turning 26,
without a future queen in sight

Each time there was an inkling of the prince finding romance, *People* was diligently there to report it, with the help of the savvy and well-connected staff in its London bureau. As Terry Smith, one of the London bureau reporters, who was also a photographer, explains, "Before Di came along the big story on Fleet Street was the current woman linked with Charles, even though Fleet Street knew full well much of that time that the women they were linking with Charles had no chance of ever becoming his bride, and indeed many of them were no more than a front for the affair he was already carrying on with Camilla Parker Bowles."

People was finally able to announce, "Prince Charles Finally Finds His Royal Bride: A Shy Teacher Named Diana Spencer," in the issue dated March 9, 1981, indeed a memorable day in the magazine's history. From that moment on, Diana Spencer's life, from her courtship through her marriage through her children and the decline of her marriage—including every detail from her shoes to her hairdressers—would be meticulously charted in the pages of *People* magazine.

The charting was not a simple matter. The principals in what was virtually the biggest story to hit *People* in its first decade were unequivocally not available for interviews; yet over the years, *People* became the magazine of record in the United States when it came to covering Charles and Diana, along with anything—or anyone—that was remotely related to them. It may not have been easy, but *People* quickly found the way to do it.

Thanks to the London bureau, every word printed in the British press— ten daily and nine Sunday newspapers—about Charles and Di was clipped, collated, and filed. That in itself was a daunting task. After Diana gave a speech in 1993 at a conference on eating disorders, Terry Smith calculated that the total column-inch coverage devoted to the speech amounted, literally, to twenty-seven feet in the daily press alone.

Besides the bureau staff's own impressive contacts—palace insiders, Charles's physiotherapist, Di's astrologer, Fergie's hairdresser, from each of whom it was always hoped an occasional unintended nugget might drop—the London reporters relied heavily on their own informants within the British press. Each one had a specific area of expertise: Nigel Dempster was said to have the hot line to Princess Margaret; Brian Hoey had well-cultivated sources within the Buckingham Palace household; James Whitaker followed Diana to virtually every one of her official and unofficial engagements at home or abroad.

With that royalty team solidly in place, along with an infinite amount of ingenuity, combined with the proficient stateside help required to get the stories tuned and shaped right for the American reading public, *People* was in gear to come up with the meticulous facts, the details, and every conceivable last ounce of trivia that would fill their stories on the royals in the roller-coaster years to come.

The first Diana cover appeared in *People* on June 22, 1981—six weeks before her wedding:

LADY DIANA
A sneak preview
of her Big Day:
the wedding gowns
(all 6 of them!),
the gifts, guests
and the royal pain
of planning it all

When it sold 2,291,000 newsstand copies—nearly all of the copies that were printed that week—the message was loud and clear: Princess Di was destined to become a staple of *People* magazine. (The previous week's issue with Alan Alda on the cover had sold only 1,751,000 copies, and he had been voted "the most popular star on television" by *People*'s readers themselves.)

In 1981 and 1982, the first two years in which she was a *People* feature attraction, Diana appeared on five full covers, accounting for an astounding total of 11,786,000 issues sold on newsstands alone (aside from the additional half-million subscription sales per week, which were increasing each year). She also appeared on the year-end double issue cover, as well as on the cover of the 1981 best- and worst-dressed issue and the 1982 Readers' Poll issue. If there was even the germ of a story, *People* would not miss the opportunity.

The fact that the actual wedding of Charles and Diana took place on a Wednesday, as royal weddings customarily do, made it impossible for *People* to cover the ceremony "live," since the magazine closed on Wednesday. Still, *People* managed to do two covers (and a total of fourteen inside pages) around it. The first Di cover featured every conceivable fact that could be gotten about the wedding plans:

Eight social secretaries had hand-addressed the two thousand five hundred gold-embossed invitations that went out. Diana got only one hundred, her parents, who were divorced, fifty each, and Prince Charles three hundred. The queen got the rest and sent them to, among others, Nancy and Ronald Reagan (she was coming, he was not), and François Mitterrand.

Diana, with her sixty-thousand-dollar sapphire-and-diamond engagement ring, needed "everything a newlywed needs," according to an aide. These items included "sofas for the living room and wooden spoons for the kitchen."

Di had chosen Royal Worcester oven-to-table ware for her china pattern, a Villeroy and Boch breakfast set with yellow-and-green geraniums on it, and a modest sixty-dollar coffeepot. She would have five attendants at her wedding (children of her friends, including Princess Margaret's daughter, Sarah Armstrong-Jones). Charles would be attended by his brothers, Andrew and Edward.

The wedding preview story profiled the caterer (the cake would be prepared by Chief Petty Officer David Avery); the church (Saint Paul's Cathedral); the preacher who would officiate (Dr. Robert Runcie); and the royal dressmakers (David and Elizabeth Emanuel), who would make five extra copies of the wedding gown, just in case anything untoward occurred.

The article discussed everything from the fact that Di bought black leotards for eighteen dollars for the pre-wedding ballet sessions she had arranged at Clarence House, where she stayed until her marriage, to the fact that an hour before the wedding Diana and her father would climb into a 1910 glassed-in coach, preceded by Prince Charles in a 1902 royal landau adorned with gold and upholstered in crimson satin. It even gave the names of the royal horses that would pull the coach (Oscar, Roland, and Lady Penelope, among them). And it detailed the couple's purported honeymoon plans (the Caribbean with a long stop at the Bahamian island of Windermere, aboard the royal yacht *Britannia*). In fact, they ended up cruising the Mediterranean (Gibraltar and the Greek Islands); the boat was being stocked, as *People* went to press, with Di's favorite dessert (cherry strudel).

The next cover, which closed *before* but appeared the week *of* the wedding in July because of the deadline problem, delicately wriggled around the fact that the wedding had not actually taken place even though the magazine would be on the stands after it had:

GOOD SHOW!
Behind the pageantry, a handful of loyal subjects
gives a magic touch to the fairy-tale wedding

This time *People* profiled the man who would drive the coach that would carry Diana and her father; the Hampshire grandmother who made Di's lace (royal) garter; the leader of the boy's chorus that would sing at the wedding; the florist who would make Diana's bouquet; the man who would coif her hair for the wedding; the lepidopterist whose silk farm produced the skeins for the cloth that would become Diana's wedding gown; the cleaning women who would dust the cavernous Saint Paul's Cathedral prior to the wedding; and the man who actually built the bed for the couple's new Gloucestershire estate, Highgrove.

In spite of the fact that the issue contained no pictures from the wedding (but plenty of others), this second Diana cover, dated August 3, 1981, sold 2,551,000 copies, nearly a quarter of a million copies more than the first one.

Three months later, the princess was pregnant. The issue was dated November 23, 1981:

THE PREGNANT PRINCESS
Nannies, nappies, names
and Lord knows what all:
Di and Charles plan for the royal heir

Again it sold more than two million copies.

People managed to squeeze in—and get out—two more Diana covers before the next year, 1982, was over. Of course, there was one for the birth:

OH BOY!
For Diana's 7 pound, 1½-ounce prince,
the palace plans a future fit for a king

There had actually been two covers ready and waiting for the royal birth, one with a pink background, should it be a girl, and the blue that was actually used when the baby turned out to be Prince William. Diana was kind enough to make up for the fact that she had gotten married on a Wednesday by having her baby on a Monday, which was ideal for *People*'s closing schedule. That issue, dated July 5, 1982, was the biggest yet, selling an astounding 2,579,000 copies on the newsstand alone.

The following month, the issue covered the royal christening:

KING OF HEARTS:
A royal christening—
and a touching moment
for Diana and her little prince

It sold well over two million copies again.

Five covers in fifteen months—an engagement, a marriage, a baby, and a christening—thanks to Princess Di. It seemed that, with good reason, *People* was at least as much in love with Diana as Prince Charles was purported to be.

LADY DI COVERS
(and Copies Sold*), 1981–1984

6/22/81 Lady Diana: A Sneak Preview of Her Wedding (2,291,000)

8/3/81 Good Show! A Magic Touch to the Wedding (2,551,000)

11/23/81 The Pregnant Princess (2,019,000)

7/5/82 Oh, Boy! (2,579,000)

8/16/82 King of Hearts: Prince William (2,346,000)

1/21/83 Diana's Ordeal (1,961,000)

10/1/84 Di's Pride and Joy: Prince Henry Is Born (1,857,000)

* Newsstand sales only—subscriptions not included

1982

1982 COVERS

Richard Thomas & Triplets
Brooke Shields & Calvin Klein
Cher & Children: Chastity & Elijah Blue
Patty Hearst & Daughter Gillian
Timothy Hutton
Olivia Newton-John
Daniel Travanti, Veronica Hamel
 & Michael Conrad (*Hill Street Blues*)
Suzanne Somers
Tom Selleck
Liz Taylor
John Belushi
Kenny & Marianne Rogers
Princess Grace
Henry Fonda & Jane
Readers' Poll
Cheryl Tiegs
Tom Selleck & Bess Armstrong
Pamela Sue Martin & John James
Anthony Geary
Jane Fonda & Tom Hayden
Stefanie Powers
Burt Reynolds & Loni Anderson
Soap Stars Melody Thomas, Tristan
 Rogers & Lisa Brown
Sylvester Stallone & Son Sergio
Henry Thomas of *E.T.*
Princess Diana
Aileen Quinn & Dog Sandy (*Annie*)

John Belushi
Mickey Mouse & Richard Simmons
Dolly Parton
John Ritter & Family
Princess Diana & Prince William
E.T.
Jill St. John & Richard Wagner
Olivia Newton-John
Robin Williams
Best- and Worst-Dressed People
Princess Grace: A Tribute
Ted Knight, Nancy Dussault & Baby Eric
 Michael Wills
Scott Baio
Falcon Crest: Jane Wyman, Ana Alicia,
 Lorenzo Lamas & Falcon Apollo
Celebrities Dating
Cat Garfield
John DeLorean & Family
Monaco's Royal Family: Caroline,
 Stephanie, Albert & Prince Ranier
Mick Jagger & Jerry Hall
Christine Ferrare DeLorean
Larry Hagman & Linda Gray
Yoko Ono & Son, Sean Lennon
Joan Collins

YEAR-END DOUBLE ISSUE:
Princess Diana, Paul Newman, E.T.,
Ted Koppel, Barbra Streisand

Films: E.T.
Rocky III
On Golden Pond
An Officer and a Gentleman
Porky's

_ar_: Gandhi

TV Shows: Dallas
60 Minutes
The Jeffersons
Three's Company
Alice

nys: Barney Miller
Hill Street Blues

Songs: "I Love Rock 'n' Roll"
—Joan Jett & the Blackhearts
"Ebony and Ivory "—Paul McCartney
& Stevie Wonder
"Up Where We Belong"—Joe Cocker
& Jennifer Warnes
"Truly"—Lionel Richie
"Rosanna"—Toto
"Gloria"—Laura Branigan

ammys: "Rosanna " (record)
"Always on My Mind" (song)

stsellers: Cujo—Stephen King
Eden Burning—Belva Plain
Master of the Game—Sidney Sheldon

North and South—Elizabeth Gaskell
The Parsifal Mosaic—Robert Ludlum
Space—James Michener
Cosmos—Carl Sagan
Jane Fonda's Workout Book—Jane Fonda

Tonys: Nicholas Nickleby
Nine
Othello

Marriages: William Agee + Mary Cunningham

Divorces Edward & Joan Kennedy
Herbert & Roxanne Pulitzer
Lee Majors & Farrah Fawcett
Elizabeth Taylor & John Warner

Deaths:

John Belushi	Ingrid Bergman
Alfred Bloomingdale	John Cheever
Henry Fonda	Anna Freud
Archibald MacLeish	Arthur Rubenstein
Lee Strasberg	King Vidor
Dave Garroway	Princess Grace
Paul Lynde	Thelonius Monk
Vic Morrow	Ayn Rand
Leonid Brezhnev	Romy Schneider
Satchel Paige	

NEWS

- Vicki Morgan sues Alfred Bloomingdale for palimony
- Scott Thorson sues Liberace for palimony
- After a three-month investigation, L.A. district attorney rules Marilyn Monroe's death was either a suicide or an accidental drug overdose
- Sophia Loren returns to Italy to serve seventeen days in jail for tax evasion
- Cyanide-laced Tylenol capsules kill seven in Chicago area
- Claus von Bülow found guilty of attempted murder of wife by insulin injection
- Nancy Reagan controversy over free outfits from designers
- Actress Dominique Dunne strangled to death by boyfriend
- John DeLorean arrested on cocaine possession charges
- _Twilight Zone_ movie-set accident kills Vic Morrow and two children
- Wayne Williams found guilty of killing young blacks in Atlanta
- Falkland Islands war erupts between Argentina and Great Britain
- Queen Elizabeth wakes to find intruder in her bedroom
- Jimmy Connor defeats John McEnroe at Wimbledon
- Princess Grace dies in car accident
- Yuri Andropov replaces Leonid Brezhnev after Brezhnev's death
- Barney Clark receives first artificial heart transplant

CHAPTER FOURTEEN

Better Read When Dead

JOHN BELUSHI
A DANGEROUS LIFE,
A TRAGIC DEATH

PRINCESS GRACE
1929–1982
A TRIBUTE

—Cover lines from People, *for two of the bestselling issues of 1982*

IT WAS THE year of *Hill Street Blues* and Tom Selleck; the year Liz and Dick got together yet again, Jane Fonda campaigned for her husband, Tom Hayden (while her workout book climbed to the top of the charts), and Burt and Loni found each other. The "soaps" were hotter than ever. So was Sly Stallone. An alien named E.T. charmed the world, John DeLorean was arrested for cocaine possession, Mick Jagger split with Jerry Hall, and Dick Stolley edited his last issue of *People* magazine, only days after *People*'s eighth birthday, in 1982.

Phil Kunhardt, who had been the editor of *Life*, had decided to retire, and Richard B. Stolley had been named to replace him. "*People* is a very healthy eight-year-old," Stolley said at the time. "I couldn't have asked for a better group of editors to work with, but it's time for somebody else to have the responsibility, the enjoyment—and the hours."

Stolley's replacement was Patricia Ryan, whose career had begun at *Sports Illustrated* (as a researcher) fourteen years before *People* was born. Ryan had worked her way up the long road to the role of top editor; now she became the first woman appointed managing editor of a Time Inc. magazine in twenty-seven years.

On the Friday preceding the closing of his last issue, Dick Stolley still had work to do. There was, after all, an issue to finish, an issue that would bear the last masthead to have his name as managing editor at the top of it. He was not about to let down now.

His last issue was laid out, to the degree that it could be on a Friday. Everything seemed to be under control. Nothing extraordinary seemed likely to throw a wrench into the operation as Dick Stolley glided toward the end of his brilliant career at *People*—until the shocking news hit the offices of *People* magazine that John Belushi was dead.

No one knew more than that. Belushi had been found dead that morning, March 5, 1982, in his bungalow at the hip Chateau Marmont hotel, which was tucked away in the gentle hills of Hollywood above L.A.'s Sunset Strip. How he had died was a mystery, although he had been alive and well the night before. He had dined on the Strip with Robert De Niro, who was casting him in his new film, and then he had driven to West Hollywood to catch a show at the Improv, a showcase for young comedians that he frequented to keep up on the work of new comics. He had even jammed some at On the Rox, a private club where stars often provided spontaneous entertainment. That was all that anyone at *People* knew.

It was ironically befitting that Stolley would have to deal with a decision about a celebrity death cover for his last issue, considering the admitted mistake he had made when Elvis Presley had died—which he still viewed as the single biggest miscalculation of his career at *People*. Now, six years later, here he was, faced with the same problem. John Belushi was no Elvis—or was he? Aside from the tragedy of the death of this young man, this very popular thirty-three-year-old celebrity and exploding star of *Saturday Night Live*, the question had to be asked: Was he big enough for a cover? Dead? The answer, Stolley quickly decided, was yes.

When he started to think about what to do for the story, knowing what he knew at the moment, he immediately thought of David Sheff. Sheff had, he remembered, spent weeks with Belushi and Aykroyd for the Blues Brothers cover and had subsequently spent additional time with them for other stories, as well. He had gotten to know them better than almost any other journalist at the time. Why not have him write his very personal recollections of Belushi as he had done with John Lennon? That had certainly worked well. More than a year later, it was still the biggest-selling cover in the history of the magazine.

Stolley asked Jim Gaines, who was still the editor of the "Up Front" section, to make the call to Sheff, who was living in San Francisco at the time. Gaines had worked with Sheff on the Lennon story—he had actually ended up prying it out of him. John Belushi's mysterious death was precisely the kind of news story that would go in the "Up Front" section.

This time they did not fly Sheff to New York. Instead, David Sheff sat down right away at home and began to write what he would later describe as "a thesis on what a great guy John Belushi was and what a great experience it had been chasing him around during those weeks." As he wrote, knowing no more than anyone else did at the time, his words and his vision of the wonder of John Belushi became more and more inflated.

Soon, however, while Sheff was hard at work retrieving his memories, clues about what had really happened to John Belushi began to surface. As it became clear at least that Belushi's death had by no means been from natural causes, Stolley assigned a whole team of reporters to dig up what they could. He had people in L.A., where Belushi died, and people in Chicago, where he grew up, and people in Martha's Vineyard, where he had a house, and people in New York, where he lived and worked on *Saturday Night Live*. It was the first of what would become known as *People*'s "swarm" technique, where the magazine literally unleashed a swarm of reporters all at once to gather as much about a given story as possible, as quickly as possible.

While Sheff wrote his recollections in San Francisco, the *People* team spread out across the country, gathering everything they could find, interviewing friends, colleagues, teachers, and relatives—anyone who could add pieces to the puzzle of John Belushi's life and sudden death. What they found was astonishing, even to Stolley. "It was a total shock," he recalls. "We didn't know any of that stuff, then. It was really ugly. This woman [Cathy Smith] had been coming in and out of the Chateau Marmont. Little by little the story got peeled off. We tracked down Gilda Radner, we got *Saturday Night Live* writer Michael O'Donoghue. We had time."

As he had been when John Lennon was killed, Stolley was lucky in terms of deadlines for the story about John Belushi's grotesque and sudden death. He had time to send his reporters out on the story, and indeed, according to some, *People* was the first to learn that Belushi had died after shooting up a "speedball," a combination of cocaine and heroin that had been provided him by the woman named Cathy Smith, who had reportedly dealt drugs of all kinds to countless celebrities. She had been with him in his room at the Chateau Marmont in the early hours of the morning that he died, sometime after he had left On the Rox, which was well past 1:30 A.M.

Dick Stolley even had time to get pictures of John Belushi's funeral into the magazine, since the funeral took place on a Tuesday. He sent a reporter and photographer to the funeral and to Belushi's burial site in Abel's Hill

Cemetery, near his home on Martha's Vineyard. There were, within the eight-page story, pictures of the pallbearers, who included Dan Aykroyd and Belushi's manager, Bernie Brillstein, and his brother Jim. A picture of his mother, Agnes, clutching a golden cross as she left the Albanian Orthodox funeral; a picture of James Taylor leading the mourners in song at Belushi's burial; a picture of a shaken Dan Aykroyd leading the funeral cortège to the grave on his motorcycle.

As it turned out, not one word of David Sheff's was used. "All I remember," he says, "is that not one word of what I wrote was printed because I was writing about the comic genius, about watching him interact with fans and watching him perform. I wrote about my great memories of being on the roller coaster with Belushi. Not a word of it was used because, of course, the real story had nothing to do with that."

Replacing what Sheff had written was a comprehensive story gleaned from the highly effective *People* swarm technique, which captured virtually everything that was known up to the time the magazine went to press about John Belushi's death from a drug overdose.

That was Dick Stolley's last cover:

JOHN BELUSHI:
A dangerous life,
a tragic death

It was extremely successful, selling nearly two and a half million newsstand copies.

An odd pattern seemed to be developing at *People* when it came to celebrity deaths. Almost every time someone famous died, one of the key people on the staff was gone on vacation. In the early fall of 1982, it was about to happen again, this time in multiples. M. C. Marden was filling in for Mary Dunn, who had just left on vacation; Landon Y. Jones, a good-looking, extremely smart Princeton graduate whose book *Great Expectations* became the defining journal of the baby-boom generation, was filling in for Pat Ryan. Adding to the game of "musical chairs," Anna Stewart, the deputy news editor, was filling in for the vacationing Hal Wingo. Those absences in themselves should have been clues that something tragic was about to happen, but the shrinking attendance list went even further—all the way to the thirty-fourth floor, the executive suite of Time Incorporated, where Ralph Graves, the editorial director of the company, was filling in for Henry Anatole Grunwald, the editor in chief.

It was late afternoon on Tuesday, September 14, and the issue was about to close with a cover of Prince Andrew, when Lanny Jones got an urgent call from Ron Holland, the head of an advertising agency that worked closely with

People. The agency was responsible for, among other things, the television ads that promoted the magazine.

As it happened, Holland, a native of Philadelphia, had close ties with Princess Grace's wealthy family there. The day before, an auto accident had occurred on a winding road in France as Grace and her daughter Stephanie returned in their Rover from Roc Agel, their mountain retreat. *People,* of course, had learned of the accident, but the reports out of France had been that Princess Grace was recovering well from her injuries, that it had been no more than a "fender-bender." Now, late on this Tuesday, as daylight was giving way to darkness, Holland was on the phone telling Lanny Jones the mind-boggling news that Princess Grace was dead. He had, he told Lanny, just heard this tragic fact from members of her own family, who had just received a phone call from Monaco.

"She just died," Holland told Lanny somberly.

"That's amazing," Lanny replied. "I can't believe it."

Holland insisted that it was true.

Lanny immediately called everyone he needed into his office. It was striking the way the staff pulled together during a crisis to accomplish whatever had to be done under what often appeared to be impossible circumstances. M. C. Marden was the first to arrive, and as she had done before with Lennon and Belushi, she instantly flew into action, organizing the picture staff for the sprint to grab up every picture of Grace Kelly they could get their hands on from the Time Inc. Picture Collection and any other place they could think of before anyone else knew what had happened. *People* beat everyone to the pool of pictures and had a complete choice of everything that was available. Virtually no one at any of the magazines had heard—nor had they even been prepared for the possibility—that Grace Kelly was dead.

Lanny called upstairs, since he was supposed to report to Ralph Graves under the circumstances, and said, "We've heard that Grace Kelly has died. Have you guys heard anything about this?"

Graves contacted Dick Stolley, who also happened to be on the thirty-fourth floor at the time, serving in a temporary executive capacity away from *Life.* Stolley offered to call downstairs and find out what he could from the news bureau at *Time.* Within moments he called Lanny back and told him, "They don't know anything about this. I can't find out a thing."

Lanny did not care. He was going to go forward in any case. It was getting later and later, and in the dark of the night he made the decision that he would definitely change the cover. He had to act fast if he were going to be able to make the change—it would barely be possible. As it was, it would be the latest cover change in the history of the magazine. They would do eleven pages, mostly pictures and captions. There would be little time for detailed text. They would use a picture of Grace taken by Harry Benson only a few months before to accompany a story that *People* had done about her life and her children.

It was not until three or four hours later that an Associated Press bulletin announced that Grace Kelly had died, and finally the word got out. Lanny Jones had already made his decision about the cover, but when the news reached Pat Ryan, who was away on vacation, she called him and grilled him hard about the cover change. She was not convinced that he was doing the right thing. It was admittedly a big risk to take, but Jones held his ground, and Ryan ultimately came to agree with him.

There was, admittedly, a lot at stake when it came to making such a late cover change. In the case of the Princess Grace issue, the number of pages the magazine would contain had to be changed, the cover had to be changed, and the presses had to be delayed. There were, however, larger concerns, as Jones explained. "You worry if you're going to get the magazine to the trucks that take it to the newsstand on time. That's an even more costly expense because if you miss the trucks, then you've missed future sales. That's a big consideration."

There were other inherent problems. "There's a full chain of events that has to take place—that's the risk," Jones explains further. "If the trucks leave too late and don't get to the wholesaler in time to be bundled and sorted and sent out to the newsstands, it's a big risk." At the same time, the right cover could account for millions of extra dollars in newsstand sales. It was a risky business, all right, especially at the eleventh hour.

The Grace Kelly issue did not close until eight o'clock on Wednesday morning. Lanny Jones did not leave for home until nine. But as it turned out, the risk was worth taking. The "Tribute to Grace Kelly" issue became the second-biggest-selling issue in *People*'s history, second only to John Lennon, underscoring the addendum to Stolley's cover theory: "And *nothing* is better than the celebrity dead."

1983

1983 COVERS

Clint Eastwood & Son Kyle
Dustin Hoffman
Roxanne Pulitzer & Marvin Mitchelson
Princess Di & Charles
Princess Stephanie & Paul Belmondo
Robert Mitchum & Ali MacGraw
Karen Carpenter
Brooke Shields
Sylvester Stallone & John Travolta
Readers' Poll
Bing Crosby
Richard Chamberlain & Rachel Ward
Oscar & E.T.
Linda Evans
David Soul
Joan Rivers
Dena Al-Fassi
Kristy McNichol
Helen Reddy
Victoria Principal
Mr. T
Carrie Fisher & Jabba the Hutt
Tony Perkins
Sally Ride
Prince William
Robert Wagner

Eddie Murphy & Richard Pryor
Roger Moore & Bond's Babes
John Travolta, Cynthia Rhodes,
   & Finola Hughes
Goldie Hawn
Diana Ross
Ryan O'Neal & Farrah Fawcett
Kenny Rogers & Linda Evans
Fall Preview
Princess Grace
Chevy Chase & Daughter Cydney
Korean Air Lines Tragedy
Best- & Worst-Dressed People
Bobby Kennedy, Jr.
Natalie Wood
Michael Jackson
After *M*A*S*H*
Pierce Brosnan
Jessica Savitch
Paul McCartney
Karen & Richard Carpenter
Jacqueline, Caroline & John Kennedy, Jr.
Jane Pauley
Barbra Streisand
Olivia Newton-John & John Travolta

YEAR-END DOUBLE ISSUE:

PRESIDENT RONALD REAGAN, MR. T, JENNIFER BEALS,
VANESSA WILLIAMS, RICHARD CHAMBERLAIN

BOTTOM 5

SALLY RIDE
AFTER *M*A*S*H*
REMINGTON STEELE (BROSNAN)
PRINCESS STEPHANIE'S NEW LOVE
BOND'S BABES

Films: *Return of the Jedi*
Tootsie
Flashdance
Trading Places
WarGames

Oscar: *Terms of Endearment*

Top TV Shows: *60 Minutes*
Dallas
M*A*S*H
Magnum, P.I.
Dynasty

Emmys: *Cheers*
Hill Street Blues

Top Songs: "Every Breath You Take"
—The Police
"Billie Jean"—Michael Jackson
"Flashdance...What a Feeling"
—Irene Cara
"All Night Long"—Lionel Richie
"Beat It"—Michael Jackson
"Islands in the Stream"
—Kenny Rogers & Dolly Parton

Grammys: "Beat It " (record)
"Every Breath You Take" (song)

Bestsellers: *Changes*—Danielle Steel
Christine—Stephen King

The Little Drummer Girl—John le Carré
Hollywood Wives—Jackie Collins
The Name of the Rose—Umberto Eco
In Search of Excellence—Thomas Peters
Growing Up—Russell Baker

Tonys: *Cats*
Torch Song Trilogy
On Your Toes

Marriages: David Frost + Lady Carina Howard
Richard Burton + Sally Hay
Paul Simon + Carrie Fisher
Princess Caroline + Stefano Casiraghi

Divorces Patricia Neal & Roald Dahl

Deaths:

Bear Bryant	George Cukor
Arthur Godfrey	Billy Baldwin
Karen Carpenter	Buster Crabbe
Gloria Swanson	George Balanchine
Jack Dempsey	Joan Miró
Buckminster Fuller	Lynn Fontanne
Ira Gershwin	Joan Hackett
Jessica Savitch	David Niven

Sir Ralph Richardson
Terence Cardinal Cooke

NEWS

- Robert Kennedy, Jr., charged with heroin possession
- David Hampton poses as son of Sidney Poitier—the incident will become the basis of the play *Six Degrees of Separation*
- Cathy Smith indicted for supplying and administering drugs to John Belushi
- Alfred Bloomingdale's mistress, Vicki Morgan, is killed by her boyfriend, Marvin Pancoast
- Diana Ross holds free concert in Central Park
- Vanessa Williams picked as first black Miss America
- Mick Jagger turns forty
- Heart transplant recipient Barney Clark dies
- Forty die in Beirut when U.S. embassy is bombed
- Sally Ride becomes first American woman to ride in space
- Benigno Aquino killed at Manila airport upon returning from exile in U.S.
- 249 civilians are killed on Korean Air Lines flight 007 when it is shot down by the Soviet Union
- *A Chorus Line* holds its record-breaking 3,389th performance on Broadway
- 216 Marines are killed when Beirut hearquarters are bombed
- The U.S. invades Grenada
- Reagan signs a bill making Martin Luther King's birthday a national holiday
- Lech Walesa awarded Nobel Peace Prize
- Former President Ford makes a cameo appearance on the TV show *Dynasty*

CHAPTER FIFTEEN

The Crash of '83

"It will be as spectacular as anything we've had
now or in the Gilded Age . . ."

—MRS. EILEEN SLOCUM
in People, *August 1, 1983, describing the Challenge Ball to be attended by
Prince Andrew in Newport, Rhode Island, that summer*

IT WAS AFTER THE blizzard hit and the small, twin-engine plane began to shake like a washing machine in the middle of its "spin" cycle, bouncing above the fog-shrouded tops of the Catskill Mountains like a Ping-Pong ball marking the words of a song, that it occurred to Susan Reed that she might not survive her first assignment as a reporter for *People* magazine.

It was not until the snowmobile in which she was riding after the harrowing experience in the plane—which, by some miracle, had actually managed to land in one piece—flipped over and dumped her out into the icy depths of the wet snow upon which it was attempting to carry her to her destination, the country home of TV star Doug Barr, that she realized she was in the midst of what she would later refer to as her first "near-death experience" in the line of duty for *People.*

The editors had thought that pictures taken at Barr's house in the Catskill Mountains would be far more interesting than pictures taken at his Manhattan apartment. They were undoubtedly right. At *People* the pictures were key. Each year, five thousand pictures were selected from a pool of more than a million submitted by hundreds of photographers. If the pictures were not good, there would be no story—the pictures were the reason for Susan Reed's trip to the Catskills in the first place.

In the end, she had emerged drenched but intact. After she was given dry clothes and a hot drink at Barr's house, she completed the interview like a trouper and made it back to New York City safely with her story in hand. The whole experience turned out to be an omen of the general nature of Reed's tenure at *People*: always unpredictable.

Susan Reed was a down-to-earth, unpretentious young woman. The daughter of a diplomat in the foreign service, she had grown up in Southeast Asia—Thailand, Japan, and Laos. She had gone to college at Vassar, had always had an interest in the arts, and had gotten a job writing about art and art dealers for *Saturday Review* magazine after she graduated. When *Saturday Review* folded, she worked as a freelance writer until a friend of hers who worked at *People* asked her if she would like to come to work there.

Although she had little interest in celebrities, she knew a good percentage of *People* was devoted to human-interest stories—stories, as the original prospectus had stated, about ordinary people doing extraordinary things. So Susan Reed (whose great uncle was John Reed, the notorious Communist buried in the Kremlin) decided to accept the job.

No reporter was guaranteed, however, which stories he or she would be assigned. Not long after she had survived the unnerving Catskills trip, Reed was assigned another story that was about as far from human interest and as close to celebrity as anyone could get. Prince Andrew was about to arrive in Newport, Rhode Island, as Her Majesty's representative at the trials for the America's Cup, the renown yachting race, where entries from England, Italy, Australia, France, and Canada were competing for the chance to challenge the United States. During his stay, he was to be the guest of honor at the British America's Cup Challenge Ball, which Mrs. Eileen Slocum, an organizer of the event, predicted would be "as spectacular as anything we've had now or in the Gilded Age."

It sounded like a perfect *People* story. Reed was teamed up with another young *People* reporter, Deirdre Donahue, to cover the event. The tricky part of the assignment was that Reed and Donahue would have no official access. Security was going to be exceedingly tight—everything from the Secret Service to the FBI to Scotland Yard would be keeping people out. Their mission was to get as much as they could about the fancy Challenge Ball in spite of the fact that they could not get into it.

Before they left for Newport, they were called into the offices of Andrea Chambers, the senior editor in charge of the story. "Try to get into this party," Andrea told them, knowing full well how difficult it would be. "It's crucial to the story. You two can go out and buy yourselves a dress before you go. A simple black sheath will do."

Reed had to laugh as she left Chambers's office. "Deirdre and I were not the black-sheath type," she said later. "We never put on a simple black sheath in our lives. But we did go out and buy dresses." Reed bought a beautiful pastel peach, silk Nicole Miller gown, which *People* paid for. And then they set out for Newport, Rhode Island, for their hoped-for but unlikely rendezvous with the prince.

When they arrived at their hotel in Newport, Reed and Donahue quickly developed a plan: They would call everyone they knew—anyone they could find—to try to get into any of the events occurring throughout the weekend that might somehow lead them to the *coup de grâce*, the elegant, black-tie Challenge Ball, which was to be held at Beechwood, a twenty-seven-room "cottage," the palatial estate once owned by Lady Astor.

They started with Deirdre's friend, the well-known debutante Cornelia Guest, whom she knew from her Harvard days. Then they went through a list of everyone else they could think of who might know anybody going to the party. "We were just working the phones when we got up there," explains Reed.

The long round of phone calls proved frustrating until they finally got the break they had been looking for. Somebody told them that a man by the name of Jimmy Van Alen, a well-known Newport socialite, might be able to help them. Van Alen was an avid tennis fan who also happened to be the man who had invented the tiebreaker. They were told they could find him at a place called the Newport Casino.

The intrepid duo proceeded to locate Van Alen and arranged to do an interview with him, purportedly about the tiebreaker, with the hidden hope of getting him to help them get into the Challenge Ball. After unleashing all of their collective charm on the unsuspecting Jimmy Van Alen, they sensed the moment was right. They asked him if he could get them into the ball.

Unfortunately, he replied no, but there was something else he could do. Some friends of his were giving a dinner party before the ball, which was not scheduled to begin until 10:30 P.M. Many people would be at the dinner party. He would get them invited to that.

That evening Reed and Donahue donned their new dresses and arrived at the very chic dinner party to which the tiebreaker's inventor had gotten them invited, right down the hill, as it turned out, from Beechwood, where the Challenge Ball was to be held. It did not take them long to uncover the fact that virtually everyone, with the glaring exception of themselves, was going to the ball directly from the dinner party.

There was little to be done, since they were not in possession of the exclusive invitations that were essential to get even close to the ball. Since the *People* photographer assigned to the story, Christopher Little, had planned to station himself outside the gate to take pictures of people arriving at the affair, which was about all he could do under the circumstances, they decided they would amble up to Beechwood to meet him and see what more, if anything, they could do to get their story.

And so the saga began—a succession of unpredictable events that had a most unexpected outcome. In their formal attire, Reed and Donahue left the dinner party and ambled up the posh avenue in Newport toward Beechwood. They had walked only a few feet when a car carrying people they had just had dinner with at the party pulled up and stopped behind them. Someone, assuming that they, like everyone else at the party, had been invited to the ball, asked them if they wanted a ride. Amazed at this unanticipated stroke of good fortune, they climbed into the backseat of the car.

When it arrived at the gate, the other passengers confidently showed their invitations and the rest of their various credentials and passes to the security guards. The car, with Susan Reed and Deirdre Donahue plunked comfortably amid the official invitees, was waved through and steadily proceeded up what appeared to be an interminable driveway that led to the "cottage."

Deirdre and Susan looked at each other, not knowing exactly what to do. They could not believe that they had actually made it inside the gate. The car continued to approach the mansion. As it pulled up to the front door, they saw the huge spotlights glaring down upon the long red runner that led from the front door to the driveway. Before they knew it, a valet took the car as attendants in uniform appeared with their arms extended to escort the arriving guests up the brilliant red runner, sparkling in the night, illuminated by klieg lights.

"Here Deirdre and I are," recalls Reed. "The [invited] people get out in front of us. We get out. We're in no-man's-land now. We're too late to turn back, and the only thing we know is that we're going to be in jail within moments when they find out we don't have tickets to this ball."

They made their way up the elegant red runner directly behind the people with whom they had come. As they moved forward step-by-step, they realized it was taking the guards who were checking the invitations so much time that a backup of about ten couples had developed. Still, they forged on. After what seemed like miles, they arrived at the door to find themselves only inches from the intimidating security guard. The people in front of them showed their invitations, and just as it was their turn to present their credentials, the guard was interrupted by one of the hostesses with a pressing need. During the split second in which he turned away to communicate with her, Reed and Donahue slipped timorously past him, and right on through the imposing doors of the mansion.

The whole scenario was beginning to feel like a James Bond movie. They were through the door, only to find themselves in yet another foyer, this one with even more security people who were asking for yet another invitation, the one required for table assignments. The jig appeared to be up.

Deirdre Donahue, however, could not find the necessary sense of surrender within herself to allow that to happen. Inspired by the stark realization that they had somehow made it this far—past the gate, up the driveway, past the guards at the door, and into the foyer just outside of their ultimate goal, the ballroom itself, which beckoned them from only a few feet away—she pretended to turn her ankle and then she shrieked, in a voice that would echo endlessly through each of the twenty-seven rooms of the rambling Beechwood cottage, "Oh my God, my shoe! *I've broken my shoe!!!*"

The scene is still vivid in Susan Reed's mind. "Deirdre became hysterical," she recalls. "She began screaming at people, abusing them. Then she yelled, 'Where's the ladies' room? *I have to go fix my shoe!*' The ladies' room was one foyer inside and she created such a scene that they let us into the ladies' room. At that point, we were home free."

After that it was easy. They entered the ballroom, and there was Prince Andrew, right beside them. They swept through the party—they had to keep moving since they had no table assignments—surreptitiously taking notes on napkins for the story that might never have been. They jotted down details of the hors d'oeuvres and the meal—"a menu that included lime and Cointreau cocktails (most guests took one sip and slipped them back on the waitresses trays), deviled kidneys, smoked haddock, kippers and other British fare." They wrote their observations of their view from within:

> The guest of honor sat primly in one of seven pink-and-white striped tents, sipping a Perrier and lime and fidgeting with the signet ring on his pinky . . . He stood military straight while the Regimental Band of the Irish Guards played military ditties . . . Only twice did the prince take rather stiffly to the dance floor . . . The local dowagers, resplendent in rustling taffeta, sidled as close as protocol and security guards allowed . . .

Finally, Reed and Donahue made their way to the walled garden for a breather, securely ensconced now within the boundaries of the ball. They were standing there among the lush and pungent flowers, taking in the rich air surrounding the mansion, when they heard a loud, reverberating thud. A tuxedo-clad body, that of a frustrated British reporter, had landed in the soft earth beside them. In a final desperate attempt to crash the alluring party, the poor chap had shamelessly vaulted the wall and landed in the garden. He brushed himself off, and as the girls watched, he casually sauntered on into the ball.

He had done it the hard way.

PEOPLE WAS ARGUABLY—and understandably—obsessed with "society" and royalty, both at home and abroad. Jacqueline Kennedy Onassis was a perfect example. In the first two decades of *People*'s life, she would appear on the cover alone eleven times, in spite of the fact that she never, without exception, even came close to granting *People* (or anyone else for that matter) an interview.

The task of pursuing the Kennedys, as it turned out, often fell to Susan Reed and Deirdre Donahue, in large part, Reed suspects, because they were both under thirty and they had both gone to Ivy League colleges. She believes this led to the assumption that they knew the Kennedys, although that was not really the case.

During the time that Reed had what she refers to as "The Kennedy Beat" at *People*, she tried repeatedly to get an interview with Jackie. "All the time," she recalls. "I would call her secretary, Nancy Tuckerman, put in the request, and always be turned down. She was very gracious, but it was impossible. And their friends are very protective so they tend to shut down. Nobody's ever gotten to her. If you ask every book or magazine editor in America, 'What is the story you'd cut off your right arm for?' they would say 'Jackie Onassis.' "

It was a beat that Reed was happy to leave behind. "I always say new levels of human degradation were reached on every Kennedy story I reported," she says. "Of course, we never had access to anybody and I would have to call up all their friends and people who knew them and they would slam the phone down and scream at me. It would take me ten minutes to squirrel up my courage for the next call after getting completely trashed on the last one."

Although nobody talked in either case, *People* did covers in 1983 on "The Kennedys 20 Years Later," a look at the lives of Caroline and John two decades after the death of their father, and on Diana's little prince William on the occasion of his first birthday.

There were other, more significant celebrity stories: Karen Carpenter died of anorexia nervosa—the first celebrity to bring the tragic problem to the public fore. The bizarre drowning death of Natalie Wood was explored in *People*'s pages by her sister Lana. Another death by drowning, that of newswoman Jessica Savitch, was also a cover that year. There was an ironic—in hindsight at least—cover story on Tony Perkins, with a cover line that read:

TONY PERKINS OF PSYCHO II
Like the mama's boy he plays,
he was scared of women
(even Fonda and Bardot),
until his good wife
turned his life around

Perkins would be dead of AIDS nine years later.

It was a year with an unusual number of stories that melded celebrity with tragedy. But a news event would occur in September 1983 that had nothing whatsoever to do with celebrity. Because of the way it was handled by Jim Gaines, the assistant managing editor under Pat Ryan, who happened to be sitting in for her the week it occurred, it would have a remarkable and lasting impact on *People* magazine: the shooting down by the Soviet Union of a Korean Air Lines passenger jet, flight 007, carrying 269 civilians.

Jim Gaines was a talented and aggressive journalist, an editor who would ultimately put his own distinct mark on *People* magazine. He had gone to work at *People* in 1976 after working as an editor at *Saturday Review*. After that he had become a reporter and producer for *The 51st State*, a news program on PBS, then a writer in the national affairs section of *Newsweek*. When he got to *People*, he had quickly risen from writer to senior editor and then to assistant managing editor. He was already the author of two books—a literary biography about the Algonquin Round Table and a collection of essays about the piano. At one time he had considered becoming a concert pianist.

Gaines was in charge when KAL 007, flying thirty-three thousand feet over the Sea of Japan on its way from New York to Anchorage to Seoul, was mysteriously shot down by a Soviet missile; Pat Ryan was on vacation in Maine with Ray Cave, the editor of *Time* magazine, with whom she lived.

It was during a telephone conversation with Ryan at her vacation home that Gaines first heard the news of the disaster. "*Time* just called Ray and said the Russians blew up a passenger airline," she told him. "I guess there's not much in it for us."

At that moment, Gaines agreed with her that it probably was not a *People* story. A few hours later, as he sat at lunch with John Saar, a senior editor at *People*, discussing the shocking tragedy, he began to see things differently. "As we talked about it," recalls Gaines, "I started thinking, my God, this is really quite remarkable." He started to ponder the ironies of how each person who was killed on the doomed flight had wound up on the plane that would take all of them to their deaths in this still-unexplained, unbelievable occurrence. Soon he began to understand that the shooting down of KAL 007 really was a *People* story, after all.

Jim Gaines was a sort of present-day Renaissance man, an accomplished author who was also a talented classical pianist, among other things. His interests were broad and he excelled at everything he did. Gaines had always believed that the success of *People* magazine was the notion of ordinary people doing extraordinary things. "That was the reason *People* was never successfully copied," he says. "The people who would copy it believed it was all the celebrities. What kept people coming back, week after week, was that they saw themselves somehow, or that they were made to feel something or understand something because they saw themselves. It seemed to me that we were becoming a news magazine. That we were in fact a news magazine. That it wasn't just gossip. That it wasn't just celebrity. That it was really serious information. People were using *People* as a news magazine."

Now, while he was sitting in for Pat Ryan, Jim Gaines was suddenly faced with the perfect opportunity to prove his point. With what he called the "Bridge of San Luis Rey approach"—how each one of the passengers and crew got on the plane, what happened to them, what accident of fate led them there—he decided to go ahead with the story. Not only that, he would make it a cover.

Not everyone agreed with Gaines's assessment. In fact, the reaction was quite the opposite. The magazine's shrewd and respected publisher, Dick Durrell, made it clear to Gaines that he thought he was nuts. "I don't think *People* had ever put anybody whose face wasn't recognizable on the cover before," muses Gaines. "I think there was some rule about how a successful cover of *People* had to be recognizable to 80 percent of the readers, so this really broke some *People* rules. There was no place in Stolley's law for such a cover."

Stolley himself was shocked when he heard what Gaines was planning to do. "I kind of gulped," he recalls. "I was stunned. But I grew up in news, and when I thought about it, I thought it was a great idea."

Pat Ryan, for her part, did not. She was understandably wary when Gaines informed her about what he was planning. "I couldn't believe he was putting it on the cover," she says. "Durrell called me and told me he couldn't believe it either. I thought it was a loser."

It was, without a doubt, a groundbreaking concept for *People*, but it involved the ever-present risk of losing a lot of money if it did not work. Still, the more Gaines thought about it, the more convinced he became that it was a justified risk and that, in terms of the way he perceived the magazine's image, it was definitely a risk worth taking. "It was a big deal," he says. "This was Reagan calling Russia the Evil Empire. People were just horrified at what happened, and pissed off."

On Friday Gaines told Mike Ryan, another editor, to go away on the weekend to "marinate." He wanted him to try to come up with a great cover billing for the story. On Saturday night, he was invited to Ryan's apartment for a party; when he arrived at the house he was stunned. "I remember he opened the door and said, 'Getting Away with Murder,' " recalls Gaines. "I said, 'Oh my God, that's great!' It was at that point that I knew we had to go with it. The line was so good."

A massive effort was already under way to report the story across the country through survivors of those who had died on Korean Air Lines flight 007. Reporters in New York, Atlanta, Washington, D.C., Detroit, Philadelphia, and Tokyo fanned out, uncovering poignant and shattering stories. The results were more astounding and mind-boggling than Gaines or anyone else could have imagined. They would ultimately prove that a *People* cover story need have nothing to do with celebrities if it were compelling enough and handled correctly.

Gaines handled it brilliantly. The copy itself began on the cover, under Mike Ryan's gripping headline, "Getting Away with Murder." Next to a picture of the widow of one of the victims holding her two young children, it said:

> The father in this family, New York businessman Jan Hjalmarsson, had planned to take an earlier flight. Instead, he stayed home to spend more time with wife Olga, daughter Olivia and their newborn son, Alexander. That night, with no time to spare, he dashed to the airport for KAL's Flight 007, and settled with relief into seat 18G . . .

In the pages that followed, the accounts of the fateful circumstances that brought each victim to death on the doomed flight were chilling: Jan Hjalmarsson, the father of the family on the cover, was originally scheduled to leave New York at 5:00 P.M. When he discovered that flight 007 would take off seven hours later yet arrive in Seoul at almost the same time, he changed his reservation so he would have a few more hours with his wife and his children. Becky Scruton was going to visit her parents in Seoul shortly after her husband, Dale, died of cancer. She arranged for her kids to be cared for and booked a flight to Korea on Saturday, August 27. But when she realized she had forgotten her passport, she returned home and booked another flight instead—KAL flight 007, which would leave the following Tuesday. John Oldham, a former Fulbright scholar, was booked to fly Monday but, sympathetic to the exigencies of the academic world, he had postponed his trip for twenty-four hours so he could help some visiting Chinese scholars find housing near New York City's Columbia University. The day of the flight, Han Tae Park took a walk with a friend of his, a fellow Korean immigrant, Hong Taek Chung, in whom he often confided. He had, ironically, talked about dying that day. The most dreadful thing he could think of, he told Chung, would be to die in a plane crash because, in that kind of an accident, even though you were in danger, you could not do a thing about it. Lawrence McDonald, the Democratic congressman from Georgia and chairman of the ultraconservative John Birch Society, had missed the flight he was supposed to take on Sunday night by just a few minutes because the flight he was scheduled to catch from Atlanta went to Baltimore instead due to a thunderstorm. He could have caught a Pan Am flight to Seoul but decided to wait in New York for a night to take advantage of a ticket on the same airline carrier that he had already paid for. Marie Culp and Hazel James missed their flight to New York from Pontiac, Michigan, when Marie's stepson took them to the wrong departure terminal, but they booked another flight and arrived in New York in time to board the doomed flight 007. Neil and Carol Grenfell and their two children had been ready to return to their home in Korea where he was the top marketing executive for Eastman Kodak until his leave was extended by two weeks so that he could host a delegation of Korean businessmen at the corporation's Rochester, New York, headquarters.

Those were only some of the "Bridge of San Luis Rey approach" stories that Gaines's inspiration uncovered. It was a unique approach to a story that the whole world was interested in—an approach that *People* magazine was perfectly and uniquely equipped to take. Without a familiar face on the cover or in any of the eight astonishing pages inside, the issue did well that year, placing among the top twenty sellers. *People* would not lose sight of the lesson of KAL 007. It was the first distinctive mark Jim Gaines would make on *People* magazine, but it would by no means be the last.

Although she had not agreed with Gaines's decision in the beginning, Pat Ryan came to appreciate the way the gamble had turned out and she later ruminated on the complexities of such decisions. "It's a very humbling experience, being managing editor of that magazine," she said. "You will quickly find out that you know nothing for sure. You go with your best gut instinct. KAL opened up new ground for me and new ground for the magazine. Had I been sitting in the editor's chair that week, I never would have done it."

PART II
INSIDE
PEOPLE

the second decade

1 9 8 4 – 1 9 9 3

TOP 5
OUR FIRST 10 YEARS!
MICHAEL JACKSON'S BRUSH WITH DISASTER
VANESSA WILLIAMS
RICHARD BURTON'S DEATH
THE BUBBLE BOY

1984

1984 COVERS

Princess Caroline
Dennis Wilson & the Beach Boys
Cher
Mr. T
Shirley MacLaine & Debra Winger
Michael Jackson
John Lennon & Yoko Ono
Bo Derek
People's 10th Anniversary Issue
Tom Selleck
Paul Newman
Gary & Lee Hart
Daryl Hannah (*Splash*)
John DeLorean and Children
Boy George
Michael Jackson
Dolly Parton, Willie Nelson, Kenny
    Rogers, Loretta Lynn, George Strait
Robert Redford
Griffin O'Neal & Ryan
John Belushi
Jackie O
Princess Caroline & Son
Harrison Ford & Kate Capshaw
Dolly Parton & Sylvester Stallone
Readers' Poll
Michael Jackson

Geraldine Ferraro
Vanessa Williams
Comedy: David Letterman, Joan Rivers,
    Bill Murray, Eddie Murphy
Richard Burton
Fall Preview
Bruce Springsteen
Vanessa Williams
Cyndi Lauper
Best- & Worst-Dressed
Princess Diana and Prince Henry
Farrah Fawcett
Sally Field
Sophia Loren & Son Edouardo
David, the Bubble Boy
Diana Sawyer
Kid Stars: Ricky Schroder,
    Drew Barrymore & Henry Thomas
Prince
Liza Minnelli
Baby Fae and Mother
Joan Rivers
Linda Evans and Baby on *Dynasty*
Mary Lou Retton

YEAR-END DOUBLE ISSUE:
Tina Turner, Bruce Springsteen, Richard Gere

BOTTOM 5
HOW TO MAKE YOUR KID A STAR
GARY HART
SUMMER PREVIEW
THE A TEAM DRAWS FIRE
SOPHIA AND SON

Films: *Ghostbusters*
Indiana Jones and the Temple of Doom
Gremlins
The Karate Kid
Beverly Hills Cop

...ar: *Amadeus*

TV Shows: *Dallas*
60 Minutes
Dynasty
The A Team
Simon & Simon

...mys: *Cheers*
Hill Street Blues

Songs: "Like a Virgin"—Madonna
"When Doves Cry"—Prince
"Jump"—Van Halen
"Footloose"—Kenny Loggins
"What's Love Got to Do with It"—Tina Turner
"Karma Chameleon"—Culture Club

...ammys: "What's Love Got to Do with It" (record)
"What's Love Got to Do with It" (song)

Bestsellers: *And Ladies of the Club*—Helen Santmyer
The Fourth Protocol—Frederick Forsyth
Lincoln—Gore Vidal
The Name of the Rose—Umberto Eco
The Witches of Eastwick—John Updike
Wired—Bob Woodward

Tonys: *The Real Thing*
La Cage aux Folles

Marriages: Elton John + Renate Blauel
Christina Onassis + Thierry Roussel
Margaret Trudeau + Fried Kemper
Patti Davis + Paul Grilley

Divorces: John DeLorean & Cristina Ferrare
Pierre & Margaret Trudeau

Deaths: Ansel Adams · Yuri Andropov
Truman Capote · Indira Gandhi
Marvin Gaye · David Kennedy
Peter Lawford · Ethel Merman
Sam Peckinpah · François Truffaut
Lillian Hellman · Andy Kaufman

NEWS

- Robert Kennedy, Jr., sentenced to probation for 1983 heroin-possession conviction
- Seven people indicted in McMartin Preschool molestation case in Manhattan Beach, California
- Singer Marvin Gaye shot and killed by his father
- Charles Manson set afire by Krishna inmate
- Penny Marshall held hostage by two burglars in L.A. home
- Burt Lancaster and Margot Kidder have fistfight on set of *Little Treasures*
- Newswoman Christine Craft awarded $325,000 in damages against KMBC-TV in Kansas City for fraudulent hiring
- Robert Stewart and Bruce McCandless walk through space on *Challenger* flight
- Geraldine Ferraro named first woman vice-presidential nominee for Democratic party
- Michael Jackson's album *Thriller* becomes the bestselling record album in history

CHAPTER SIXTEEN

The Reporter and the Bubble Boy

"Love but don't touch. That was the rule for the dozen years of
David Phillip's life. He spent 12 years in plastic bubbles, isolated
from germs or bacteria. Isolated, too, from any human touch or kiss.
But never isolated from love, and he knew that."

—DAVID'S MOTHER,
Carol Ann, in People, October 29, 1984
(eight months after his death)

THERE WAS NO way of knowing for sure if the child about to be
born would be the victim of the same disease, Severe Combined Immunodeficiency syndrome, that had killed its little brother a year before. So every precaution that was humanly possible was being taken at the
impending birth. Now, as the mother arrived at the hospital ready to deliver her baby, the scene was chillingly surreal. The small hospital room,
which had been scrubbed from floor to ceiling five times and then kept
locked until she got there, was completely stripped of draperies and all
unnecessary furniture.

Filled with understandably intense apprehension, she undressed slowly,
deliberately, and donned the sterile hospital gown. Instantly she was rushed
into the germfree room for a shower, bath, and shampoo. From that moment
on, there would be no communication with the world outside of the room
except by phone. No risk of any virus or bacteria could be taken.

She was bundled like a mummy in sterilized sheets to avoid any contact
with airborne sources of infection. The doctors moved in slow motion and in
silence. The process had been painstakingly rehearsed. During the birth, the
patient was given instructions only by a slight pressure on her shoulders.

Everything humanly possible was done to avoid stirring any air that could cause a germ to float toward her.

When it was over, she saw the doctor lift her newborn son, holding him in his double-gloved hands. The mother glimpsed her son for less than ten seconds before he was placed in a plastic isolator bubble. He had thick black hair, and his eyes were so dark that they were eerily piercing. She watched as the little boy was baptized with the sterilized holy water that had been placed inside his bubble.

Nurses at the Clinical Research Center at Texas Children's Hospital had been practicing for two weeks with a doll to get used to the cumbersome built-in gloves required to hold, feed, and change the baby inside the bubble. Three days would pass before Carol Ann, the mother, would see her child David Phillip again. The doctors were still conducting tests on him. What she saw when she got to the door of his room for the first time overwhelmed her. There was a large isolator bubble for her son and another for his supplies, each with a pair of the unwieldy floppy black gloves attached. Hoses were pumping in filtered air as if they were moving in time to the hum of the motors that drove them. Little David was sound asleep, oblivious to the spectacular circumstances of his birth.

He was two weeks old before the doctors determined that David, like his brother who had died (at the tender age of seven months) just ten months before David was born, had SCID, Severe Combined Immunodeficiency syndrome. No one had been certain what the parents' chances were of having a second child with the disease, but the doctors had told them that the odds of its happening again were only one in ten thousand *if* the cause of their first child's illness had been a mutant gene. But, if the cause had been a defective X chromosome, their chances of having another child with the same problem would be one in four. There had been no way of knowing more; there had been no record of SCID in either family. They already had a healthy daughter, Katherine, who was three; both wanted more children. They decided the risk was worth taking.

When the young couple learned their second son had SCID, they were devastated. "My husband spun on his heels in helpless anger, doubled up his fist, and struck the wall," the boy's mother said later in *People*. "My own heart was breaking as we embraced and reminded ourselves of the pledge we had made that whatever happened we would do what was necessary to secure for our baby the best life he could have."

They did everything in their power to keep that promise. David's first two months were spent in the hospital, but when Thanksgiving came, he was allowed to go home for a visit. He would alternate between home and the hospital, where the doctors monitored him closely, for the rest of his life. On his first visit home, Carol Ann was ecstatic. "I could cradle him with the gloves at feeding time, and sometimes I kissed him through the plastic," she later wrote. "If I held him long enough, I could feel the warmth of his skin, and I was certain that he could feel mine. I liked to position him so he could feel my heartbeat . . . often he would nap in my arms as I held him with the gloves."

To maintain maximum privacy for David, his parents never revealed their last name or their home address, but that did nothing to diminish the world's interest in the miraculous child. When David was four months old, in January 1972, Carol Ann and her husband (who was also named David) allowed a *Life* magazine reporter by the name of Kent Demaret to visit the child at their home. Ultimately, David, the Bubble Boy, would have an unimaginably profound effect on Kent Demaret's life.

Demaret had been working on a story in Mexico when *Life* asked him to return to Texas to do the story of David and his family. He did not know if he would be able to get them to cooperate. "They wanted to have a very normal life," he says. "They were good, solid folks from Texas, and they had their own ideas about how life ought to be lived. They were not reclusive by any stretch of the imagination. They were very gregarious, but they didn't want their names printed in front of millions of people."

The hospital had agreed to contact the family for Demaret with his request, and the family had agreed to let him come. "David was home by then and in his bubble," Demaret recalls, "and it was just an awesome kind of thing to see."

The reporter was not altogether comfortable with newborn children—let alone a baby in David's unique circumstances. "Little kids scare me, unless they can hold on," he says. "I really didn't carry my grandkids much until they got to the point where they could hold on to me. I'm afraid if I hold them too tight I'll hurt them, and if I don't hold them tight enough, they're going to slip out of my arms like a wet bar of soap. So I'm thinking about little David, this tiny little baby in his bubble and I'm thinking about how difficult it must be to just do ordinary things like change his diapers. But then I realize there's a lot more than that—feeding him, bathing him, all the things that have to be done. Cutting his hair, his little fingernails. Here was this young couple who were accepting this enormous burden with great beaming smiles, with pride and a sense of mission of some kind. There was something almost spiritual about it."

The monumental task facing the couple understandably took time for them to adjust to. "At first I couldn't bring myself to touch him with the black, floppy gloves," Carol Ann later admitted. "They intimidated me, and I had a strange sense of foreboding."

She quickly learned how to care for David in the bubble. She would later say that holding and feeding and changing her son with the big rubber gloves became second nature to her. The hardest thing was buttoning the tiny buttons of his clothes when he was an infant. "They were almost impossible to fasten with those gloves," she explained. "So I would remove an adhesive tab from one of his disposable diapers and fasten the shirt with that. Sometimes it worked and sometimes it didn't."

On his first visit, when Carol Ann and her husband asked him if he wanted to touch the baby, Kent Demaret became acutely aware of the magnitude of the problems involved in caring for David. "They had these big gloves and I remember being pretty scared," he says. "I took off my watch and my rings because I sure didn't want to punch a hole in that glove. And I could feel the heat of the baby's body and I was just very struck by it."

What impressed Kent Demaret the most was that Carol Ann and her husband never complained. "Old Dizzy Dean had an old Southern saying it reminded me of," he says. "The pitcher would rear back and throw the ball and it'd be going somewhere between ninety and one hundred miles an hour and it would hit the batter. And Dizzy Dean would say something like, 'Well, it hit him right there on the arm, folks, you can see where it hit him. It just knocked him back about two feet. But watch him. He won't rub.'

"Here was a family," he says wondrously, "and they wouldn't rub. They were faced with an enormously uncertain kind of future, in many ways. It was mind-boggling having to deal with an infant who was only a few weeks old, laying there sleeping, but what was going to happen later when he was running around like little boys do?"

Demaret wrote the story for *Life*, and Harry Benson took the photographs. There was something about the lead picture that Harry took of Carol Ann holding the tiny baby in the bubble when he was only four months old that would stay with Kent Demaret for the rest of his life. "She was looking down on her child with a Madonna-type motherly look," he says. "She looked kind of like a little deer. She's that way around children. Her big brown eyes would get all watery and her lips kind of swell up and you think she's going to lick them. It was a very striking picture."

The story about the boy in the bubble ran in the January 21, 1972, issue of *Life* magazine, but Kent Demaret's relationship with David and his family did not end there. As the months went by, Demaret, who lived in Houston, only a short distance from David's house, would visit from time to time. "I'm crazy about kids," he says, "and sometimes I'd drop off a present for little David. I didn't see them on a super-regular basis, but once in a while he'd have a birthday party and they would invite people that they considered close to them and I would always be very flattered to be invited."

Although David was consigned to a life eternally bound by the plastic bubble that kept him alive, under the circumstances he did very well. "From a distance I watched him grow up," says Demaret. "I watched his bubble get bigger and his body get bigger. I saw his little dog when he got it and his parakeet. As he got a little older and could talk, I'd sit on the floor next to the bubble and chitchat with him."

Over time, the unimaginable limitations on the Bubble Boy became more apparent. Even some of the gifts that Demaret brought him posed serious problems. "I took him a pair of binoculars once," he recalls. "There was a window by his bubble and he could look out a little better. But the binoculars could not be properly sterilized because of the heat and working parts, so they had to be pressed up against the plastic for him from outside of the bubble."

Another time Demaret brought David a little remote-controlled car. It had been possible to sterilize the remote device that David needed to hold to make the car go. "He could sit in his bubble and chase the car all over the house," says Demaret. "But everything that went into that bubble had to undergo a pressure sterilization system in a supply bubble. And there were some things that you just couldn't sterilize," he says. "It was a long time, for example, before David could use anything to draw with because you couldn't reliably sterilize the lead in pencils, and crayons would melt. They finally developed a way to do that."

Food posed a different problem. "He never ate a hot meal because you couldn't get any kind of fire inside there," says Demaret. "So all his food was sterilized in advance and stored in the supply bubbles. They had a system where they could prepare it for him from the outside. Later he learned how to do it himself." There were two foods that David heard about on television that he longed for but never got to try: ice cream and Coke. The ice cream had a high fat content and it could not be sterilized because it would melt. The heat required to sterilize the Coke would have broken down the carbonation and ruined the taste.

It had been determined when David was only three that his intelligence was almost two years ahead of his age. Later, his parents learned that his IQ was 126. He did not go to school, school came to him, and David made a lot of friends. At first he was taught by visiting teachers, but by the second grade, a speakerphone was hooked up to his classroom, which was two miles away, and he could talk back and forth to the students and teachers from his bubble.

David's perception of the world, because of the bubble, was unique. As time went on, Kent Demaret came to acquire a greater understanding of the nuances that formed David's singular world. "He had a one-dimensional view of the world," he explains. "If he looked at the house across the street, he could not imagine that there was a back side to it. It would be like a dummy Hollywood set. He was isolated from a lot of things, like the realization that the world was round. And he wondered about a lot of things. He ran barefoot inside of his bubble or with socks on his feet, because shoes were not something that were needed. He used to wonder what it would be like to walk barefoot in the grass."

There was always the inner, undeniable knowledge, however, that there was a limit to how long David could live in isolation, in spite of the supreme efforts that were keeping him going. Carol Ann and her husband knew that. They simply had no idea when that limit would be reached. Of course, there was always the underlying hope that some cure or treatment would be discovered to allow David to leave his bubble and lead a normal life.

When David was eleven, as he was approaching puberty, his family learned more about the bone marrow transplant procedure for combating his disease. The technique had improved greatly and become much more sophisticated in the decade that had passed. Twelve years earlier, his brother had undergone a bone marrow transplant from their healthy sister, Katherine, who was nearly four years older than David. Now the doctors treating David believed that at worst, even if the procedure failed, it would do David no harm, and there would be nothing to lose by trying it. If it worked, it would stimulate the growth of a healthy immune system. Carol Ann and her husband discussed the possibility with their son. "We also told David that there was no danger to him and that we couldn't wait to hold him tightly, without a wall of plastic between us, and to kiss him," she said later. "David just looked at all of us with those large dark eyes and finally said, 'Okay, but I don't think it's going to work.' "

Once again, Katherine was to be the donor. In the fall of his twelfth year David underwent the operation. Weeks went by, and still the doctors could not tell if the technique was working. More than two months later, as Christmas approached, his family begged to take David home, and they did. Christmas went fine, but on New Year's Day, David, who routinely had to check his temperature, found that he had a slight fever. Within a few days he grew violently ill and his temperature soared.

Even then, he stayed in touch with Kent Demaret. "David had had a birthday not too long before that," says Demaret, "and I had given him an encyclopedia . . . he had it at the hospital with him . . . he called to tell me thank you and he even asked me to come and see him."

Thinking of the family, Demaret declined. "I decided not to try and go see him because the parking lots were full of reporters," he recalls. "I'm well enough known that I knew, if I walked through that crowd, I might be recognized, and I didn't want the hospital to be rushed. I didn't want the family to be rushed and crowded or anything like that. Anyway, I decided not to go. At that time David had not become critically ill, and that was something that later haunted me because I made the right decision for the right reason, but I felt bad about not seeing him. I don't know how much he really wanted to see me or how much he was being polite. But I was very torn by that later on."

David's condition continued to deteriorate. The doctors were baffled, unable to do anything for him as he became increasingly ill. They were faced with a terrible choice: leave him in the bubble, where they were unable to treat him, or take him out, where it was certain that terrible dangers awaited him.

The family decided to remove David from his bubble on February 7, 1984. "Even though he was groggy," Carol Ann later recalled, "he seemed fascinated by the different view of things outside the bubble, and he ran his fingertips over the furniture and lifesaving equipment."

Outside of the bubble, David's condition worsened immediately. He became weaker as more complications set in, and he slipped in and out of a coma. Within days, Carol Ann and her husband were told by the doctors that their son would soon die, and David, the incredible little boy who had lived his whole life inside a plastic bubble, was given the last rites.

As her son lay dying, Carol Ann asked the doctor if she could remove her surgical gloves and touch him for the first time in both of their lives. She was told that she could. "It was the first time, ever, that I touched his hand," she later said. "I lifted my mask. I kissed him. It was the first time, and the last time."

After David's death, on February 22, his family was astounded at the outpouring of emotion, and the depth of the public's love and caring and interest in David's life. "When he died I think they were quite surprised by the impact," says Demaret. "They heard that people were crying in the streets. They never told the press, but the president made a private call to the house. Their grief was very personal."

They asked Kent Demaret to help them handle the press coverage of the funeral services for David. "They didn't want it to be a press circus," he explains, "but they felt an obligation to these reporters—most of them happened to be women who were medical reporters—who over the years had done medical stories." On behalf of the family Demaret arranged for those reporters to attend the services. He picked them up in his car and brought them to the home of the family afterward. That was the extent of the family's involvement with the press.

Interest in the family did not diminish, however. Kent Demaret had been working for *People* since the magazine had begun ten years earlier, shortly after the demise of *Life*. During the years of David's life, Hal Wingo had often brought up the subject of doing a story on the Bubble Boy. "About once a year Kent and I would have a conversation about it," recalls Wingo, "and I would ask him if there was any way we could ever, ever tell the story of David, the Bubble Boy—what's happened to him since he was this little child as reported many years ago in *Life*. By then David was nine or ten."

As Demaret had come to know the family, he had grown very protective of them. He never wanted to push them into cooperating with *People* in spite of the fact that he worked for the magazine, and Hal Wingo could clearly see that. Wingo was a kind, sensitive, and gentle human being, and he refrained from pushing the issue. "Carol Ann just wasn't going to have anything to do with us at the time," he says. "She was a very private person. She was sympathetic, but really not interested in doing much more than was ever allowed—distance shooting, that was all."

When David died, Wingo broached the subject with Kent again. "There are times when being close to the story really hinders you, and I told Hal I just knew the family's need for privacy," Demaret says. "I knew their agony and the grief they were going through. If Hal wanted to ask them, I would help him make contact, but I just didn't have the heart to bring it up."

About a month after David's death, when Hal Wingo, who was a Texan himself, was in Houston, he invited Kent, Carol Ann, and her husband out to dinner. "It was the first time she had gone out since the boy died," Wingo recalls. "She had really withdrawn. We went to a really nice restaurant, and we were just visiting, the three of us: David's mother, Kent, and I. His father either couldn't go or did not want to come.

"At one point while we were having dinner, Kent got up and excused himself, and I said to Carol Ann, 'I know this is very painful for you to think about, but if you ever feel like there's a time when you can share with other people what it was like to be David's mother and the bravery that he reflected all through his life, we would love to be the ones to tell that story, and have you tell it in your own words through Kent, who you can really trust and feel good about.' She kind of got all teary eyed and said she appreciated that, and that she would certainly always keep that in mind."

No more was said about the story until a few more months had passed. Demaret never brought the subject up, but Wingo did not forget about it. "Hal asked again some months after David died, and the deepest part of the shocking grief was subsiding," says Demaret. "Carol Ann discussed it, I think, with her husband and they said yes. But they asked that I do it. I had very mixed emotions about it. I didn't think anybody else could do it as well. I knew nobody else could do it with the same feeling that I had, and I knew that nobody else could do it with the same information I had. Even though there wasn't constant contact, I knew more than anybody else. Not only did I have the most facts, but I had a better chance of the nuance and the rhythms of life of these extraordinary people."

And so Carol Ann's story of her son David's life got under way, with Kent Demaret, for *People* magazine. It was a long and arduous process, and it proved to be emotionally draining for everyone involved. "It was extremely difficult," recalls Demaret. "I didn't really know how to do it. I never in my life ever liked that part of the reporter's job. The idea of sitting down with grieving people and having to say, Well, what was your child's favorite toy? and to take them back into the tragedy just almost made me physically ill."

The family had decided that the *People* story would be Carol Ann's story, written in her words, with her distinctive voice and her pacing. It was up to Demaret to accomplish this. As they began to work together, he saw her pain. "She was putting up a very brave kind of face," he says. "She wasn't breaking down and sobbing but I could see that she was having problems, and I would have to stop."

They worked on it for endless hours in the weeks that followed. At the *People* offices in Houston, Kent showed Carol Ann how to use a computer, and he devised a system he thought would make the whole process easier for her. "I would give her total privacy to sit there and just write whatever came into her mind," he says. "Sometimes she did break down and cry, but you don't impose on somebody else's dignity."

Working on the story proved to be as difficult for Kent as it was for Carol Ann in many ways. "After she would write, quite often just to decompress, we would chitchat. Usually, the night before, I had worked on what she had written, and I would also type up a list for her to think about. I would put the kinds of things on the list for her to look or not look at, at a time when she wanted to. The kinds of things I didn't want to say out loud. The kinds of things that I didn't want to reignite her despair: David's toys, the baby years, the discipline, the joys, the anecdotes of life. The things I would ask her to think about until the next time she was going to start. Then she would give me a printout of whatever she had written. And I would give her a list of new things to think about."

When Carol Ann gave Kent what she had written, he would often work into the night. "I would pick up her thought patterns," he says, "and I would usually go back and put down what she had done with an overall idea of where the story was going. There were many times I would be working late at night and I would be crying into the keyboard. I just can't tell you how deeply affected I was."

By the time they had finished, there were enough pages for a book, and Demaret sent them on to the magazine in New York. In addition to the words, there were pictures—two or three hundred of them, which he took great care with, captioning every one himself. But there were still difficulties ahead. The story was exceedingly long, and its style was not typical of *People*. When Kent spoke with Hal the next day, he asked if he had finished reading it. "He sounded like he was a little put off," Kent says. "I said, 'Well, just read it all, Hal. When you get through you'll cry.' Sure enough, he called back several hours later and he had been crying."

Pat Ryan decided to run the story in two parts, but in spite of that it was still too long. Cutting it down to size would not be easy. Wingo believes Kent's emotional involvement in the story made it even more difficult. "He would almost take Carol Ann's side," says Wingo. "He would be protective of her and say, 'You can't push too much on this woman.' There was a lot of friction in pulling that story together. But, as I said, she was a very private woman. For her to open up as much as she did and tell what she told and relive what she lived with Kent was amazing. I must say, he was her support night and day. For him, it was more important that she be protected than to even get a story. At that point, it was more important for him to be sensitive at a human level than for the magazine to get a story. I respect that. As it turned out, it was a very powerful story."

. When the story ran, it became one of *People*'s top ten bestselling issues. But the story of Kent and Carol Ann did not end there. The tremendous strain of the difficult, emotionally wrenching years of David's life finally took their toll on her marriage. About a year after the *People* story ran, she and her husband were divorced. Demaret called her later and they went to dinner and a movie together. Two years later, Carol Ann and Kent were married.

"I just had a lot of respect for and a lot of admiration for her," he says. "She is an extremely smart person, but she lived *her* life in captivity, too. It has been marvelous. It's kind of like running around with a little martian. I'm showing her parts of the world she didn't know existed. I took her to the mountains and showed her a rock hammer and showed her a creek that might have gold in it. She went up that creek like an otter."

More than twenty years after he first met Carol Ann and a decade after the intense experience they shared when they wrote the story of David's life together for *People*, Kent Demaret is clearly in awe of the Bubble Boy's mother, the woman who became his wife. "She has a way of overwhelming you," he says. "She is a beautiful woman, but more than that, there is something magical that comes from inside. I have people tell me that they shook her hand and they felt like they had touched a saint."

1985

1985 COVERS

New Brides: Jamie Lee Curtis, Olivia
   Newton-John, Mariel Hemingway,
   Bette Midler, Sally Field
Princess Di & Prince Harry
30 Hardest-Working Celebs
Ted Kennedy & Tara & Teddy, Jr.
Mel Gibson
Sharon Gless & Tyne Daly
Molly Ringwald & Zach Galligan
Diana Ross, Michael Jackson, Bruce
   Springsteen, Lionel Richie,
   Willie Nelson
Bob Dylan
TV Rerun Madness
Madonna
Cher
Are They Worth It: High-Salaried Celebs
Jacqueline Bisset & Alexander Godunov
Christie Brinkley & Billy Joel
Dr. Ruth Westheimer
James Garner
Cathleen Webb
Bette Davis
Madonna
Prince Charles & Princess Di; President
   & Nancy Reagan
Julianne Phillips & Bruce Springsteen
Sylvester Stallone
Sam & Patt Frustaci & Quints
Claus & Cosima von Bülow
Joseph Mengele

Cyndi Lauper
Jack Nicholson & Anjelica Huston
Tina Turner
Princess Di
Mick Jagger, Tina Turner, Madonna,
   Keith Richards, et al.
Ali MacGraw
Rock Hudson's Other Life
Ann Jillian
Simon Le Bon
Sean Penn & Madonna
Priscilla Presley
Rock Censorship: Prince, Madonna
   & David Lee Roth
Olivia Newton-John & Matt Lattanzi
Don Johnson
Arnold Schwarzenegger
Marilyn Monroe & Rock Hudson:
   His Last Days
Best- & Worst-Dressed
Cybill Shepherd
Princess Di
Aidan Quinn
Barbara Stanwyck & Linda Evans
Raisa Gorbachev
Phillip Michael Thomas
Mikhail Baryshnikov
Don Johnson

YEAR-END DOUBLE ISSUE:
Don Johnson, Michael J. Fox, Princess Diana,
Bruce & Julianne Springsteen

Films: *Back to the Future*
Rambo: First Blood Part II
Beverly Hills Cop
Rocky IV
Cocoon

Oscar: *Out of Africa*

Top TV Shows: *Dynasty*
Dallas
The Cosby Show
60 Minutes
Family Ties

Emmys: *The Cosby Show*
Cagney & Lacey

Top Songs: "Say You, Say Me"—Lionel Richie
"We Are the World"—USA for Africa
"Can't Fight This Feeling"
   —REO Speedwagon
"The Power of Love"—Huey Lewis
   and the News
"One More Night"—Phil Collins
"Born in the USA"—Bruce Springsteen

Grammys: "We Are the World" (record)
"We Are the World" (song)

Bestsellers: *The Accidental Tourist*—Anne Tyler
The Cider House Rules—John Irving

The Hunt for Red October—Tom Clancy
Lonesome Dove—Larry McMurtry
Dancing in the Light—Shirley MacLaine

Tonys: *Biloxi Blues*
Big River
Joe Egg

Marriages: Billy Joel + Christie Brinkley
Cristina Ferrare + Anthony Thomopoulos
Bruce Springsteen + Julianne Phillips
Madonna + Sean Penn
Steven Spielberg + Amy Irving
Victoria Principal + Harry Glassman
Sylvester Stallone + Brigitte Nielsen
James Taylor + Kathryn Walker

Divorces: Muhammad & Veronica Ali
Carl Bernstein & Nora Ephron
Johnny & Joanna Carson
Marie Osmond & Stephen Craig

Deaths: Anne Baxter   James Beard
Marc Chagall   Dian Fossey
Rick Nelson   Rock Hudson
Nelson Riddle   Orson Welles
Nathan Pritikin   Ruth Gordon
             Yul Brynner

NEWS

- General William Westmoreland drops his $120 million libel suit against CBS
- Mikhail Gorbachev chosen to lead the Soviet Union when Konstantin Chernenko dies
- Capital Cities buys ABC for $3.5 billion
- Bernhard Goetz indicted for attempted murder of four youths in New York subway
- Richard Ramirez, L.A. "Night Stalker," arrested and charged with 68 criminal charges of murder and sexual asssult
- Philadelphia police bomb headquarters of radical MOVE group, setting off a two-block firestorm, killing 11 people
- Claus von Bülow acquitted in retrial of attempted murder of wife Sunny
- Anthropologist Dian Fossey found slain in Rwanda
- Gary Dotson rape sentence commuted after Cathleen Webb recants her story
- TWA plane hijacked by radical Shiite Muslim terrorists resulting in a 17-day hostage crisis
- Palestinian terrorists seize the *Achille Lauro* cruise ship, killing American tourist Leon Klinghoffer
- The body of Dr. Joseph Mengele, "the angel of death" of Auschwitz, is identified
- Reagan has a malignant tumor removed from his intestine
- Ted Turner drops his bid to take over CBS
- Earthquake in Mexico kills thousands
- The hulk of the *Titanic* is found south of Newfoundland
- Rock Hudson dies of AIDS
- G.E. to buy RCA for $6.3 billion

CHAPTER SEVENTEEN

To Di For
(The End of the Dream)

"Charles and Diana—the Prince and Princess of Wales to their subjects and storybook lovers to the rest of the world—will celebrate their fourth wedding anniversary on July 29. Yet little more than halfway toward that fabled seven-year itch, there are signs of growing conflict in the royal household . . ."

—*From* People's *cover story, "Malice in the Palace," July 22, 1985*

THREE YEARS AFTER Louise Lague had come to work for *People* as a writer, she was on maternity leave after the birth of her first child, when she received a phone call at home. It had just been announced that Princess Di was pregnant. "We know you're on maternity leave," said the editor who called her. "But could you come back and just write this story about the princess expecting? Because you're the only one who can spell 'amniocentesis.'"

Louise had returned to write the story. Ten years, two royal pregnancies, and forty-four Diana cover appearances later, she explained the magic of Princess Di in a speech she made in New York.

"I did come back and had a wonderful time," she said of her return to *People*, "and the princess and I have both since become staples of the magazine. She has been on the cover forty-four times in the last ten years and she never fails to sell out. The day Diana took a solitary walk on the beach on New Year's Eve, a one-page story with a fuzzy paparazzi photograph was something like the best-read story ever in the history of the magazine.

"Do you remember this story?" Lague asked her audience. "Poor Di. It's New Year's Eve. She's been with her in-laws for ten days. You know that feeling? She's in Balmoral, Scotland. She hates it there because it is cold and

Dirty Dancing's Patrick Swayze has come a long way from his
ballet days. He took a break from shooting *Youngblood* in
Toronto in 1984. (*Raeanne Rubenstein*)

This 1974 picture that Dick Swanson shot of Gerald Ford hung on the wall of *People*'s layout room for years, with the caption "Is that really his foot?"

(*Dick Swanson*)

A happy Drew Barrymore posed for *People* in 1982 during her *E.T.* days, before her problems with drugs and alcohol began. (*Tony Costa*)

On the October 28, 1974 cover (40¢): People weekly — In this... Wilbur... an ele... go-going... John... sin... Paradis... BURT REYNOL & DINAH SHO The supersta said Isabel P Argenti cagey r

On the February 13, 1978 cover (60¢): The Electric Light Orchestra turns on — Amityville Horror: its specter grips a second family — Joe Namath's retirement blues — People weekly — Clint Eastwood & Sondra Locke — He and his new star ride out a Gauntlet of gossip

Burt Reynolds first appeared on *People*'s cover (with Dinah Shore) on October 29, 1974. He was thirty-eight years old at the time and she was nineteen years his senior. (*Neil Leifer*)

Clint Eastwood and Sondra Locke appeared on *People*'s cover in 1978 while vehemently denying rumors of a relationship. They lived together for thirteen years after that. (*Steve Schapiro*)

MAY 18, 1987 • $1.50

People weekly

ART STOPPER

The brainy
rida beauty
who rocked
Presidential
ont-runner

Donna Rice
in Cannes

The first *People* cover
of Donna Rice ran the
week after the scandal
with Senator Gary Hart
broke in 1987. The photo
was taken several years
earlier on the beach
in Cannes.
(*Peter C. Borsari; inset Ben
Weaver*)

Harry Benson shot this photograph
of Clarence and Virginia Thomas
at their Virginia home shortly
after the Thomas-Hill hearings
in 1991. It ran as the cover for
the Virginia Thomas story, on
November 11 of that year.
(*Harry Benson*)

SUZANNE SOMERS: *Step By Step's* real-life stepmom

NOVEMBER 11, 1991 $1.95

People weekly

EXCLUSIVE VIRGINIA THOMAS TELLS HER STORY

"HOW WE SURVIVED"

The wife of
Clarence Thomas
describes the "hell"
of the hearings, her
own experience with
sexual harassment
and her belief that
Anita Hill "was
probably in love with
my husband"

After photographer Steve Kagan took this picture of Julia Roberts and Lyle Lovett during Lovett's concert the night of their wedding, the film was confiscated. *People* sued and won the case.
(*Steve Kagan*)

Glen Campbell and Tanya Tucker's on-again, off-again relationship was on-again when this picture was taken in 1980.
(*Harry Benson*)

This intimate picture captured a side of Hillary and Bill Clinton that had rarely been seen publicly. It was taken by Harry Benson in 1992 for the story on the Clintons by Lanny Jones.

(*Harry Benson*)

TROUBLE

Greta Garbo had no idea she was being photographed from a boat in Antigua Harbor with a telephoto lens after she had taken her clothes off to go for a swim in 1975.

(*Harry Benson*)

John Candy's
yellow Lab,
Keema, would
not get off his
master's back
in 1981,
when Candy
was a player
on the popular
TV show
SCTV.
(*Mimi Cotter*)

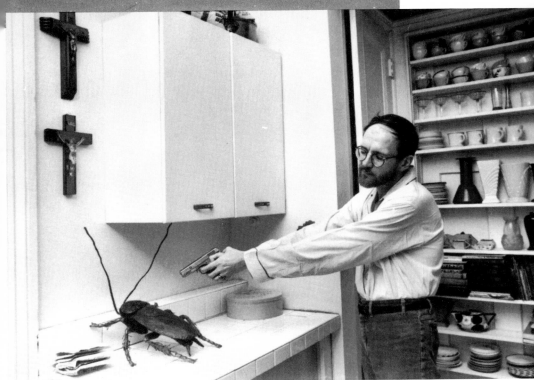

Saturday Night Live writer Michael O'Donoghue demonstrated his problem
with roaches in the kitchen with typical flair. (*Mimi Cotter*)

Muhammad Ali posed as the slave Crispus Attux for *People*'s Bicentennial issue in 1976. He gave photographer Harry Benson some real problems in the process.
(*Harry Benson*)

When Margaret Trudeau, the wife of Canadian prime minister Pierre Trudeau, took off on a weeklong getaway in 1977, she spent much of her time with the Rolling Stones. She is seen here with Ron Wood (*left*) and Mick Jagger at a Rolling Stones recording session that week. It was the beginning of the end of her marriage to Trudeau. (*Ken Regan/Camera 5*)

Harry Benson's dog, Lucy, with Shana Alexander and her daughter, Kathy, during what would turn out to be a disastrous shoot in the Hamptons in 1975. (*Harry Benson*)

Truman Capote made
a futile attempt to get
in shape for a *People*
story by reporter
Patricia Burstein
in 1976.

(*Jessica Burstein*)

Dustin Hoffman, 1982. The quintessential example of picture editor
Mary Dunn's vision of what made a *People* picture unique.

(*Raeanne Rubenstein*)

These chilling photographs of John Lennon's murderer, Mark David Chapman, were taken at Attica State Prison in 1987 for Jim Gaines's three-part story about Chapman.

(*Harry Benson*)

ANGRY

Robin Williams is still furious with *People* as a result of the story
about him that ran in the magazine in 1988.
(*Mark Sennet*)

like the old Indian proverb SAYS
Do not judge a Man until you've walked
2 moons in his Moccosins.
Most people don't Know Me, that is wHy they write
such ~~other~~ things in wich Most is not TRue
I cry very very often Because it Hurts and I
worry about the children all my children all over the
World, I live for them.
If a Man could SAy nothing AGAINST a
character but what he can prove, HISTORY COULD
NOT Be written.
Animals sTRike, not from Malice, But because they
want To live, it is the same with those wHo
CRITisize, they desire our BLOOD, NOT our
pain. But STILL I MUST achieve I MUST seek
TRuth in all things. I MUST endure for the power
I was sent forth, for the world for ~~the~~ children
BuTHAVE Mercy, for I've been Bleeding a
long Time Now. MJ.

Michael Jackson on stage
in Tokyo during his 1987
world tour. He wrote
the letter to reporter
Todd Gold in answer to
Gold's written questions
to him. The letter landed
him a cover headlined
MESSAGE FROM MICHAEL.
(Neal Preston)

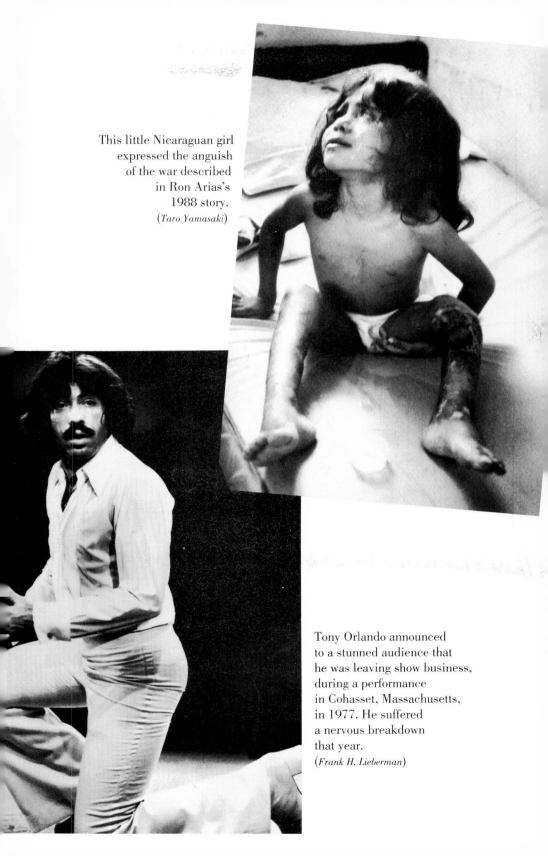

This little Nicaraguan girl
expressed the anguish
of the war described
in Ron Arias's
1988 story.
(*Taro Yamasaki*)

Tony Orlando announced
to a stunned audience that
he was leaving show business,
during a performance
in Cohasset, Massachusetts,
in 1977. He suffered
a nervous breakdown
that year.
(*Frank H. Lieberman*)

Michael Douglas and Jane Fonda, who were starring in *The China Syndrome*, had already been photographed for a *People* cover in 1979 when the nuclear disaster at Three Mile Island occurred. (*Tony Costa*)

When the *People* teams fanned out to cover the nuclear disaster, they caught this picture of a tourist taking a picture of his wife in front of the cooling tower. (*Michael Abramson*)

Human drama in Harrisburg: Who's to blame?

Marvin Hamlisch: the love song he lives

Larry (Dallas) Hagman, an off-camera oddball

Oscar de la Renta's $2,000,000 mistake

APRIL 16, 1979 · 75¢

People weekly

A Disaster Movie Comes True

Michael Douglas: After 'China Syndrome,' he isn't just Kirk's son anymore

Priscilla Presley went riding with her daughter, Lisa, for a *People* story in 1978. It was the first interview she had given since Elvis's death, more than a year earlier.
(*Frank H. Lieberman*)

Tony Orlando made a comeback performance, the first since his nervous breakdown, in Las Vegas in 1978. He is pictured with the author, who covered both stories.
(*Tony Korody*)

Farrah Fawcett, who has appeared on *People*'s cover fourteen times since its debut, in a picture taken for a story in Poundridge, New York, in 1975. The author (*at right*, with Fawcett) was the reporter. Fawcett's hairdresser, Jose Eber, made a rare appearance without his trademark hat. (*Ken Regan/Camera 5*)

This *People* picture
captured the delight
of popcorn king
Orville Redenbacher
at the height
of his success.
(*Thomas S. England*)

Singer Sly Stone,
of Sly and the Family Stone,
was flying high during a
People shoot in 1980.
(*Neal Preston*)

TRIBUTE

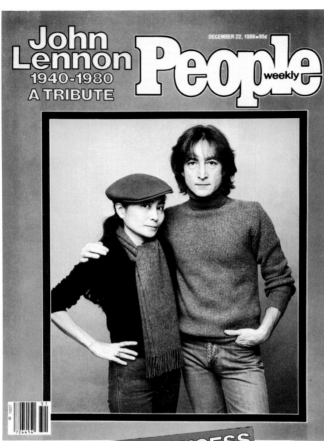

The cover that ran the week after John Lennon's death in 1980 remains the best-selling cover in the history of the magazine. (*copyright Jack Mitchell*)

The picture of Grace Kelly, used on the cover after her death in 1982 (*below left*), was taken by photographer Harry Benson for another *People* story months before her death. It remains the second-best selling cover in the history of the magazine. (*Harry Benson*)

The *People* cover that ran after John Belushi's death that same year (*below*) was also a top seller. (*David Alexander*)

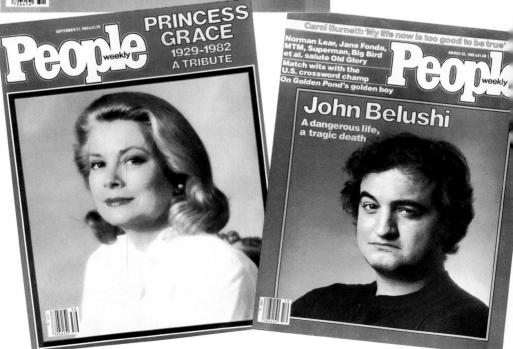

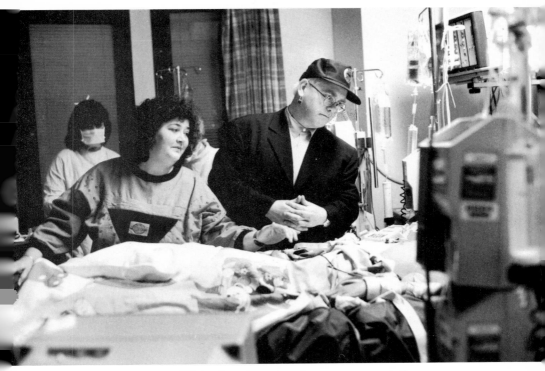

Elton John and Jeanne White, Ryan's mother, kept a constant vigil over
Ryan in the hospital during Ryan's last days in 1990. (*Taro Yamasaki*)

INSPIRATION

People reporter Bill Shaw (*left*) and photographer Taro Yamasaki
(*right*) with Ryan White in 1988. (*Taro Yamasaki*)

PARENTS

Paul McCartney and daughter at the piano in 1975.
(*Harry Benson*)

NBC producer Dick
Ebersol with his wife,
Susan Saint James, and
their son, in front of their
Connecticut home.
(*Christopher Little*)

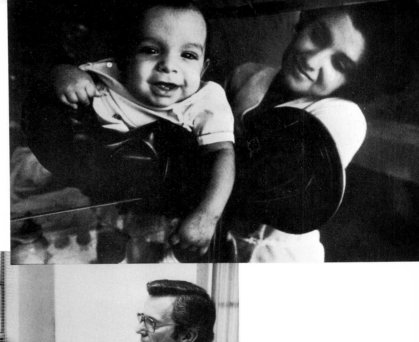

David, the Bubble
Boy, and his mother,
Carol Anne, in the
picture that ran in
Life magazine
shortly after his
birth in 1971.
(*Harry Benson*)

Carol Anne and reporter
Kent Demaret working
on the story of David's
life for *People* in 1984.
They later married.
(*Ben Weaver*)

Carly Simon and her son, Ben Taylor, were caught in a joyful moment
in front of their home on Martha's Vineyard in 1980.

(*Ken Regan/Camera 5*)

Princess Diana on the cover of *People* after the birth of her first child, Prince William, in 1982. (*Terry Smith*)

People photographer Ian Cook was in the throng of photographers after Diana in 1982. (*Press Association*)

Photographer Jayne Fincher caught up with Diana in the Outer Hebrides in 1985: "You don't see Diana dressed like that very often," Fincher said. "It was pouring, but her makeup was perfect."
(*Jayne Fincher*)

Diana attended the royal premiere of *Back to the Future III* in 1989.

Prince Andrew
gave Fergie a
royal hand with
her train after
their wedding
in 1986.
(*Ken Goff*)

The new royal
couple in the
wedding carriage.
(*Ian Cook*)

People's first editor, Richard B. Stolley, with actress Ann-Margret at his farewell party at Studio 54 in 1982. He left to become editor of *Life*. (*Robin Platzer*)

STAFF

People staff members laying o[ut] a picture spread: Dick Burghe[r] (*second from left*), Hal Wingo, editor Dick Stolley, and Mary Dunn. (*Evelyn Floret*)

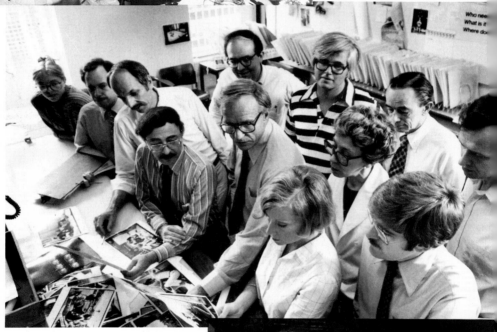

Pat Ryan (*left*) replaced Dick Stolley as *People*'s editor in 1982.
(*Robin Platzer*)

People editor Lanny Jones
with President Clinton, Hillary,
and Washington bureau
chief Garry Clifford
in 1992. (*Harry Benson*)

Managing editor Jim Gaines
at work on the magazine, 1987.
(*Raeanne Rubenstein*)

Reporters Susan Reed (*right*) and Deirdre Donahue with photographer Christopher Little at Maria Shriver's wedding in 1986. (*Christopher Little*)

People's photographers at the Black and White Ball in 1988 at the Plaza Hotel. They include, first row: Mark Sennet (*second from left*), Tony Costa (*center*), Ian Cook (*third from right*); second row (*from left*): Raeanna Rubenstein, Steve Schapiro, Mimi Cotter (*second from right*); third row (*from left*): Ben Weaver, Christopher Little, M. C. Marden (*fifth from left*), Harry Benson (*sixth from left*); fourth row: Terry Smith, Taro Yamasaki (*right*); fifth row: Ken Regan (*left*), Dick Stolley (*sixth from left*), Maddy Miller (*seventh from left*); sixth row: Tony Korody, Peter C. Bosari (*right*); last row (*from left*): editors John Saar, Jim Seymore, and Hal Wingo.

damp and there's no place to shop. So on New Year's Eve afternoon she rips off her location beeper and slides out the back gate and goes for a lonely walk on the beach, pondering her life. The palace guards are going insane. The princess has disappeared! And you know who finds her? A photographer finds her. He was hiding in the bushes waiting for just this to happen. So this was the best-read story in our magazine. That is the pull of the princess . . ."

About the time that Lague interrupted her maternity leave to help out with the pregnant princess and the spelling of "amniocentesis," another writer was hired who would also become instrumental in *People*'s stateside royal coverage in the years to come. Carol Wallace was on the staff of the New York newspaper *The Daily News* when she was offered a job at the magazine. She had recently won an award for best feature writing from the Women's Press Club in New York, and she agonized about whether to take the job at *People*. She was, after all, a newspaperwoman and did not know much about the way magazines functioned, but she was intrigued with the possibilities and decided to give it a try.

On her first day at *People*, before Wallace even had a chance to take off her coat, an editor came up to her with her first assignment. "My first story," she recalls, "was to write twenty lines about a cow that got his head stuck in a barrel. I was just mortified. I said to myself, What have I done?"

She had barely finished the twenty lines about the unfortunate cow, however, when the course of her career at *People* took a 180-degree turn. The staff at the time had been split regarding how much attention should be paid to the royals. "A lot of people thought this was just far too trivial for us to cover," says Wallace. "Why does anybody care about the royals? Why should we care if Di takes a walk or gets a new hat?"

Carol was on the side that thought a lot of attention should be paid to the royals, and the magazine would soon come to believe that it was impossible to pay too much attention to them. Wallace had always been intrigued by Princess Di. "I was fascinated by what was happening with the royals," she says. "I always viewed it as a true-life soap opera. Everybody I knew couldn't get enough information about Diana and had strong opinions about the family, about the princess, about the younger royals, about the queen and her purse. Before Diana came along, it was just this frumpy, dowdy family. All the women looked like Mamie Eisenhower and the queen always carried this purse. She would never let her purse out of her sight. It was like she was carrying an IV in it."

Within days the cow had transformed into a princess when Wallace was assigned the royal beat. "There was such interest at the time in this young woman who was living out a fairy tale," she says. "I remember when they got married. I was up early in the morning watching and here she was sacrificing any privacy she would ever have for the rest of her life. Everyone was debating about, Would you do it? and, What did you think of her dress? . . . there was just so much fascination. Not since Jackie Kennedy had everybody been so fascinated."

The fascination continued to grow, even as the fairy-tale façade began to show signs of cracking shortly after Prince William's christening in the summer of 1982. The following January, the royal couple had gone to Liechtenstein, just across the border from Zürich, for an Alpine ski holiday. Somehow, as *People* reported (in a cover story titled "Diana's Ordeal"), an intrepid reporter had started the trouble on that trip when he played a hunch and placed a phone call to the residence of Prince Franz Josef II in Liechtenstein. "What will happen when Prince Charles stays with you this week?" the reporter had asked.

"How did you find out?" the astonished Franz Josef had replied.

From that moment on, for the rest of their ski holiday, Charles and Diana had been pursued, dogged, and hounded by the press. For the first time, the twenty-one-year-old princess showed her anger. As *People* put it:

> Shy Di was no longer bashful about her preference for privacy. On and off the slopes, Diana was uncharacteristically icy to the pursuing paparazzi. As she pulled down her ski cap and hid her face behind gloves during one close encounter with the press, even Charles found her behavior frustrating and pleaded: "Please, Diana, don't do that. You're being stupid."

Charles was not the only one to admonish Diana. Nigel Dempster of *The Daily Mail* complained, "She's behaving like a petulant, spoiled brat."

Others tried to shed light on the difficulties Diana faced, pointing out that in the twenty-three months since she had become engaged, she had assumed in rapid succession the weighty roles of media personality, royal princess, and mother. "It's not easy," conceded an editorial in another London newspaper, which also admonished her for her behavior, "being thrown in at the royal deep end at the tender age of twenty-one."

By the summer of 1985, nine months after the birth of their second son, Henry, it became apparent that there was more than a hint of trouble in the marriage of Charles and Diana. As their fourth anniversary approached, *People* revealed that there were signs of conflict in the royal marriage. "Charles and Diana—the Prince and Princess of Wales to their subjects and storybook lovers to the rest of the world," the magazine reported, "will celebrate their fourth wedding anniversary on July 29. Yet little more than halfway toward that fabled seven-year itch, there are signs of growing conflict in the royal household."

According to *People*, Diana was "no longer the blushing kindergarten teacher who snared the world's most eligible bachelor." She was displaying a new assertiveness and self-confidence. She was not only venturing out socially without her husband, but her public engagements would outnumber her husband's that year for the first time in their marriage, while Charles was tiring of his "relentlessly repetitive royal chores" as he waited to succeed the throne.

With the solid reporting that *People*'s London bureau afforded the magazine—in large part because certain staff members had impressively strong, but by their very nature extremely confidential, connections to the palace as well as to many of the players in the royal arena—*People* did not hesitate to go forward with their story about the apparent marital woes.

Carol Wallace came up with the memorable cover line "Malice in the Palace." The story would stand up as one of the most substantial pieces the magazine would ever do on the royal couple, demonstrating not only the accuracy of *People*'s pipeline to the palace but the reliability of their royal reportage as well.

"Malice in the Palace" sold more than two million copies. By then, Carol Wallace was doing everything in her power to find anything that would provide even a germ for a possible story on the royals. "We were as hungry for this stuff as we could get," she explains. "When Diana sat on Charles's car and he made her get off, we made that into a one-page story. Anything goes."

Anything went. One cover had already preceded "Malice in the Palace" that year:

HARRY
How his christening
fueled the royal feud
between Diana and Princess Anne

It addressed the tensions between the two women, which became obvious after Princess Anne had failed to show up for the christening. The piece explained that Anne was upset that she had not been among the godparents named for the child, and the issue sold 1,890,000 newsstand copies.

After "Malice in the Palace," Charles and Di actually shared a cover with Ronald and Nancy Reagan as the magazine managed to concoct a story about the amounts of money the couples spent. The cover line was

TALK ABOUT POWER TRIPS!

and underneath:

**An inside report on the yacht,
the jets, the banquets,
the gowns and the gaffes . . .
as Charles & Di & Ron & Nancy
do Europe on $1 million
a day—at least**

Even that sold 1,491,000 newsstand copies, and there was another later:

WHAT'S DIANA WORTH TO BRITAIN?

alongside a picture of Princess Diana wearing a hat from which a
$500,000,000 price tag hung. Inside, the headline read

DI: Birth of a Saleswoman

Underneath, the subhead:

**Princess Diana, hood ornament to an empire,
may be the best advertisement for Britain
since the Beatles**

Perhaps the question should have been "What's Diana worth to *People*?"
    The answer to that was "a lot." It was eventually calculated by *People*'s
publishing office that a cover with Princess Diana on it would sell 18 percent
more copies than an average cover without her.

AS THE PROVOCATIVE malice in the palace continued throughout
1985, there were other occurrences of great significance that would have a
lasting impact around the world: A TWA plane with 239 passengers aboard
was hijacked and held for more than two weeks by Iranian terrorists; the
Achille Lauro cruise ship was seized by Palestinian terrorists in the eastern
Mediterranean, resulting in the death of an American, Leon Klinghoffer;
primatologist Dian Fossey was found murdered at her research camp in
Rwanda; and Rock Hudson disclosed that he was dying of AIDS. As the first
well-known Hollywood star to die of the disease, he would bring both public
awareness and attention to the crisis that was in the process of becoming
widespread and devastating.
    People brought all of these stories to its readers—an astounding thirty
million people a week. After it was disclosed that Rock Hudson had AIDS,
the *People* cover "The Other Life of Rock Hudson" sold 2,318,000 newsstand
copies. After Hudson's death, the magazine put him on the cover with Marilyn Monroe, as a new book about her death was published. "Their Last Days:
Rock & Marilyn" sold 1,919,000 newsstand copies.

In 1985, the four Diana covers sold a total of 7,073,000 newsstand copies, which meant that—with the subscription rate adding more than a million copies by then, and with *People*'s pass-along readership of ten—more than 100 million people read those issues alone (a number that allowed the magazine to charge $105,000 for a one-page ad at that time). A total of more than 150 million issues of *People* were sold—reaching more than a billion readers.

Even after eleven years, with the help of the royals, the magazine's circulation continued to climb.

LADY DI COVERS
(and Copies Sold*), 1985–1993

1/14/85	Harry's Christening Fuels a Royal Feud (1,890,000)
5/20/85	Talk About Power Trips (1,491,000)
7/22/85	Malice in the Palace (2,079,000)
11/11/85	What's Diana Worth to Britain? (1,613,000)
10/13/86	Fergie & Di: The Merry Wives of Windsor: (1,905,000)
6/8/87	Save the Wales! (2,105,000)
7/20/87	Naughty, Naughty, Follies of Fergie & Di (2,278,000)
11/9/87	The Big Chill: Charles & Di Confront a Dead-End Marriage (2,057,000)
4/25/88	Growing Up Royal (1,809,000)
8/1/88	Seven-Year Hitch (2,083,000)
10/31/88	Charles Builds a Private Life Without Di (1,737,000)
7/16/90	The Woman Who Will Be Queen (1,857,000)
10/9/90	The Decade of Diana (1,495,000)
2/11/91	Diana: Rich, Royal and Home Alone (1,732,000)
6/17/91	Wounded Prince (1,558,000)
7/22/91	Charles & Di: Where Has Their Love Gone? (1,692,000)
4/13/92	Diana in Mourning (1,844,000)
6/22/92	Exclusive! Diana (2,310,000)
6/29/92	The Other Woman: Diana's Rival (2,040,000)
8/3/92	Diana's Diet Ordeal: Battling Bulimia (2,726,000)
9/14/92	Diana's Secrets (2,725,000)
11/30/92	It's Over (2,691,000)
12/21/92	Diana Makes a Deal (2,691,000)
4/12/93	Diana On Her Own (2,641,000)

* Newsstand sales only—subscriptions not included

1986 COVERS

Donna Dixon	David Letterman
Ingrid Bergman	Prince
Ricky Nelson	Rodney Dangerfield & Danny DeVito
Mark Harmon	Prince Andrew & Sarah Ferguson Wedding
Bette Midler	Pierce Brosnan
Christa McAuliffe	Meryl Streep & Jack Nicholson
Diana Ross's Wedding	Vanna White
Patti Davis	Farrah Fawcett, Carol Burnett,
Imelda Marcos & Michele Duvalier	Eddie Murphy, Lucille Ball, Barbra
Whoopi Goldberg	Streisand, Tina Turner
Caroline Kennedy	Priscilla Presley
George Harrison & Madonna	Frank Sinatra
Old Maids: Donna Mills, Sharon Gless,	Ava Gardner, Mia Farrow, Victoria Principal
Linda Ronstadt, Diane Sawyer	Nancy Reagan, Natalie Wood, Frank Sinatra
Prince Andrew & Sarah Ferguson	Patrick Duffy
Lionel Richie	Elizabeth Taylor & Robert Wagner
Ed & Victoria McMahon	Princess Diana & Sarah Ferguson
Sgt. Ken Ford	Charlie's Angels
Dolly Parton	Joan Rivers
Duke & Duchess of Windsor	Kathleen Turner
Readers' Poll	Princess Stephanie & Rob Lowe
Joan Rivers	Julie & David Eisenhower
Summer Trash: Donna Mills	Carol Burnett
Rock Hudson	Best- & Worst-Dressed
Rock Hudson & Linda Evans	Bruce Springsteen
Unmarried Men: John Kennedy, Jr.	Cary Grant
Uncle Sam's Dirty Book	
Prince William	

YEAR-END DOUBLE ISSUE:
Paul Hogan, Whitney Houston, Tom Cruise,
David Letterman, Vanna White, Pat Robertson,
Sarah Ferguson

Top Films: *Top Gun*
Crocodile Dundee
The Karate Kid Part II
Back to School
Star Trek IV

Oscar: *Platoon*

Top TV Shows: *The Cosby Show*
Family Ties
Murder, She Wrote
60 Minutes
Cheers

Emmys: *The Golden Girls*
Cagney & Lacey

Top Songs: "That's What Friends Are For"
—Dionne & Friends
"Walk Like an Egyptian"—Bangles
"On My Own"—Patti LaBelle
& Michael McDonald
"Greatest Love of All"
—Whitney Houston
"True Colors"—Cyndi Lauper
"Addicted to Love"—Robert Palmer

Grammys: "Higher Love" (record)
"That's What Friends Are For" (song)

Bestsellers: *The Bourne Supremacy*—Robert Ludlum
The Handmaid's Tale—Margaret Atwood
It —Stephen King
The Prince of Tides—Pat Conroy

Tonys: *I'm Not Rappaport*
The Mystery of Edwin Drood
Sweet Charity

Marriages: Lee Iacocca + Peggy Johnson
Patty Duke + Michael Prince
Debra Winger + Timothy Hutton
Maria Shriver + Arnold Schwarzenegger
Diana Ross + Arne Naess
Barbara Walters + Merv Adelson
Caroline Kennedy + Edwin Schlossberg
Prince Andrew + Sarah Ferguson
John McEnroe + Tatum O'Neal

Divorces: Chris Evert Lloyd & John Lloyd

Deaths: Desi Arnaz   James Cagney
Simone de Beauvoir   Cary Grant
Ted Knight   Vincente Minnelli
Georgia O'Keeffe   Otto Preminger
Duchess of Windsor   Ray Milland

NEWS

- Cathy Smith sentenced to prison for her role in drug-overdose death of John Belushi
- Billionaire Boys Club trial opens in L.A.
- Griffin O'Neal cleared of manslaughter but convicted of negligence in boating-accident death of Gian Carlo Coppola
- Preppy murder defendant Robert Chambers, Jr., uses "rough sex" defense in killing of Jennifer Levin

CHAPTER EIGHTEEN

Adding Fergie to the Fire

"The queen has a soft spot for Sarah. She has known
her since childhood and is delighted Andrew has taken
such an interest in her . . ."

—*a friend of Sarah Ferguson's, in* People, *January 27, 1986*

*P*EOPLE HAD BEEN planning a cover story on Joan Collins the
week the *Challenger* blew up. The space shuttle had exploded into a
massive orange fireball only seventy-three seconds after liftoff on
January 28, 1986, while millions of viewers watched their television screens
in horror. The beloved schoolteacher Christa McAuliffe was among the six
crew members killed, and McAuliffe had replaced Joan Collins on *People's*
cover that week. Collins had not been pleased.

The year had already begun with a tragedy in the skies when Ricky
Nelson died in a fiery plane crash with his band and his fiancée only weeks
before the *Challenger* exploded. Ironically, but predictably, the two covers
had sold extremely well—once again the golden combination of celebrity and
tragedy.

It was welcome news for the magazine—not to mention Queen Elizabeth—when it was announced, also in January, that Sarah Ferguson would
marry Prince Andrew in April. Princess Di had proved beyond a doubt that
nothing was better than royalty for *People*. To make matters even better,
Fergie was one of Di's closest friends. She told a BBC interviewer that she
sought out Diana's advice on practically everything because, as she put it,
there was nobody better than the Princess of Wales.

The queen was relieved to see the matter of marriage in her son Andrew's love life resolved. He had been making an unsavory public display

in the queen's eyes, with the likes of model Koo Stark; Carolyn Seaward, Miss United Kingdom of 1980; Vicki Hodge, a woman thirteen years his senior with whom he frolicked in the Bahamas, and who later sold the story to the tabs; and Katie Rabett, an obstetrician's daughter who had managed to lose randy Andy when Fleet Street had unearthed nude photographs of her.

Fergie was another story, in spite of the fact that she had lived openly with two other men in her life: Paddy McNally, a former manager to racecar driver Niki Lauda, and Kim Smith-Bingham, a twenty-nine-year-old businessman. Things were changing in the palace as they were in the world outside of it. According to *People*, he "could do worse than to settle down with Sarah Ferguson, the 26-year-old daughter of Prince Charles's polo manager, the cousin of Elizabeth's assistant private secretary and possibly the sexiest descendent of King Charles II."

The article pointed out that, according to an intimate friend of Sarah Ferguson's, "the Queen has a soft spot for Sarah. She has known her since childhood and is delighted Andrew has taken such an interest in her."

Not only had Diana set up the romance between Fergie and Andrew, she had already paved the way for her friend in *People*, and Fergie was a natural. By the time the magazine was twenty, Fergie would appear on its cover almost as much as Princess Di.

The magazine managed to squeeze in two more royal covers before the wedding even took place. First, there was

ANDY'S LUV
(and Di's delight)
Sarah Ferguson

It was a piece that contained juicy tidbits about all three of them.

"Thirty years ago," *People* pointed out, "this marriage would never have been allowed to happen. Fergie, as her friends and now the world know her, is a woman with a past . . . At Buckingham Palace, where divorce is still enough to get a servant kicked out, Fergie might once have been blackballed for that . . ."

The piece also unveiled the fact that Diana had engineered the romance between Sarah and Andrew and that the loyal princess had buoyed Sarah's spirits when Andrew was at sea or seemed unresponsive to marriage; that Fergie was a well-liked prankster while she attended boarding school; and that her social life seemed always to have been as important to her as her career. It also took the opportunity to enumerate Andrew's succession of women, and it could not resist documenting the British tabloids' coverage of his affair with Koo Stark:

SECRET LOVE OF THE PRINCE
AND A NUDE STAR

and

I SAW ANDREW LEAVE HER FLAT
IN THE MORNINGS. HE ALWAYS
LOOKED RATHER TIRED.

and finally

QUEEN BANS KOO

and

IF NOT KOO, WHO?

People was not about to miss out on any of this tantalizing royal stuff. They even managed a cover on Prince William and his parents' worries over how he would behave at the upcoming nuptials. "His official debut at Andy's wedding has Charles & Di in a tizzy," the cover cried. "Will his antics steal the show?"

They did not.

But there was no doubt that the wedding would be the *pièce de résistance*. For once, the magazine would be able to cover a royal wedding with live pictures and still get the issue out just under the deadline, in spite of the fact that it would take place, as all royal weddings do, on a Wednesday. This time *People* would not lose out.

The deadline was pushed back one day, until Thursday. M. C. Marden was used to this by now, and she knew that she had to arrange as much as she could beforehand. This was not her first royal wedding. She also knew it was not going to be easy to get what she needed. She flew to London herself to edit the film on the spot and to see that it was transmitted instantly so it would come in under the deadline. "We kept the magazine open a day later," she recalls, "and we had to transmit the picture, because that was the only way to get it there fast enough."

This was going to be a big moment for M.C.—the opportunity of a lifetime, so to speak—and she was going to do everything in her power not to blow it. She hired three photographers for the job. The London bureau's Terry Smith was the first, and he was stationed right outside Westminster Abbey, hoping for a clear shot of the newest royal couple as they emerged from the church; Ian Cook was the second. He was stationed up on a moat with a view of the spot where the carriage carrying the royal couple would turn the corner on its route from the church to Buckingham Palace. A third photographer, Ken Goff, was stationed farther away, at Buckingham Palace, for the last possible chance when the carriage arrived.

That was all M.C. could do for the moment. She stationed herself in a pub, which had been converted into an editing room, next door to the lab where the pictures would be developed. She was not alone. There were representatives of all the other magazine and photo agencies waiting for exactly the same thing.

For the media, it was like a well-orchestrated circus. Runners were scurrying everywhere, picking up the film as it was shot, hustling it over to the lab as quickly as they could get there to have it developed. Once done, the people from the lab would run the pictures next door to the pub, where everyone was waiting to see what they had gotten.

It was a curious scene: an English pub filled with picture editors, all with portable light tables in front of them so they could examine the transparencies of the photographs of the royal wedding as they were delivered from the lab next door.

M.C. sat there nervously awaiting her photographs. God, she was hoping, out of three takes from three different photographers she should get *something*! But you never knew with pictures. That much she was sure of after working at *People* in the picture department for nearly a decade. This situation was less than optimal.

While M.C. waited nervously in the pub–converted lab, Terry Smith stood poised with his camera, ready to shoot, sandwiched between hundreds of other photographers on shaky bleachers that had been set up for that purpose outside of the church. He positioned himself as best he could, and as he was bumped and jostled, he stood his ground and waited for the right moment. Finally, it came. The royal carriage appeared, moving closer. He knew he would have only a second or two to shoot. Steadily he waited for the precise moment as the carriage carrying the newlyweds got closer and closer to him. There it was, getting nearer, nearer. It was almost time. And then *BAM!* The carriage passed in front of him. Terry shot. Just as Smith's camera shutter clicked down to immortalize the newly married couple in the one chance the photographer had to capture his picture for *People*, a horse walked smack in front of Fergie and Andy. "That was the picture," M.C. recalls sadly. "I had a picture of the horse in front of Fergie and Andy."

Still there was hope. That had only been take number one. Up the hill, with a different view, Ian Cook waited, poised and ready for his shot. Looking down from his perch, he saw the carriage approach. Then—what? What was going on? Just as he was ready to shoot, the horses drawing the carriage picked up speed. They started to run. He could not believe what was happening! "The carriage goes *BA BOOM BA BOOM BA BOOOOOM!*" says M.C. "All those pictures were wasted."

M.C. was beginning to despair as she walked through the pub looking at everyone else's pictures of the wedding. It seemed as though the whole world was in the pub. "There were Italian magazines and Swiss magazines, and agencies from all over," says M.C. "I was surrounded by pictures, but none of them were mine."

There was still one remote possibility: Ken Goff, the photographer she had stationed at Buckingham Palace. If the pictures that had already been missed had been long shots, she did not hold out much hope for the photographer stationed farthest away from the wedding. When that take came in, it was even worse than the rest. "It was shot from hundreds of miles away, so that didn't work either," says M.C.

Now she really had a problem. "By this time," she says, "I'm walking around the pub, asking everybody, 'What are you going to do with those pictures?' Because I had to get a cover. It was not the fault of any of the photographers. These guys had schlepped outside on the street. They had done everything. It was just that the gods weren't with us."

While the picture disaster was playing itself out, the reporters in the London bureau had fanned out to do everything in their power to get what they could, and thankfully they got a lot. Meanwhile, back in New York, Carol Wallace had arrived at the office at four o'clock in the morning on the Wednesday of the wedding, which was 9:00 A.M. in London, to begin writing the piece directly from the TV coverage of the wedding. "We had about 80 percent of the story and coverage of the wedding reported and written ahead of time," she says, "because this is really the kind of stop-the-presses, rip-out-the-front-page, minute-by-minute story."

The deadline was looming larger and larger. The magazine still closed on Tuesdays, but with Pat Ryan's decision to hold it open an extra day, they had until the end of Wednesday. Fergie and Andrew's wedding was by all standards a dream cover for *People.* M. C. Marden had actually arranged for the use of a satellite to transmit the pictures, which she still did not have, so they would arrive in time for the closing. A live picture was that crucial for this wedding issue.

Carol Wallace worked away at her desk in New York, writing the top of the story from the television coverage (which was seen by an estimated three hundred million viewers in thirty-nine countries). "By then the London bureau reporters were in the streets and reporting it," says Wallace, "and it was just a minute-by-minute thing that we had to get closed."

The writing was not the problem. There could be no cover if there was no cover picture. In fact, M.C. had foreseen that danger, and as Carol wrote the story in New York, M.C. was working on the backup arrangement she had set up. She had made a deal before the wedding with a well-known picture agency, Gamma-Liaison, that in the worst-case scenario—if, God forbid, *People* did not have a usable wedding picture of their own—the agency would sell one frame to her. That was all. But if it was good, that would be enough. It turned out to be a stunning picture of Fergie, in her wedding gown, waving from her carriage, as her new husband, Prince Andrew, looked at her lovingly. The tag line:

NICE WORK, LUV

It was. The Fergie and Andy wedding issue sold 2,590,000 newsstand copies.

Ironically, though, there was a slight hitch. If the timing had not been what it was, *People* could have had two big wedding covers instead of one. As it happened, Caroline Kennedy married Edwin Schlossberg the weekend before Fergie married Andy. Since both of those weddings had to close in the same issue, the Kennedy wedding became an inset on the cover. Down the left-hand side were pictures of Senator Ted Kennedy and Jackie, Caroline with her husband, Maria Shriver and Arnold Schwarzenegger. Considering the fact that, according to *People*'s research, weddings are among the most widely read topics in the magazine, it is no wonder the issue did so well.

It was the beginning of the Fergie era in *People* but certainly not the end. By the time *People* celebrated its twentieth anniversary only eight years later, Fergie, along with Di, would have appeared on the cover more than almost anyone else. Two months after the wedding cover, there was another cover, this time a joint effort:

FERGIE & DI:
THE MERRY WIVES OF WINDSOR

"Eleven weeks after she wed Prince Andrew and nine weeks after their honeymoon in the Azores, the newest member of the House of Windsor has become a wildly popular co-star in the royal road show," said *People*. "In fact, if performances by members of the House of Windsor carried credits, Sarah, Duchess of York, would already be sharing top billing with Diana, Princess of Wales."

Indeed, by the end of her first year as an official member of the royal family, Sarah Ferguson, the new princess of York, would appear on *People*'s list of the most intriguing people of 1986.

FERGIE COVERS
(and Copies Sold*)

4/7/86	Andy's Luv: Sarah Ferguson (1,643,000)
8/4/86	Nice Work, Luv: Andy & Fergie Marry (2,590,000)
10/13/86	Fergie & Di: The Merry Wives of Windsor (1,905,000)
12/29/86	25 Most Intriguing People of 1986 (3,047,000)
7/20/87	Naughty, Naughty Follies of Fergie & Di (2,278,000)
9/21/87	Here Comes Fergie! (1,835,000)
11/16/87	1987's Best & Worst Dressed (2,665,000)
1/11/88	Here's to a Great '88 (1,571,000)
8/29/88	Fergie's Little Princess (1,941,000)
12/26/88	25 Most Intriguing People of 1988 (2,990,000)
1/9/89	Here's to a Fine '89 (1,617,000)
11/20/89	Why the Brits Are: Fed Up with Fergie! (1,664,000)
4/16/90	Exclusive: Bringing Baby Home (1,520,000)
10/9/90	The Decade of Diana (1,495,000)
3/11/91	Fergie and the Playboy (1,463,000)
3/30/92	End of a Fairy Tale (2,066,000)
9/7/92	Fergie's Final Folly? (2,726,000)
3/8/93	Fergie: The Ugly Truth (1,552,000)

* Newsstand sales only—subscriptions not included

TOP TEN BESTSELLING COVERS EVER*

John Lennon 1940–1980: A Tribute (12/22/80)
(2,644,000)

Princess Grace 1929–1982: A Tribute (9/27/82)
(2,623,000)

Nice Work, Luv: Fergie and Andy Marry (8/4/86)
(2,590,000)

Oh Boy! The Palace Plans a Future for (7/5/82)
Diana's Baby (2,579,000)

Good Show! (Charles & Diana's Wedding) (8/3/81)
(2,551,000)

Olivia Newton-John: Greased Lightning (7/31/78)
(2,508,000)

Karen Carpenter: Death Comes at 32 (2/21/83)
(2,506,000)

Brooke Shields in *The Blue Lagoon* (2,494,000) (8/11/80)

Priscilla Presley Talks (2,481,000) (12/4/78)

Why Farrah Split (2,461,000) (8/20/79)

*Newsstand sales—excluding year-end, anniversary, and Readers' Poll issues

BOTTOM TEN WORST-SELLING COVERS EVER

Hillary Clinton: The First 100 Days (976,000) (5/10/93)

American Hostages in Lebanon (1,009,000) (7/18/88)

Michael Caine (1,039,000) (5/4/87)

Jay Leno (1,088,000) (11/30/87)

Avenging Sgt. Kenneth Ford (1,112,000) (4/28/86)

The Return of David & Shaun Cassidy (1,128,000) (11/1/93)

Jacqueline Bisset & Alexander Godunov (1,133,000) (4/1/85)

Broadcast News (1,139,000) (2/1/88)

Fabio (1,150,000) (10/4/93)

Dustin Hoffman and Warren Beatty (1,159,000) (5/25/87)

1987

1987 COVERS

Bruce Willis
Oprah Winfrey
Huey Lewis
Prince Edward
Susan Dey, Corbin Bernsen (*L.A. Law*)
100th Birthday of Hollywood:
   Marilyn & Others
Liberace
John Lennon (Inset, Mark Chapman)
Pam Dawber
Charlie Sheen
Cybill Shepherd's Wedding
Mary Beth Whitehead, Elizabeth Stern
   & Baby M
Harry Hamlin (Sexiest Man)
Russia Issue
Teen Sex: Dermot Mulroney
   & Patricia Arquette
Michael J. Fox
David Crosby
Michael Caine
Ted Danson
Donna Rice (Inset, Gary Hart)
Warren Beatty & Dustin Hoffman
Rita Hayworth
Princess Diana
Donna Rice (Inset, Lynn Armandt)
Summer of Love by Peter Max
Bess Myerson & Andy Capasso

Fred Astaire
Jackie Gleason
Princess Diana & Sarah Ferguson
Oliver North: *People* Poll
AIDS: Ryan White
Joan Collins & Brigitte Nielsen
Elvis Presley
Jackie Onassis
Joan Rivers & Edgar Rosenberg
Mark Harmon & Sam Nelson
Michael Jackson
Sarah Ferguson
Princess Caroline with Baby Charlotte
Jessica Hahn
Michael Jackson
Surrogate Mother Pat Anthony
Fatal Attractions: Glenn Close
   & Michael Douglas
Baby Jessica McClure
Princess Diana
Best- & Worst-Dressed
Don Johnson & Sheena Easton
Jay Leno
Donald Trump
Madonna & Sean Penn
Cybill Shepherd & Twins Ariel and Zack

YEAR-END DOUBLE ISSUE:
Princess Diana, Baby Jessica McClure,
Michael Douglas, Brigitte Nielsen,
Oliver North, Gary Hart

Top Films: *Beverly Hills Cop II*

Platoon
Fatal Attraction
Three Men and a Baby
The Untouchables

Oscar: *The Last Emperor*

Top TV Shows: *The Cosby Show*

Family Ties
Cheers
Murder, She Wrote
The Golden Girls

Emmys: *The Golden Girls*
L.A. Law

Top Songs: "Faith"—George Michael

"Livin' on a Prayer"—Bon Jovi
"La Bamba"—Los Lobos
"I Wanna Dance with Somebody"
—Whitney Houston
"Bad"—Michael Jackson
"Open Your Heart"—Madonna

Grammys: "Graceland" (record)
"Somewhere Out There" (song)

Bestsellers: *Beloved*—Toni Morrison
The Bonfire of the Vanities—Tom Wolfe
Misery —Stephen King

Presumed Innocent—Scott Turow
Call Me Anna—Patty Duke
and Kenneth Turan
His Way—Kitty Kelley

Tonys: *Fences*

Les Misérables
All My Sons

Marriages: Diahann Carroll + Vic Damone

Tom Cruise + Mimi Rogers
Mark Harmon + Pam Dawber
Johnny Carson + Alexis Maas
Tom Selleck + Jillie Mack
Bruce Willis + Demi Moore
Cybill Shepherd + Bruce Oppenheim

Divorces: Joan Collins & Peter Holm

Lee Iacocca & Peggy Johnson

Deaths: Fred Astaire   Michael Bennett
James Coco   Jackie Gleason
Jascha Heifetz   Danny Kaye
Liberace   Dean Paul Martin
David Susskind   Andy Warhol
Lee Marvin

NEWS

- Mike Tyson charged with assault & battery for allegedly trying to kiss a female parking attendant in Hollywood
- *Twilight Zone* trial defendants acquitted
- Jim Bakker resigns in sex scandal
- Gary Hart/Donna Rice scandal

CHAPTER NINETEEN

Shooting the Shooter: Mark David Chapman

"I never wanted to hurt anybody. My friends will tell you that. I have two parts in me. The big part is very kind; the children I worked with will tell you that. I have a small part in me that cannot understand the world and what goes on in it. I did not want to kill anybody and I really don't know why I did it."

—MARK DAVID CHAPMAN
*to the police after killing John Lennon, as reported
in his first interview since the murder, by James R. Gaines
in* People, *February 23, 1987*

ALMOST EVERY DAY, Jim Gaines's route to work would take him past the Dakota, the building where John Lennon had been murdered, and every time he saw the dark, imposing building Gaines would think about Mark David Chapman, the man who had shot him.

James R. Gaines was a curious man. He was intrigued by the fact that Chapman had never given even the semblance of an interview, that he had made only two public statements since the murder. One was a terse letter he had written to *The New York Times* in which he had said the reasons for the killing could be found in J. D. Salinger's *The Catcher in the Rye*, the book Chapman was holding when he had been arrested in front of the Dakota on the night of December 8, 1980. The other was a passage he had read from *The Catcher in the Rye* just before his sentencing; in the passage, the fictional character Holden Caulfield says to his younger sister, Phoebe:

"Anyway, I keep picturing all these little kids playing some game in this big field of rye and all. Thousands of little kids, and nobody's

around—nobody big, I mean, except me. And I'm standing on the edge
of some crazy cliff. What I have to do, I have to catch everybody if they
start to go over the cliff—I mean, if they're running and they don't look
where they're going I have to come out from somewhere and catch
them. That's all I'd do all day. I'd just be the catcher in the rye . . ."

The bearded, dark-eyed, inquisitive Gaines was also mystified by the fact
that Chapman had pleaded guilty to Lennon's murder. "The fact that the guy,
who had an obvious insanity defense, pleaded guilty against his lawyer's
wishes," Gaines later explained, "made it even more intriguing."

At this particular moment, however, eighteen months after Mark David
Chapman had been found guilty of killing John Lennon and sentenced to
twenty years to life, as Jim Gaines sat across a bare table from him inside the
forbidding walls of Attica State, a maximum-security prison in upstate New
York, what he was more curious about than anything else was why in the
world the thirty-one-year-old, born-again Christian staring back into his face
had committed the shocking murder.

"John Lennon's death was a stunning loss because he carried so many
dreams with him," Gaines wrote in the introduction to the three-part piece he
wrote on Chapman for *People* in February 1987. "My wish to know the
reasons for his murder was like the wish, when a family member dies, to
know exactly how, at what time, of what. It doesn't help to know but it is
somehow necessary. In the Chapman case, no clinical or legal theory was
adequate. I found myself saying, but why?"

In the nearly two hundred hours that Gaines spent with Chapman at
Attica in the days and months to come, he had found out as much as was
seemingly possible to find out about John Lennon's killer and the details of
his life—his upbringing, his family, his education—the complex and bizarre
components of Chapman's psyche, the jagged pieces of his life that had
conspired to motivate him to murder John Lennon.

Besides the time he spent talking with Chapman, Gaines had interviewed
everyone he could find who could add to the intriguing puzzle. Among them
were Chapman's mother, the police officer who arrested him, his lawyers, the
psychologists who had been brought in to evaluate him, expert witnesses for
the defense, a young woman who had been at a YMCA camp with him where
he was a counselor, and Chapman's wife, Gloria, whom he had married in
1979—eighteen months before he murdered John Lennon.

Gaines had even spoken on the phone with Chapman's father, David, but
he had refused to meet with Gaines unless he would arrange for a brain scan
for his son. Gaines had explained to him the New York State law that
prohibits a criminal from receiving any benefit from written works about him,

and he had offered to show the father the results of numerous EEGs and other neurological tests already performed. David Chapman had declined. He had refused to be interviewed until his son had been cured of the physical ailment he believed had caused him to do what he had done. "You just find out what's wrong and have it fixed," he had told Gaines on the phone. That had been their last conversation.

As he dug deeper, Gaines uncovered revealing and captivating details about John Lennon's killer: Mark David Chapman's parents had had an unhappy marriage, ending in divorce. His father, who worked for an oil company, had beaten Chapman's mother during Mark's childhood; when this happened, she would often scream her son's name in the middle of the night. His father had been cold and undemonstrative, while his mother had looked upon her son more as her best friend than as her child. From the time he was an infant until he was almost a teenager Chapman would shake, and in bed as a baby he would rock so hard that his parents had to take the casters off his crib because he would rock it right across the room. He had an obsession with little children and often fantasized that he was a king in a world in which they were his subjects. He fancied himself the "Catcher in the Rye" of his generation and had wanted, and actually had tried at one point, to change his name to Holden Caulfield, the protagonist of Salinger's book. He had an IQ of 121, which was on the lower end of the superior range. In the ninth grade he had slipped away from his family and into drugs, using everything from glue and marijuana to cocaine, LSD, and even heroin. He had become a born-again Christian and refused to play Beatles songs on his guitar thereafter because John Lennon had once said that the Beatles were "more popular than Jesus." Before killing Lennon, Chapman had considered killing Hawaiian governor George Ariyoshi (because he was popular), Johnny Carson (because he was also popular), Jackie Onassis (because he admired John F. Kennedy and she had disgraced his memory by marrying Aristotle Onassis), Paul McCartney (until he found out that Lennon was more accessible), Elizabeth Taylor (he despised people who flaunted themselves), George C. Scott (he did not know why), and Ronald Reagan (he just wanted to disrupt the inauguration by firing a few shots). He had thought about killing his father, too.

Gaines also learned that Mark David Chapman had tried to kill himself. He had been in Hawaii when he had driven to a deserted location and fitted a vacuum-cleaner hose to the exhaust pipe of his car. He had opened the hatchback and put the hose inside. Then he had packed the gap by the lid with old clothes and towels and got back in the car to die. Fifteen minutes later, a Japanese fisherman had knocked on the window, startling Chapman, and he had not been able to figure out why he was not dead. When he got out of the car, he saw that the exhaust had burned a hole in the hose.

It was an irony as poignant as the stories Jim Gaines's curiosity had uncovered about the passengers who had died on Korean Air Lines flight 007: The fact that Mark David Chapman had survived the attempt to take his own life that night would ultimately result in the untimely death of John Lennon.

It had taken two years for Gaines to get Chapman's wife to agree to meet with him. When she finally consented, she made it clear that it was not Jim Gaines, but God, who had convinced her.

"We talked several times on the telephone," wrote Gaines.

> I thought her reluctance was driven by guilt: Having shown flagrant signs of mental illness, Chapman had told her he intended to kill John Lennon and she had done little to stop him . . . Unexpectedly, the most sensitive subject for Gloria turned out not to be her failure to get help for her husband in time to prevent his crime; rather, she worried that their friends would be shocked to discover that Chapman (a man, I was reminded, who already stood convicted of murder) had sometimes struck her.

Like Lennon, Chapman had married a Japanese woman. After their marriage he had worked as a security guard. Often, late at night after Gloria had gone to bed, he would listen to Beatles records through headphones, she told Gaines—but with the volume set so high that she could still hear the music in the next room. Her husband was troubled by migraines and night sweats. After they had seen two movies—*Dracula* and *Freaks*—Chapman had told his wife (as Gaines wrote in *People*): "Sometimes I get so frustrated and bottled up I just want to blow somebody's head off." It was Gaines's conclusion that Chapman's identity was battered by "what he perceived as betrayal by his father and abandonment by his mother and by a vivid sense of his own failure."

Chapman had learned that John Lennon was living in New York from books he got at the library. Gloria told Jim Gaines, "He would get angry, saying that Lennon was a bastard. He was angry that Lennon would preach love and peace but yet have millions."

Later, Chapman himself told Gaines, "I remember being caught up in these fits of anger and euphoria at the same time. I'd look at the picture [of Lennon] and say: 'You phony, I'm going to get you.' "

In his three-part story on Chapman, Jim Gaines told for the first time the meticulous details of Chapman's trip to New York for the purpose of John

Lennon's murder. He told how Chapman had arrived in Manhattan on a Saturday morning and checked into the YMCA on Sixty-third Street, just off Central Park West, only blocks from Lennon's apartment; how he had dropped off his bag and set out for the Dakota, waiting for hours for Lennon to appear, finally giving up and leaving to go to dinner and a movie; how he had taken a hotel room in midtown Manhattan the following day and set his few possessions in a tableau that he believed would later provide the police with the motive for the crime he was about to commit: a Todd Rundgren tape, a picture of Judy Garland wiping away the Cowardly Lion's tears in *The Wizard of Oz* (inscribed by Chapman "To Dorothy"), his Bible (inscribed "Holden Caulfield"), his passport, a picture of himself with refugee children, and a photograph of his '65 Chevy. ("Each thing had its special meaning, also placement," he later told Gaines. "I was leaving my past behind.")

Gaines explained in the *People* piece how Chapman had returned to the Dakota with Lennon's just-released album, *Double Fantasy*, which he planned to use as an excuse for being there—to ask John Lennon to autograph its cover; how he had waited futilely for the famous Beatle to appear once more, this time for ten hours, before giving up; how while waiting he had read, ironically, the Lennon interview with David Sheff that had just been published in *Playboy* (which, he later told Gaines, had further convinced him "how right he was to think Lennon a phony, how right it would be to kill him"); how he had met Lennon's son Sean that day and had actually shaken his hand; and how finally John Lennon himself had appeared and Chapman had asked him to autograph his album.

Lennon politely accommodated him. "Is that what you wanted? Is that all you want?" he had asked Chapman, looking him straight in the eyes. Chapman told Gaines that at that point he had had second thoughts about the murder he had planned. "I kept saying, you know, you have his autograph, you can just go home now . . . instead of taking his life, just take away his autograph . . . I wanted to go home. I really did."

Chapman, of course, did not go home, and over the course of all the hours he spent with Jim Gaines, he explained to him in minute detail why—and how—when Lennon's limousine appeared just before 11:00 P.M. on Monday, December 8, 1980, he was sitting inside the archway of the Dakota, waiting for him:

> "I knew it was his [limousine]. I knew it. I felt it. My soul reached out to that car and I knew he was out there. I said, 'This is it.' So I got up, and the car rolled up, and the door opened and Yoko got out . . . Yoko was about thirty or forty feet in front of him—weird. It was all meant to be. If they were together, I don't know if I could have shot

him or not. But see, he was alone . . . He looked right at me, and I didn't say anything to him. And he walked by me. I know he remembered me because I had this hat . . . and I had my coat on, you know, I looked the same. I'm sure he [remembered me], but he didn't say anything."

Then Mark David Chapman had pulled the trigger.

Later that night, around dinnertime in Hawaii where she lived, Chapman's wife had been horrified when she heard on TV that John Lennon had been shot. Surprisingly, she admitted to Jim Gaines that she had had a second reaction as well. "I felt a kind of joy for Mark," she said. "A happiness. Just like a fleeting thought, you know, I felt relief for him, like 'Horray.' I mean, I know it sounds crazy, but . . . I just felt kind of relief for him, that he had accomplished something he set out to do."

In the third and final installment of the *People* piece, Jim Gaines skillfully analyzed the psyche of Mark Chapman, the aftermath of the murder, and how and why Chapman had finally decided to plead guilty in spite of the fact that he could probably have easily been found to be insane.

Finally Gaines wrote about his own feelings and the effect doing the piece had on him:

> In the years since I met Chapman, I have twice received what he calls his "catcher" letter—an ostensibly final sign-off that reads simply, "Please read *The Catcher in the Rye*." Both times he has reestablished contact, but I will not be surprised if a time comes when he does not, and I take his talk of suicide seriously. He has, after all, killed a man, and in the years I have known him he has talked of killing others, notably his father. Someday, perhaps after he reads this, I suspect he will think of killing me. Among the side effects of undertaking a story like this one are the dreams and waking fantasies of such an achievement.

Another drama occurred in the process of putting the Chapman story together for *People* that has never been reported: the shooting of Mark David Chapman—not with a gun, but a camera. This time the shooter was Harry Benson. "It was the most amazing thing," says Jim Gaines, "that I've ever seen a photographer do."

Two years and hundreds of hours of conversations between Gaines and Chapman had passed before the latter agreed to be photographed. "I knew I was going to write a big piece for *People*," says Gaines, "so of course I was going to have to have pictures." Knowing everything he knew by then, he figured that Harry Benson would be the perfect man for the job. Benson had, after all, first come to America with the Beatles and had photographed them extensively. "Harry was like the fifth Beatle," says Gaines. "I sold him to Chapman, but he insisted on losing a lot of weight before he had his pictures taken."

Mark Chapman was a man obsessed, and now he behaved in keeping with his character. He lost fifty pounds because the man who shot the Beatles was going to take his picture and he wanted to look his best. Chapman could not wait to meet Harry Benson.

When the day of the photography session finally came, Gaines and Benson arrived at Attica State Prison at the appointed time and went directly to the visitors' room where it had been arranged that Chapman would be photographed for *People* magazine. There was, however, an inherent and obvious problem here. This was *People* magazine, not *Time* or *Newsweek,* and Jim Gaines was planning one of the longest pieces ever to run in *People*: fifteen thousand words, in three parts, a total of twenty-nine pages. That would require a lot of pictures to support the story, and the pictures that Harry Benson could take would all be confined to the cramped visitors' room, a bare room painted prison green, with one window (with bars on it), one scarred table, and two nondescript metal chairs. That was all. The setting was in no way conducive to pictures that would have to support a three-part story, and Gaines knew it. "I'm thinking, How are we in this one room going to get enough situations to cover thirty pages?" he recalls.

Oddly enough, Harry Benson did not seem worried. He knew exactly what he was doing. "I was with Chapman for over an hour before I even made a move toward the camera," he says. "In fact, I knew this was the way to take him. Take him very slowly. Chapman was trying to impress me," he says, "waiting for me to make any move. I didn't make any moves at all. I just watched him, and even Gaines was beginning to think I wasn't going to take any pictures."

He immediately went to work as he always did, putting the system professionally in place. The minute he entered the visitors' room, while Gaines kept Chapman occupied by talking with him, Benson's assistant set up his lights and everything else necessary for the shooting of the man who shot John Lennon.

In the midst of the activity, Chapman turned to Gaines. "At some point, Jim," he said to him, "I need to talk privately to Harry. I want to apologize to him for killing his friend, John Lennon."

"Well, Mark," Gaines replied, "there's not much privacy here. Why don't you just go into the corner and talk to Harry there?"

As Chapman walked over to the corner to talk with Benson, Gaines did not know what to think. "I expected Harry to be really gruff with Chapman," he says. "I was worried about it because Chapman is schizophrenic and schizophrenics are very sensitive."

Harry Benson was not to be underestimated. "He was like another person," says Gaines. "I didn't recognize him." The usually ebullient Benson was, in Gaines's words, charming, sweet, and quiet. "He picked up what was going on with Chapman and went with it," says Gaines.

Harry Benson and Mark Chapman stood in the corner and talked while Jim Gaines stood on the other side of the room. As Gaines watched, mesmerized, Chapman looked Benson in the eye and said, "Harry, I don't know how to say this, but I just wanted to tell you I'm really sorry for killing your friend, John Lennon."

Jim Gaines was baffled by the scene that was unraveling before him. "I'm listening to this, thinking, My God, this is so weird," he recalls. "And I hear Harry say, 'You know, Mark, I think John went just the way he wanted to go.' And Chapman said, 'You really think so?' And Harry said, 'Oh yeah. He went out as a martyr, in the prime of his life.' "

Jim Gaines was stunned. "I thought, How could he say such a thing?" says Gaines. "Actually, in certain ways I think Harry believes it, which is probably how he can say it."

In fact Benson says to this day that he meant what he told Chapman. "I'm sure," he reiterates, "that John Lennon got out the way he would like to go out." Trying to explain, he says, "I knew that . . . he was going to go out dramatically. If John Lennon had not been killed then," he says with certainty, "he would not be alive today—so many drugs . . ."

Harry Benson saw something right away in Mark Chapman. "He fit the profile of the murderers I've met before," he says. "Wanting you to see the other side of him, the good guy. Looking you straight in the face, in the eyes, always. People who lie to you always look you straight in the face."

The fact that Benson said what he said to Chapman, virtually exonerating him—in Chapman's mind, at least—from murdering John Lennon, turned the photography session around. "This obviously cheered Chapman up," says Gaines, "and Harry started taking pictures."

Benson indeed seized the opportunity. He shot away as fast as he could, getting everything he could get for about fifteen minutes. Then, taking advantage of his momentary hold on Chapman, he decided to push it one step further. Knowing that Chapman was a born-again Christian, he asked him to kneel under the window as though he were praying.

No, Chapman replied, that was a real cliché. Everybody who goes to prison converts. He was not going to do that. Harry Benson shrugged his shoulders without an argument and said to his assistant, "I think we're done. Let's pack it up. I think we're finished."

The very thought of Benson's departure pushed exactly the right button in Chapman. Having seen that his visitor was about to leave—undoubtedly the only visitor he would have for the month—he instantly began posing for the camera to do what he could to get Harry to stay. It was the beginning of a series of pictures that would never be forgotten. Chapman put his finger to his head as though it were a gun and he were going to shoot himself; he pulled up his T-shirt, posing as a robber. He took his shirt off and started making muscles for the camera.

Jim Gaines just stood there watching. "It was the most amazing manipulation I had ever seen," he says. "Harry is an amazing person."

Indeed, Harry Benson had managed to shoot the man who shot John Lennon in a most remarkable way.

CHAPTER TWENTY

The Real Hart Stopper: The Selling-Out of Donna Rice

"There was a stakeout and then the very next morning was the story
in *The Miami Herald*. When I realized there was a stakeout, I said
to Lynn [Armandt], 'Get those pictures and destroy them.' She said
'okay,' so I thought she had . . ."

—DONNA RICE,
*referring to the pictures her friend Lynn Armandt sold
to* People *after the Gary Hart scandal in May 1987*

ONLY WEEKS BEFORE it was announced in the spring of 1987 that
Pat Ryan would be leaving to become the new managing editor of *Life*,
People was awarded the National Magazine Award for General Excellence for magazines with circulations above one million. It was the first time
the magazine had won the prestigious honor.

In her five years as managing editor of *People*, Ryan had made some
important contributions: She had improved conditions for the staff, raising
salaries almost across the board. She had also done what she could do to
improve the hours, although, because of the very nature of the magazine and
its need to conform to a story when it happened—which so often was just
under the deadline—that was not always possible to control. Now that *People*'s identity was firmly established, she had also brought in writers of note,
writers she believed would improve the quality of the magazine. She gave
Dick Stolley some of the credit for her accomplishments. "He had already
done the heavy load," she admits, "so it was easy for me to come in . . .
suddenly I had more money to spend because they made the money. And I

wasn't battle fatigued, so I could stand back and look at it, and say, Yeah, there are other ways to do things."

But Ryan's tenure had not been without controversy. Ever since the Korean Air Lines disaster cover that Jim Gaines had done while filling in for her in 1983, differences of opinion had often arisen between Ryan and some of those working under her, not only about what *People* covers should be but also about the general direction that the magazine should take. Pat Ryan had not been nearly as captivated by entertainment as Dick Stolley had been. Things like television did not interest her much, and in fact, while she was editor, television covers were proving to be less successful than they had been up to that point. Ryan was more interested in social issues—women in the workplace, anorexia, abortion, weight loss and exercise videos.

Jim Gaines and two of his colleagues, Jim Seymore (senior editor) and John Saar (the senior editor of "Up Front"), often disagreed with Ryan. They believed that *People* should be geared more toward news, that even celebrity stories should have a strong news angle, while Ryan often chose to stay away from them altogether.

"The guys," as they had come to be known, had been beside themselves, for instance, when Pat Ryan had turned down an exclusive story on Mick Jagger and Jerry Hall when she had been busted for marijuana possession in Barbados in 1987. Hall had called to offer *People* an exclusive. Seymore, a warm teddy bear of a man, a perceptive and talented editor whose well-honed instincts were usually right on target, had gotten the phone call. "She said she was set up," recalls Seymore. "She said it wasn't true. She said they wanted to tell us all about it. She told me, 'If you can get somebody down here, we'll give you the story.' "

Seymore and Gaines were all for it. They saw the value of Jagger and Hall, especially since there was a news story involved, which they were being offered exclusively. "We said, 'Great. Let's do this story,' " Seymore recalls.

But Ryan had no interest in either Jerry Hall or the story she wanted to tell *People,* exclusively or not. She did not care what Hall had to say and she made her feelings very clear. "We didn't do the story," says Seymore.

In spite of their disagreements, Ryan valued "the guys" and often respected their opinions. Seymore credits Ryan with valuable contributions. Among other things, she personally offered him one of the great opportunities of his life when she gave her blessing to a special issue, "*People* in Russia," in 1986. The issue was the culmination of a story-finding tour of the Soviet Union—covering twenty-five thousand miles over a six-week period—which Jim Seymore had overseen.

Emotions were running high in the offices of *People* magazine by the time word of Ryan's new appointment got out. What no one knew right away was who would be named to replace her. Among the likely candidates, there were two leading contenders: Lanny Jones, who had been wrested away from *People* in 1984 to become managing editor of *Money* magazine, and Jim Gaines, who had been second in command under Pat Ryan.

Anxious to have the unfettered opportunity to show what he could do, Gaines was dying to have the job. A week had passed since he had heard the news about Ryan going to *Life* and he had been doing a lot of worrying about whether he was going to get it. "By the end of the week, I had been through a state of anxiety so complete and thorough that it's like you're underwater," he says. "It's like your brain is in a vise . . . I was just a complete mess."

On Friday morning of that week Gaines awoke with a feeling in his gut that this was going to be the day he heard about Ryan's successor. He just knew it, and he was beside himself. "I didn't have a clean white shirt," he recalls, "and I thought, It really doesn't matter . . . I'm not going to lose the job because I don't have a white shirt. And if I don't get the job, I won't need a white shirt." So he got dressed without one and went into the office, where a message from Henry Grunwald, the editor in chief of *Time*, awaited him. Just as he had suspected, this was going to be the day.

When Gaines walked into Grunwald's office on the thirty-fourth floor of the Time & Life Building, Grunwald was sitting behind his desk with his foot propped up, while Jimmy "the shoe-shine man"—who had been a fixture at Time Inc. for so many years that he was never asked to leave even the highest-level meeting—buffed his brown leather shoes to a glow. Grunwald started talking, but Gaines was already in such a daze that he did not hear a word out of his mouth—until Grunwald said, "Congratulations."

"Oh, my God," Gaines replied.

Grunwald looked at him quizzically. "Why don't you sit down?" he said.

Jim Gaines sat down and Henry Grunwald kept on talking. Gaines still had no idea what he was saying. He had wanted this so badly. He thought, Is this real? Is this some kind of weird dream that I'm having? He really was not sure. Grunwald finished talking, finally, and asked Gaines to step outside so that he could give his assistant the necessary biographical information to write up the memo announcing his appointment.

When Gaines got back to his office, he still was not sure that what he thought had just happened had really happened. Could it really be? he was thinking, when Jimmy the shoe-shine man showed up to shine *his* shoes. "Jimmy," Gaines said to him, "I don't remember a thing that happened when

Grunwald told me that I was the new editor of *People*. He was talking and I was so freaked out that I don't remember a word that he said. What did he say? You were there." Jimmy the shoe-shine man looked up at Gaines and said, "He told you not to fuck up."

That is precisely what Gary Hart, the leading candidate for the Democratic presidential nomination did the very week that Jim Gaines started his new job as the editor of *People*. It was the first week in May, and late on Friday night, as Jim Gaines left the Time & Life Building for home, thinking that his first cover would be Dustin Hoffman and Warren Beatty, who were starring in the movie *Ishtar*, Gary Hart was in his Washington, D.C., town house with a woman who was not his wife, and reporters from *The Miami Herald* were watching from outside.

While Gaines spent the weekend recuperating from the anxieties of the preceding weeks, Hart was dodging that group of reporters, and although there had been no big surprises for Jim Gaines during his first five days on the job, that would all change momentarily because of what was about to happen to Gary Hart.

On Monday, Gaines happily set out for the office to close his first issue as the official editor of *People*. He made his way through the lobby toward the elevator that would take him to his office, passing the newsstand as he went. That is when he saw the headlines plastered all over the place: The giant scandal had broken the night before in the Miami paper. Gary Hart, the notorious womanizer who had recently dared the press to catch him, had been caught with a blonde in his Washington home. She was Donna Rice, a beautiful Phi Beta Kappa graduate of the University of South Carolina who had dated Prince Albert of Monaco and chummed around with the likes of Don Johnson of *Miami Vice* and the racecar driver Danny Sullivan.

When Gaines saw this news, he uttered the words that most aptly expressed his feelings—the same exact feelings he had had during the Korean Air Lines disaster, and even more recently when Henry Grunwald had told him that he was the new editor of *People*: "My God," he said, "this is amazing."

He arrived in his office just in time for the regular Monday-morning meeting at ten o'clock. He stepped into the conference room and said, "We've got to change the cover."

There was not, at that point, much to go on. All that was known was that some reporters from *The Miami Herald* had gotten a tip the previous Friday night that a Miami woman was going to be spending the weekend with Hart in Washington at his town house. They had quickly flown in from Miami and staked out Hart's apartment.

They claimed they had seen Rice go into his apartment on Friday night (around the time Gaines had left his office for home). They claimed she had spent the night there with him. Hart and Rice would later claim that she had not spent the night there, that she had left out of a back entrance.

Whether she had left or not, and which door she had used, had not stopped the newspaper from going with its story:

> WASHINGTON—Gary Hart, the Democratic Presidential candidate who has dismissed allegations of womanizing, spent Friday night and most of Saturday in his Capitol Hill townhouse with a young woman who flew from Miami and met him. Hart denied any impropriety.

Now it was Gaines's turn. This was big news and he knew that everybody would be on it. As it happened, it was Monday. Perfect timing for the cover—except for one problem. There was no picture of Donna Rice, and Gaines knew he did not want to put Gary Hart on the cover by himself.

M. C. Marden was already on the case. There were a few pictures of Rice around, as it turned out, but what M.C.—and *People*—wanted was a picture that nobody else had of her. Although M.C. did not know much about Rice, she did know that Rice had been a catalogue model. Holly Holden, a picture researcher who had worked in the Los Angeles bureau at one time, suddenly realized that she knew somebody who just might have photographed Rice.

Peter Borsari was a well-known photographer who had done a lot of work for *People* in the past. He often photographed catalogue models; Holly, who was both thorough and persistent, knew that he kept extensive files. She called him right away and asked if he had any pictures of Donna Rice. She did not hold out much hope that he would, but she figured she would try him anyway. She virtually forced him to look through his files. "Peter," she said to him, "we'll pay you five hundred and fifty dollars, just look under *R*." He did, and there was Donna Rice.

The picture had been taken in the south of France, in Cannes, nearly eight years earlier when Rice was twenty-one, fresh out of school, on vacation with a friend. They had been lying on the beach and a photographer had come up to them and asked if he could take their picture. Why not, they thought. They were wide-eyed young women. They did not see any harm in it at all. In fact, they cut up for him, played to his camera. He was smoking a cigarette, and when he was taking Donna's picture, he had handed it to her and said, "Here, take this. Give me a campy kind of look." And that is what she had done.

When she got back to the States, Rice looked Borsari up because she and her friend wanted copies of the pictures he had taken. Sure, he replied, asking them to sign releases when he gave them the pictures. "If you ever become famous," he said, "then I'll have pictures of you." Rice laughed at that; she thought the whole notion of becoming famous was funny. Little could she have imagined that one of the pictures she had in her hands would end up on the cover of *People* magazine.

Now Jim Gaines and Jim Seymore were staring at the picture in the layout room. It was incredibly *perfect*. There was Donna Rice, a pretty blonde with a thin, braided, bandana-like tie around her forehead, in a bikini, lying on her stomach on the beach, holding a cigarette in her right hand, looking right smack into their faces! Looking just exactly the way they had wanted her to look, hoped she would look. Unbelievable!

By this time, Gaines had already unleashed his reporters around the country to pick up anything they could on Rice. One of them had actually managed to get to her mother, Miriam, in South Carolina and had been invited in for tea. Miriam told the reporter that Donna was "a fine Christian girl," and she talked about her past. She had been in a gymnastics group called the Tumbling Tots, was active in church missionary groups, sang in the church choir, participated in church youth activities, became a Girl Scout, worked summers in a pizza parlor, and once had ambitions of becoming a doctor. She had been making commercials since she was thirteen. She took modeling lessons, and her mother tried to explain why. "You have to live in Columbia [South Carolina] to understand that," she told the reporter. "All the girls were taking modeling. I thought the basic course would be good for her to learn to walk properly and have poise." Donna later said she was shocked that the *People* reporter had gotten to her mother before she could even warn her not to talk to anyone.

BY TUESDAY, Jim Gaines was ready to close the issue with a story put together from *People*'s own reporting—what little they had been able to get—and a lot of clips of what had been reported by The *Herald* along with everything that could be found about Gary Hart, Donna Rice, and Lynn Armandt (a friend of Rice's who had been with the couple and another man, Bill Broadhurst, that weekend). When Cutler Durkee, a senior writer, came up with the perfect cover line—"Hart Stopper"—Jim Gaines was ready to go.

His first cover as editor was a great success, one of the bestselling covers of the year. "It was an augury of the future," Jim Seymore said later. "Can you imagine a better story to begin with?"

As it turned out, it was only the beginning of the Hart-Rice scandal. Nobody knew exactly what had happened that fateful night in the nation's capitol, and everybody was dying to know more. Besides that, Gary Hart was still in the running as the Democratic presidential nominee. Shortly after the *People* cover ran, the *National Enquirer* published a picture of Donna Rice sitting on Gary Hart's lap. It had been taken two months earlier during a trip to the island of Bimini on a boat called, ironically, the *Monkey Business.*

The story that ran along with the picture in the *Enquirer* mentioned an "undisclosed source," but that did not fool Rice for a minute. She knew exactly who the source was. There was only one person it *could* be, and that was Lynn Armandt, supposedly her pal. Armandt had been on the Bimini trip with Hart, Rice, and Broadhurst, and she had actually taken those pictures— with Rice's camera, no less! A few weeks after they had returned from Bimini, long before the scandal that was now exploding, Armandt had asked Rice if she could borrow the pictures to show her boyfriend. Rice had agreed, saying, "Well, Lynn, I'm going to loan them to you, but I want you to give them back."

"Of course," Armandt had replied, stashing the pictures in her purse. At least Rice had kept the negatives.

When the scandal broke, in the midst of the chaos, Rice thought of those pictures she had lent to Lynn. She was not really worried, though. Armandt was, after all, her friend. "When I realized everything was coming down the way it was," recalls Rice, "when I realized there was a stakeout, I said to Lynn, 'Get those pictures and destroy them.' She said 'okay,' so I thought she had. When the *Enquirer* piece ran, she did it as an undisclosed source, but the photos were there, so I knew who it was. There was only one other person who had the photographs besides me. I was absolutely devastated."

Jim Gaines and Jim Seymore, who had by now become the executive editor under Gaines, went crazy when they saw the picture of Rice on Hart's lap. They knew a hot story when they saw one, and this story was really hot—unlike the bumped *Ishtar* cover, which ran later and turned out to be a bomb, as did the movie.

Like virtually every other publication, they had tried everything they knew to get Rice to talk to *People.* As it turned out, *Life* had gotten her, which was hard for Gaines to swallow. That meant Donna Rice would also be Pat Ryan's first cover—*Life* was a monthly—but Rice had agreed to talk to *Life*, giving that magazine's story a cachet not shared by the *People* piece. Gaines maintains that *Life* got her because "they didn't ask her to write about anything other than what it's like to be a Southern belle."

Rice would later explain that she had made a careful choice. She was desperately concerned about her reputation and hurt by the way she was being portrayed. She felt that everything she had worked so hard to accomplish in her life had gone down the drain in the blink of an eye. "My reputation had been very important to me and I had had quite a good one," she explains. "I saw it all slip away. I had worked very hard academically and I was being called a bimbo. I had worked very hard professionally and I was being called a party girl. Because of that, at any cost, I did not want to be perceived as anyone who would exploit this situation."

Donna Rice was smart enough to see that she was being portrayed, in her words, as the kind of girl who wanted to cash in. "That's what the bimbo, party-girl, *femme fatale* personality would do," she says. "That wasn't who I was but that was the way I was being portrayed and that's the way I believe I was being perceived by the public."

A friend of hers at the large and well-respected public relations firm, Rogers & Cowan, suggested that she talk to *Life*, arguing that it was upscale, classy, and not gossip oriented; even though she says she did not want to do it, Donna had agreed. Pat Ryan had, in a sense, pushed her into it, she felt, convincing her that it would be her only chance to set the record straight; since *Life* was a monthly, if she waited, she would no longer be of interest to the American public. Rice had agreed to the standard writer's fee of four thousand dollars. The only stipulation was that she could not speak to any other publication during the month that the *Life* piece was on the stands. "I thought that would be the end of it," she says. She had just made another grave miscalculation.

Then Gaines got a phone call. After Rice had done the *Life* piece and during the period when, under the condition of her agreement, she could not talk to any other magazine, a woman telephoned Gaines and said she had some pictures—and a story—that she wanted to sell to *People*. Of Gary Hart and Donna Rice. On the *Monkey Business*. Pictures—as it turned out—from the same roll of film from which the now-famous "lap" picture that had run in the *Enquirer* had come. She was, she told Gaines, the other woman on the *Monkey Business*.

Well, she should come up to the office and show him the pictures, Gaines had replied. Jim Seymore could not believe it. These pictures were just dropping out of the heavens. He never ceased to be astounded by Gaines's unbelievable good fortune when it came to these kinds of things.

Jim Seymore and John Saar were with Jim Gaines in his office when Lynn Armandt arrived with her bounty. Seymore could not believe his eyes. She was wearing what he described as an orange tubelike shift that seemed to have been sprayed on her body. "It was the most tantalizing, sexually charged outfit I've ever seen on a woman," he says. "She was quite attractive. She wasn't *gorgeous* gorgeous. She maximized her assets. Quite frankly, most of the men on the staff were just tripping over their tongues after she came to the office."

Gaines and Seymore and Saar looked at the pictures. It did not take them long to agree that they wanted them. Yes, they told Armandt. They wanted to make a deal.

They agreed to pay her $150,000 for the pictures and her story. She would give them her account of the affair between Donna Rice and Gary Hart before, during, and after the *Monkey Business*. It was not the first time *People* had paid for a story. It had not happened during the Stolley years, but later under Pat Ryan there were times when it seemed appropriate—certainly for the book excerpts that the magazine published, and occasionally for a first-person account of a story, like the one by Carol Ann, the mother of the Bubble Boy. This, however, was the first time in the history of *People* magazine that a secondhand source would be paid to talk about someone else. It would also be the last time. It was a mistake that Jim Gaines would come to regret.

At that point, Lynn Armandt checked into the Dorset Hotel on Fifty-fourth Street in Manhattan, only a few blocks from the Time & Life Building, courtesy of *People* magazine, where a writer by the name of Michelle Green began to debrief her for the story.

The reason she was coming forward, Armandt told Green, was that she was beginning to weary of the whole mess after keeping herself in seclusion for weeks. "Armandt," said the *People* story, "decided last week to tell what she knows on the theory that 'the story would never be laid to rest and my life would never return to normal until I made a statement.' " Then she told what she knew of the bungled Bimini excursion and, in *People*'s words, "the scandal that toppled Gary Hart." The borrowed picture that ran was of the happy foursome—Rice, Hart, Armandt, and Broadhurst—in a bar in Bimini, singing "Twist and Shout." There was also a picture of the group in Bimini taken by Bill Broadhurst.

Just before the piece was to close, Donna had heard from Pat Ryan at *Life* that *People* was planning the story. Before the *Life* piece, *People* had been hotly pursuing her. Now, come to think of it, they had stopped calling and

Rice was starting to see a pattern. The *Enquirer* had also been hotly pursuing her; thinking back, she realized they had stopped shortly before Armandt had sold them the picture. It was obviously happening again.

She called the magazine and told them that the photographs that Armandt might be trying to sell them were her photographs, that they had no right to print them. They told her they were going forward.

The issue was a blockbuster, outselling "Hart Stopper" by nearly one hundred thousand copies, earning back for *People* many times the fee that had been paid to Lynn Armandt:

EXCLUSIVE
DONNA RICE
Her pal Lynn Armandt was there
throughout the Gary Hart affair.
Now she tells what really happened.

Again, Donna Rice was on the cover. Again, she was wearing a bathing suit, this time a scantily cut, very revealing black bathing suit. In a small inset next to her on the cover was a head shot of her "friend" Lynn Armandt.

When the second *People* piece ran and Donna saw the cover, she felt her life was really out of control. The bathing-suit picture was a perfect example of how people were exploiting her. It had been taken some time ago by a photographer whom Rice had considered a friend in a series of test shots for her modeling portfolio. The photographer, Mark Woodbury, knew how Donna felt about them—she hated them, partly because they were too revealing. She hated them so much, in fact, that not only did she not use them for her portfolio, she told him to throw them out. He said he would, and she assumed that he had. She never signed a release of any kind, so he did not have her permission to sell them, but that had not made much difference. Lynn Armandt and Mark Woodbury were some friends.

After the *People* piece ran, Rice knew she had to do *something* to defend herself. As she watched what was left of her reputation being destroyed by people who were making money from doing it—some of whom she had trusted in her personal life—she agreed to do an interview with Barbara Walters on *20/20*. She wanted to explain about her "friend" Lynn Armandt selling Rice's own pictures to *People* and the *Enquirer*, among other things.

Rice knew that things had sunk to an all-time low when she boarded the plane to fly to New York for the Walters interview. Her hair was pulled back, she was wearing sunglasses and no makeup, and she was traveling under an assumed name at the request of *20/20*. The TV show paying her way did not want anyone recognizing her—nor did she herself desire any more attention either.

As Rice took her seat in the first-class section she saw that the man sitting next to her, dressed in expensive clothes and looking quite distinguished, was engrossed in *People* magazine—the one with the sleazy picture of her in the black bathing suit on the cover. He did not even look up when she sat down. She glanced over and saw that he was reading the Lynn Armandt story. "Excuse me," she said, doubting that the man would recognize her. "What do you think of that story?"

"Well," he said, "it's very interesting. This one gal seems really sharp and intelligent. I really appreciate what she's gone through and what she has to say."

Rice breathed a sigh of relief and for a fleeting moment she started feeling positive about herself for the first time in what seemed like forever. Oh, she thought thankfully, this man can see what's going on. This is good! People aren't falling for this! Then the man turned to her and said, "But the blonde! God, if this . . ."

She was devastated. Oh, no, she thought, as she began defending the blond bimbo. The man had not recognized her yet, as Donna went into a tirade about how much the other woman had probably gotten paid for the story, how he did not necessarily have the right perspective, how she knew someone who knew the blonde and that she was really rather sharp. She began to defend herself vigorously in the third person until he finally said to her gently, "I'm sure she's a very nice girl, after all. Maybe I didn't see things the right way."

Rice did the *20/20* interview and afterward she felt that Walters had helped straighten out the damage caused in part by Armandt's story in *People*. When the TV show aired, the gossip actually died down for a while. Maybe, she hoped, this would really be the end of it.

Jim Gaines had never given up on Donna Rice. He had always wanted her story. He continued to talk with her on the phone a lot, trying to convince her to do a long piece for *People*, and they kept in touch. He had even taken her to an Overseas Press Club event, which was, as he puts it, her social unveiling after being cornered by the *People* story. They had become friendly, and had talked about Armandt once over lunch.

In time, Gaines came to believe that maybe Armandt had set the whole thing up for her own enrichment. Maybe she had tipped off *The Miami Herald* before the stakeout of Hart's D.C. home while Donna was there—the event that started the scandal in the first place.

He began to feel that he had made a mistake, and after extensive soul-searching and discussion, much of which took place with Jim Seymore and John Saar in meetings in their offices—and at the steakhouse downstairs in the Time & Life Building, now and then—they made a rule. It was one thing, they decided, to pay for someone's own story or photographs, but in the future they would not pay anyone for being a source, as they had with Lynn Armandt.

Seymore admitted that they felt "a little sleazy" when the piece came out. He later explained, "If you're paying someone to talk about someone else, you're really subverting the whole journalistic enterprise. That's what the tabloids do regularly. We made a rule that we would never do that again, and as far as I know, the magazine hasn't."

The Hart-Rice scandal would not go away, though. Everything was fine for a while until Gary Hart reentered the race, and the frenzy began anew. Once again, everyone was after Donna Rice. She had not said a word since the Walters interview. This time the press was really running amok. *Playboy* offered her a blank check. She describes it this way: "They said, 'You have been so smart.' Like I was playing this, and I wasn't. I was just trying to do the right thing by myself and by everyone else. *Playboy* came to me and said basically, 'Look, you have kept silent. We believe that an interview with you or anything with you in our magazine would prove to be the best-selling issue we've ever had, outselling our top-seller, which was the Jimmy Carter interview, and we're willing to pay you any amount of money for it."

According to Rice, they knew that she would not pose. Like Gaines, they had been after her for a long time, and she had absolutely refused to pose. Now, along with the blank check, they gave her an alternative: "You can do a swimsuit layout and an interview," they said. "You don't have to take your clothes off. The more you're willing to say, the more we'll pay you and we'll start at a million dollars. You've basically got a blank check."

Playboy was not alone. *Newsweek* made a cover offer. As she describes it, they told her, "We will basically do a pro–Donna Rice piece if you will say certain things." Of course, *People* came back, offering her more than the $150,000 they had paid Armandt—somewhere between that and $500,000. And *Parade* offered her their standard writer's fee—$10,000—to tell her story.

Rice said no to everyone, including *People*. She explained why to the *Newsweek* writer. "You are going to attempt to exonerate me in the public's eye to some degree," she told her, "if I'll say whether or not Gary Hart was telling the truth. That's all you want me to say. You know," she continued, "my grandmother gave me a piece of advice. She said, 'Donna, you've already been blamed for the downfall of this man once. Don't be blamed for it again. Say nothing.' If Gary Hart fails," she told the *Newsweek* writer, "nobody can blame it on me. Being on the cover of *Newsweek* magazine and your exonerating me, as much as I want that for myself, I have to sit this one out."

In the end, in terms of the media, Donna Rice made her point. No one had wanted the Donna Rice story more than Jim Gaines, but years after the scandal, he says, "I kept trying to get her to write her own story, and to this day she hasn't done it. I respect her a lot for that."

CHAPTER TWENTY-ONE

The Days and Nights of Ryan White

"How does it feel knowing you're going to die?"
"Someday you'll die, too. Things could always be worse.
It's how you live your life that counts."

—*a conversation between a young boy and AIDS patient
Ryan White at a meeting at Boys Town to educate people
about the disease, as reported in* People, *May 30, 1988*

THERE WAS SOMETHING about Jim Gaines's uncanny ability to feel the real pulse of America that changed the course of *People* magazine during the time that he was editor. He understood the value of celebrity, but he also instinctively sensed those less-obvious stories that had the potential not only to touch people's hearts but to change their lives as well. *People* was reaching around thirty million people each week; stories in the magazine often had enormous impact on this huge audience.

During the summer of 1987, before AIDS had made its way significantly into the public consciousness, Gaines decided to do a cover on the subject. This was quite extraordinary, considering the fact that *People* had never done a cover without recognizable people until he had insisted on the Korean Air Lines disaster cover back in 1983, before he became editor. And even after the KAL 007 issue, such covers had been rare.

Now he was going to put AIDS on the cover:

**24 HOURS IN THE CRISIS THAT IS
BREAKING AMERICA'S HEART
Every day is a challenge for people
with AIDS and those who love them.**

What follows
is the story of one such day.

Gaines asked his reporters to sweep the country to report every story they could find about AIDS. He wanted to bring the tragedy of AIDS to the public, and he accomplished his goal in an unheard-of, fifteen-page diary of the plague in America.

The story went from a gay couple on Bourbon Street in New Orleans to the corridors of a hospital in Santa Monica, California, where Dr. Michael Gottlieb, a foremost AIDS expert (and Rock Hudson's physician) practiced. It showed a prostitute in Salt Lake City who was HIV positive, saying good-bye to her five-year-old son as she turned him over to her parents while she sought treatment. It discussed patients everywhere: Battle Mountain, Nevada; Detroit, Michigan; Spokane, Washington; and Tulsa, Oklahoma.

It entered the House of Representatives in Baton Rouge, Louisiana, where a bill had been passed permitting the arrest and quarantine of any person with AIDS. It introduced a fireman who had tended a pregnant woman shot in the abdomen, becoming soaked with her blood in the process; he later learned she had tested positive for the disease. It featured a mother who, having contracted AIDS from a bisexual lover, had just learned that two of her four children had the disease. New York, Philadelphia, Long Beach, Atlanta, Kansas City, Chicago—single women, gay couples, heterosexual couples, children—this story told what AIDS was about.

On the cover was, perhaps, the most poignant face of all: beautiful, sweet young Ryan White, the fifteen-year-old hemophiliac from Kokomo, Indiana, who had contracted the disease from a tainted blood transfusion when he was twelve. Ryan had been forced to go to court in order to stay in the school that had tried to kick him out because he had AIDS. He had fought the ugly fight and he had won.

Until then, not many people knew about Ryan White—not many people except those in his school in Kokomo who had tried to get rid of him; or the townspeople who had slashed the tires on the family car and pelted it with eggs; or the schoolmates who had taunted him and jumped out of his way as he walked down the hall; or the people who called him "homo," "faggot," and "queer," and scribbled obscenities on his locker; or the person who fired a bullet through the living room window of his home. That is, for the most part, what Ryan White's life had been like up to the time he appeared on the cover of *People* magazine.

Bill Shaw was *People*'s stringer in Indiana. Ironically, his acquaintance with the NBC newswoman Jane Pauley had led to his job at the magazine. A reporter from *People* had interviewed him about Jane, who happened to be

Shaw's former girlfriend, shortly after she got the job as coanchor of *Today*. A few years later, after Shaw quit his job on a newspaper in Phoenix and decided he wanted to freelance, he suggested a story idea to the *People* reporter, who put him in touch with Hal Wingo. That query led to his first assignment, and he had been working for the magazine out of Indiana ever since.

When Shaw got word of the AIDS story, he immediately thought of Ryan White. The saga of Ryan and his family had been largely a local story until then, confined mostly to people in Kokomo, and in Cicero, where they had finally moved. It was perfect, Shaw thought, for what Gaines wanted to do.

He tracked down Ryan White's mother, Jeanne, and in spite of the misery that they had been through—not the least of which had been caused by the press—over the horrifying events of the past few years, since they had learned that Ryan had AIDS and he had been treated as a pariah, she agreed to let him come. The opportunity to inform people about the widely misunderstood disease was that important to her, in spite of the fact that for them, things were at an all-time low. The Whites had just moved to Cicero. Even though the court had ruled that Ryan could return to school in Kokomo, after what he had been through there he no longer wanted to stay. "I didn't want to die there," he later explained to Bill Shaw. "I really didn't want to be buried there."

Jeanne's husband had left the family long before Ryan was diagnosed with AIDS, wanting little to do with his wife or his hemophiliac son, sending a small payment from time to time to keep from going to jail. She could not find anyone to buy the house in Kokomo. People felt it was contaminated, that it was filled with "AIDS bugs." No one would even get near it. The bank was ready to take it back. Ryan was extremely ill. It did not seem as though things could get much worse. But still she said that Shaw could come.

Shaw called M. C. Marden in New York. Part of her skill as picture editor was finding exactly the right photographer for the story; for the Ryan White piece she assigned a sensitive and talented man by the name of Taro Yamasaki. Together, Bill and Taro went to Ryan's new home in Cicero, Indiana, a trip that would be the beginning of an experience that would last nearly three years, an experience that would have a profound and lasting impact on both of their lives.

It was oppressively hot and humid in Cicero that summer day when Bill Shaw and Taro Yamasaki arrived at the Whites' new house for the first time. They had just moved in after the disgraceful events that had occurred in Kokomo and there were boxes all over the place. Bill and Taro were dripping with sweat from the stifling heat. They chatted with Jeanne for a few moments, then she took them downstairs to the basement, where they were to interview and photograph Ryan for the *People* story.

What they saw when they entered his room was heart-wrenching. The young boy was extremely ill, shivering uncontrollably under the thick blankets in which he was wrapped. In spite of the heat, he was freezing cold. He could not stop shaking. He could do nothing to get warm. During the day, when he got up he warmed his hands at the stove. Bill and Taro were overwhelmed. They spent several hours with Ryan and his mother.

The reporter and the photographer from *People* were extremely sensitive to the situation with which they were faced. Not only was Ryan White a very sick boy, but because of the stand he had taken in Kokomo, he had already had a lot of experience with journalists—and most of it had not been very good. He had rarely been treated fairly. He had been pushed and prodded again and again and asked to do many things he did not want to do.

Bill Shaw and Taro Yamasaki were not about to repeat those indignities. "We were straightforward and honest," says Taro. "We were very concerned about what was best for Ryan and his family and we did not want to push him or exploit him in any way or make him do anything he didn't want to do. Having a photographer and reporter with you is a real draining thing. I would never subject myself to that."

It was clear to them at the outset that there were certain things that Ryan White did not want to do. "I shot very little film that first day," recalls Taro. "He didn't want his picture taken a lot. There were certain times he didn't want to talk."

A sort of unspoken ritual began between the *People* team and Jeanne and Ryan White. Although each had an individual agenda, in the end they all wanted one thing: to get a very important message about AIDS across to the world outside of the room in which they had all come together in Cicero, Indiana.

Jeanne White acted as the mediator. She would tell Taro and Bill when Ryan did not want to do something and they would respect his wishes. Still, she always did what she could to bring the two sides together. "You know, Ryan really does like to assert his power to some extent," she would tell them. "If you really think photographing him in this situation is important, maybe you can ask him again." She worked like that tirelessly, over and over, but not in front of her son. She would pull them to the side and say, "You know, this is something that he wouldn't be opposed to doing."

Taro was touched by her actions. "She knew what was bad for Ryan," he says. "She knew that Ryan also thought it was really important to get this message out, that people should get to know people that are afflicted with this. We should not be thinking of AIDS—we should be thinking of people.

She knew how important it was to Ryan for people to start thinking about this thing in a slightly different way—in a very different way."

Still, Taro and Bill held out little hope. Ryan seemed so sick, so close to death that day, they doubted that he would live long enough to see the *People* story come out. "I felt very sad," recalls Taro. "He was trying so hard and it seemed like he was so weak that I didn't think he would be able to keep going much longer. I was watching this young boy—it was like he was dying before my own eyes. As sad as I felt, at the same time I felt I had really gained something from him in the short time I was with him. Being a teenager is the hardest time in your life to be different. Here he was willing to say, 'I know myself and I'm going to do what I think is right and I don't care what you think.' "

Bill Shaw felt the same way. "It was awful, sad and terrible," he says. "We did the story and liked them so much—I was so drawn to them and so was Taro—that I made a mental note that I was going to stay in touch with them. Jeanne struck me as so vulnerable. I thought, Jesus, we're doing this story and it's going to sell zillions of copies and this lady just did this because she wants people to know about her son and help other people with AIDS. I thought, shit, the least I could do was stay in touch and let her know I just wasn't sweeping in there to do a story and move on to the next."

The *People* story ran on August 3. Things began to change immediately after that. Suddenly millions of people were aware of the plight of Ryan White, and they were horrified to learn what he had been through. There was an outpouring of support—overwhelming support—for the young boy with AIDS, the fifteen-year-old with a sensibility far beyond his years, who wanted to live long enough to teach the world what he could about the disease that nobody understood. Almost overnight, Ryan White became a hero.

What had happened since he moved to Cicero, combined with the effect of the *People* story—the unbridled love that replaced the dehumanizing hatred that had been so pervasive in Ryan's life up to that point—had a miraculous influence on the brave young boy. He made an incredible transformation, becoming so much stronger physically that even his doctors found it hard to believe.

By the time Olympic diving champion Greg Louganis made his professional debut as a dancer with a company in Indiana in November and invited Ryan to attend, not only was Ryan able to go, he was able to enjoy himself immensely. When Bill Shaw and Taro Yamasaki went along to cover the heartwarming story, they were astounded at the change in the kid they had thought only two months before they would never see again.

Like many others, Greg Louganis had been drawn to Ryan White. Louganis had his own reasons. As a child he had dyslexia, and he, like Ryan, had suffered a lot of abuse at school. Upon first hearing of Ryan's troubles in Kokomo and the prejudice facing him, Greg had wanted to meet him; at his invitation Ryan and Jeanne White had watched him compete at the Pan Am Games. After he won the championship, he gave Ryan White one of his gold medals.

As Taro photographed the two of them together, he was astounded by what he saw. Sitting backstage with Louganis after the dance performance, Ryan White looked like a different person. "He was so much stronger and so much happier," Taro recalls. "One thing that really struck me was how much your emotions have to do with your sickness. His life was so much better. He had met so many people that were so warm to him."

Like the doctors, Taro attributed Ryan's newfound physical strength in large part to the recent turn of events. Jeanne believed it too. "The *People* story got an incredible response," says Taro. "Both Jeanne and Ryan told us that when he stopped thinking of himself in such a negative way, when they started getting real reinforcement for what he was doing instead of just criticism, and when he saw how people around the world now viewed him as kind of a hero, it gave him much more strength and resolve to keep doing what he was doing."

As time went on, the life of Ryan White took some amazing twists and turns. A striking array of people, some of them famous, took an interest in the young man who had come to symbolize so many different things. "The first story apparently really touched a chord with people like Michael Jackson and Elton John," Bill Shaw says. "They started calling Jeanne saying, 'What can we do? This is an outrage what has happened to your family.' Being the kind of person she is and Ryan being the kind of kid that he was—they were so self-effacing and unimpressed with that sort of thing . . . people like Michael Jackson and Elton John were taken by that. Ryan and Jeanne were not starstruck in the least. They'd been through awful stuff and the last thing in the world they were impressed by was a movie star."

Shaw recalls that "their simple decency" had a lasting effect on Elton John. "You get drawn into their lives. Elton John and Michael Jackson did. They would help them with financial assistance once in a while, and a lot of moral support."

Jeanne White appreciated every ounce of the love and support she got, but from whom it came had little meaning to her. "Her reaction was the same as if the guy at the gas station had offered to help her," says Shaw. "She appreciated help from anybody. She put no greater value on it just because they were big and important."

The relationship between Ryan and Jeanne and Taro and Bill continued to get stronger. Shaw kept his promise to himself and he stayed in touch with them. From the beginning, Ryan had had a profound effect on the freelance writer from Indianapolis. "He was an extraordinary kid who you were just kind of drawn to because of his strength and courage," says Shaw. "After being around him, I always felt better. I always put my life in perspective. He and his mother always had that effect on me. I just liked being around them."

Taro felt the same way. "With Ryan I felt like I was always taking something back with me," he says, "learning something, resolving to be a better person or to fight harder for the things I believe in."

The feeling seemed to be mutual. Ryan liked and trusted both of them. In the time they spent together, Bill and Taro saw all sides of Ryan White and that only made them like him more. Like any teenager, he was far from perfect. Unlike most teenagers, he was faced with an enormous uphill battle. Sometimes when he was extremely ill he could be cranky and tough to deal with, which only made him even more appealing in the eyes of the *People* team. "When you're not feeling good and you're faced with your own mortality, being nice to reporters and photographers is not high on your list," says Shaw.

Taro agreed. "Bill and I were really fortunate," he says, "because we saw a lot of his weak side, too. He wasn't just a strong and courageous boy. He had many weak moments. Sometimes he was pretty tough on his mom and his sister. I guess that made him seem much more human to me, which just made me admire what he was doing that much more."

Ryan White almost died that January, two months after the Louganis story. He had been rushed to the hospital with pneumonia, but the amazing boy pulled through again, and as soon as he was well enough, he went out on the road in his never-ending quest to educate people. In Omaha, Nebraska, he spoke to a variety of audiences: to reporters, to a religion class at Father Flanagan's Boys Town, to one hundred adults at the Joslyn Witherspoon Concert Hall. When a young boy at Boys Town asked him, "How does it feel knowing you're going to die?," Ryan replied, "Someday you'll die, too. Things could always be worse. It's how you live your life that counts."

Bill Shaw, of course, had known of Ryan's close brush with death, and now that he was better, with Jim Gaines's blessing, Bill and Taro began a major cover story about Ryan White. The two of them had been there listening to Ryan in Omaha. They never ceased to be amazed at the grace with which he handled the complexities of his situation. Indeed, when the story was finished, the cover line read:

AMAZING GRACE
In the shadow of death from AIDS,

hemophiliac Ryan White, 16,
has found a great gift for living.
This is a boy you'll never forget.

Ryan White himself had by then become a celebrity. He had come to know not only Elton John, but Brooke Shields, Tom Cruise, Bobby Knight, Yoko Ono, Sean Lennon, Elizabeth Taylor, and Charlie Sheen, among others. He had also become well known and loved in the offices of *People* magazine. He and his mother had visited the Time & Life Building when they had been the magazine's guests at a party *People* co-sponsored at the United Nations. M. C. Marden remembers the visit well. "When he got here, it was like the biggest star in the world had come up to the floor. Everybody on the staff was going, 'Do you know who's here? That's Ryan White!' Everybody wanted him to come into their offices. He had a great time because people were giving him record albums and everything else they had from 'Picks and Pans.' There would have been nobody that this staff would have reacted to more."

It was not the least bit surprising when, early in 1990, Taro Yamasaki was asked by Maddy Miller, by then a full-time associate picture editor, to photograph Ryan White for a special *People* issue: "The 50 Most Beautiful People in the World." Taro was actually in Cicero at the time doing a story with Bill Shaw about Ryan's mother for the "Coping" section of the magazine about her taking care of Ryan throughout his hemophilia from birth. Ironically, Ryan was feeling very ill then. Under the circumstances he was not enthused about being photographed for an issue about beautiful people of any kind. Taro was about to leave for Thailand and Vietnam to work on another story and he suggested to Ryan that they hold off on the picture taking, if he preferred, until Taro returned. Ryan had said that was fine with him. "I'll probably feel better by then," he had said.

He indeed felt better when Taro returned, but Taro himself did not. He had come down with a bad case of bronchitis after the trip and the last thing he wanted to do was expose Ryan White to his germs. He called Ryan and told him that he could not photograph him until he felt better.

The following week, Ryan and Jeanne White were scheduled to go to California where Ryan was to appear at the Academy Awards ceremony. Jeanne called Taro to tell him they were going and she suggested that Taro photograph him for the special issue before they left. Taro was still very ill with bronchitis; he regretted telling her no, but he felt he could not risk getting close to Ryan. "I feel really sick," he had said to Jeanne. "I would feel terrible if I gave him my infection, so I can't."

Ryan was already in a weakened state when they left for California. After they had been there for a few days, Jeanne called Taro again and suggested that he come there and photograph Ryan, that he could wear a mask. "I just can't do it," Taro told her.

He has been sad to this day that he had to say no, but has never regretted his decision. "I still wasn't feeling well," he says sadly. "If he had normal health and normal resistance, I could have done it. I was thinking, I just can't expose him to this. If there was going to be a major picture of Ryan, I wanted to be the one to take it," he admits, "but I just couldn't. I'd rather have somebody else take it than risk giving him anything."

Soon after that, another photographer, a man by the name of Kim Komenich, took Ryan's picture in color for the special *People* issue "The 50 Most Beautiful People in the World." That picture would turn out to be the cover photograph for the issue of *People* two weeks later that chronicled the last days of Ryan White.

Shortly after the California picture was shot, Ryan took a very bad turn and was rushed back to Indianapolis, where he was admitted to the intensive care unit of Riley Hospital, at the Indiana University Medical Center. It was then that Jeanne White called Hal Wingo in a panic because she could not find Bill Shaw. She knew that Ryan was dying and she wanted Bill to be there. She called Wingo at home early in the morning. When he answered the phone, she burst into tears. "I don't know how to reach Bill," she told him. "But Ryan's in the hospital and I don't think he's going to make it."

Wingo was able to reach Shaw, who had been away on another assignment. He and Taro rushed to Ryan's bedside. For the next six days they stayed there, along with Elton John, Jeanne, Andrea (Ryan's sister), his grandparents, and Dr. Martin Kleiman, who five years ago had told Jeanne that Ryan would probably die in three to six months. When Bill Shaw had asked him to explain Ryan's longevity, he had said, "Because he's Ryan White. He's got a great attitude and that plays a big part. He's optimistic. He's not a quitter."

After the long battle, Ryan was failing. He was hooked up to a respirator. During these last days and hours, it was Elton John who seemed to be in charge, who provided Jeanne White with the comfort she sought. "Ryan lit up my life," he told her.

Elton John had confided to Bill Shaw the reason for his initial attachment to the miraculous boy he had come to care about so deeply. "One night when we were talking," says Shaw, "Elton told me that he had a really difficult childhood and he could identify with a lot of the stuff Ryan went through— kids picking on him, that sort of thing."

Jeanne had agreed to Shaw and Yamasaki's chronicling the last days of her son's life, to their presence as reporter and photographer. Much more than that, though, they were there as family and it showed. There was no question in Taro's mind where his priorities lay as Ryan's life faded. "It was really grueling emotionally," he says. "Ryan never regained consciousness the entire time. We were never able to say good-bye to him. At the same time it was this kind of amazing week where we became so much closer with everybody in the family. That whole week it was really tough to be a photographer because there were so many things that I felt were too personal to photograph. So I didn't photograph them."

Yamasaki was not even tempted. "I knew my part of the story could be so much stronger if I did certain things," he says. "I thought, These editors are going to be really pissed at me. But I just couldn't do it. I knew photojournalists who would have—there are so many pictures of people crying over the coffin of murder victims . . . I just couldn't do it."

As Elton John stood by Ryan's bedside watching his life slip away, he remembered the concert he had given the previous summer. He had called Ryan to the stage and sat him down on the piano bench. Then he had sung "Candle in the Wind" to him. Now, as he stared at Ryan White, he could not believe the candle was flickering, about to die. And after the heart monitor had gone flat and the room was silent, the minister called everyone together to join hands and pray. Taro and Bill were part of the circle. Again Taro thought of the pictures. Again he did not budge. "Those would have been amazing photographs, as I sit here and think about them," he says. "I just felt like I shouldn't photograph them. We were really totally emotionally drained. Everybody had been up all night and he died early in the morning."

Elton John was the one who held things together. "He was amazing," says Bill Shaw. "When he first showed up, Taro and I both thought, What is this? After the first several hours, it was obvious that he was there because he really cared about Jeanne, he really cared about these people. He had become a member of their family."

Back at the *People* offices, the staff was totally involved with what was happening with Ryan. It was not a usual occurrence at *People*; rarely, if ever, had there been anyone to whom the entire staff was attached. Ryan White was different. Everyone was waiting for any little bit of news about how he was doing—the picture department, the copy department—everyone at *People* was concerned.

After Ryan died that day, it was Elton John who did everything that had to be done. "What he did for those people during that week in the hospital was amazing," says Shaw. "He saw to it that there were portable phones, and when it was time to organize the funeral, he did it. He did it. He got on the phone and he was calling churches and he was calling funeral homes because Jeanne couldn't do it. She was beside herself. Elton John did it—right down to negotiating with the minister."

Taro stayed around the hospital after everyone else had left. He walked over to look at Ryan's room. "It was full of cards from around the world," he says, "and big banners that school kids had written. His picture was hanging on the wall. It's really hard to explain that experience of being in that room. There was a time when I knew that he was finally at peace and the room was very peaceful. You could feel that Ryan White was not gone. You knew that he had accomplished exactly what he had tried to do."

CHAPTER TWENTY-TWO

Michael Jackson: The Man Behind the Mask

"Most people don't know me, that is why they write
such things in wich [*sic*] MOST is not TRUE
I cry very very often Because it hurts and
I wory [*sic*] about the children. All my children
all over the world, I live for them."

—*MICHAEL JACKSON,*
in a letter answering a written question from Todd Gold
of People, *while on tour in Japan, October 12, 1987*

BY THE END of 1987, when Michael Jackson's album *Bad* was released—his first since the blockbuster *Thriller* five years earlier—some very strange rumors were circulating about the singer's eccentricities. Among them: He had proposed to Elizabeth Taylor; he had had plastic surgery on his eyes, nose, lips, cheeks, and chin; he had taken female hormones to keep his voice high and his facial hair wispy; he had had his skin chemically bleached; he had offered to pay one million dollars for the remains of the famed "Elephant Man"; and he slept in a hyperbaric oxygen chamber because he thought it would prolong his life.

An endless stream of tabloid publicity gushing from the depths of Jackson's long silence only fueled the speculation. He had not given an interview in years, since the one he gave to *Ebony* magazine in 1984. Even after he had signed the unprecedented endorsement deal for more than ten million dollars with Pepsi in 1986, his words were brief: "This is a great honor. Thank you, Mr. Enrico and Pepsi associates. Ladies and gentlemen, thank you." That had been his last public statement.

People was no less anxious than everyone else to get to the bottom of these provocative accusations. Now, it seemed as though *Bad* would be a good opportunity to do that. The press people involved in the album's release were dying for a *People* cover and so was Michael Jackson. Jackson had a thing about magazine covers—namely, he liked being on them. There was one simple problem: He refused to do an interview.

Since Jackson lived in Los Angeles, this particular conundrum fell into the hands of *People*'s L.A. bureau—more specifically onto the capable shoulders of Todd Gold, a boyish, dark-haired, bespectacled, twenty-nine-year-old writer and editor (and the father of a young child), who not only had a wide range of substantial *People* stories to his credit, but had written a book as well. Gold understood the dynamics of the Jackson situation well. He knew that both sides—Jackson and the magazine—wanted a cover. The question was how to do the story. "We had heard about the surgery, the oxygen chamber, and all the rest, and yet along with the weirdness there was a finely crafted album on the other side," says Gold. "The problem became, Who do you talk to?"

It was a problem that, after much negotiating, Todd Gold was able to solve. Arrangements would be made for him to talk with many of the major people in Michael's life—musicians, background singers, and songwriters, among others, who had worked with Jackson. He would also be able to interview Jackson's record producer, Quincy Jones, and his manager, Frank Dileo. "The point," says Gold, "was being able to ask people about Michael Jackson who supposedly really knew what was going on."

As he spoke with the people who had been made available to him, it became quite clear that the carefully premeditated spin being put on the story from that end was that Michael Jackson was absolutely normal. Quincy Jones, for one, assured Todd Gold that Michael was one of the most normal people he had ever met. "He is grounded and centered and focused and connected to his creative soul." He may have been grounded and centered and focused and connected, but what about Liz and the surgeries and the Elephant Man's bones and the oxygen chamber?

It was Frank Dileo who finally gave Todd Gold the concrete answers that he needed: Had Jackson proposed marriage to Elizabeth Taylor? "No." Or offered one million dollars for the Elephant Man's bones? "Maybe, but doesn't everyone have a skeleton in their closet?" Had he had his eyes done? "No." His lips? "No." His nose? "Yes." Had his skin been chemically bleached? "No." Had he had hormone shots to keep his voice high? "Ridiculous." Had a cleft been put in his chin? "Yes." Why? "Because he wanted one."

Dileo had seemingly answered everything to the best of his ability. Had

Jackson quit Jehovah's Witnesses? (He had.) Had he attended the "Captain Eo" premiere at Disney World dressed as a nurse? (Maybe—Dileo wasn't sure which of Michael's many disguises he had worn.) Did he sleep in the hyperbaric oxygen chamber? (Well, he had one, but Dileo was not sure if he actually slept in it.)

When the story ran, both sides were reasonably happy with the outcome. *People* had been fair. The story had taken a middle-of-the-road stance. It had been left to the reader to decide: "Michael Jackson," the cover read. "He's back. He's *bad*. Is this guy weird, or what?"

Whether he was weird or not, one thing was certain: *Bad* was sizzling hot and so was Michael Jackson. When he hit Japan during the middle of his world tour, two months after the *People* story had run, the resultant "Michael-mania" had only one precedent—the Beatles craze. Scalpers were being paid seven hundred dollars for forty-dollar concert seats. There was memorabilia everywhere—even a Michael Jackson store selling stuffed animals patterned after Michael's real ones. Jackson's face was plastered over everything from shopping bags to the broadcast tower of NTV, a major Japanese television network. Michael's beloved chimp, Bubbles, had drawn thousands of people to a personal appearance. Two Japanese amusement parks had been shut down when Jackson let it be known he and his entourage wanted to "play" there. Young girls were stalking him—passing out in front of his hotel. "Typhoon Michael," as he was named by the Japanese press, had blown in with the force of a hurricane.

When the *People* editors in New York got wind of this, they called Todd Gold in L.A. In spite of how recently the last Jackson cover had run, they wanted to do another story on the Michael Jackson phenomenon in Japan. It would not be a cover this time, but a two-page story for the inside of the magazine.

Todd Gold was more than happy to comply. He informed Frank Dileo of the plan. Dileo agreed to get him tickets to the concert. With that, Gold set out immediately for Tokyo.

Although he knew it was futile, Todd put in the requisite request for an interview with Michael Jackson when he got to Japan. It was something you had to do as a reporter—you always had to ask. As he expected, Dileo's response was negative. An interview would be impossible, he said, and Todd had let it go at that. "But by the way," Dileo had informed him, "Michael wants to meet you."

That night, before the second show, Todd Gold was escorted by Frank Dileo into Michael Jackson's dressing room, where Michael awaited them, wearing what struck Todd as an overabundance of thick, heavy makeup, looking a bit nervous, and sipping—appropriately—a cup of tea. When he reached out and shook Todd Gold's hand, the reporter was surprised at the firmness of his grip.

The visit had not lasted long. After a few minutes of small talk, Todd noticed that Jackson had glanced up at his manager, subtly signaling the end of the rendezvous. Even then, although Todd Gold understood that Frank Dileo had thrown him a bone, he did not really mind. He had met Michael Jackson.

Later that night, Frank Dileo's ulterior motives became apparent. "Well," he said to Todd, "You got to meet him—now do we get a cover?"

"I don't think so," Gold replied. But he promised he would call New York and ask.

Todd Gold was an experienced and good reporter. He knew Frank Dileo well—he had spent a lot of time with him and they liked each other a lot. Now, for some odd reason, he had the vaguest feeling deep inside that somewhere out there in the Japanese ozone lurked the slightest possibility, if he played his cards right, maybe—just maybe—he could somehow finagle an interview with the publicity-shy Jackson.

After he spoke with Cutler Durkee, the editor in New York in charge of the story, whatever delusions he had about a cover were instantly dispelled. There was no way there would be another Michael Jackson cover unless he somehow came up with two things: not only an interview with Michael, but some new pictures of Jackson in Japan, as well.

Although it seemed impossible, his nagging hunch persisted. Gold just had this *feeling*. He knew how much Michael wanted a cover, so he decided to try a different tactic. Forget the interview for the moment. This time, he thought, he would push Frank Dileo for pictures. Maybe that would be easier. He found Dileo again. "A photo session, Frank," he told him. "Just get us a photo session."

To his surprise, the following afternoon before the show, Dileo told him yes. If it meant the possibility of a cover, Michael Jackson was willing to do pictures. That news was good and bad. The good news was that he said yes, but the bad—no, make that almost impossible—news was that Jackson could barely show his face in Japan without being virtually demolished. He could not even step off the elevator in the hotel without his big burly security chief and his six behemoth bodyguards. Now Todd Gold and the photographer, Neal Preston, had to figure out a way to get pictures of Michael Jackson in Japan—pictures that really showed the *flavor* of Jackson in the country he had taken by storm—the kind of pictures that *People* demanded, without killing him in the process.

Since Jackson had said yes to the pictures, Gold decided to push the envelope one millimeter further. He went back to Frank Dileo. "Frank, he's doing the photos," he said. "Why won't he give an interview?"

"He doesn't give interviews," said Frank.

"Then, how about if I give you some written questions for Michael to answer?" he asked. "You know, we've got to have something to go with the photos or otherwise it's stupid. We might as well not have the photos."

"I don't know," Dileo said skeptically. "Give me a list. I'll see what I can do."

Gold immediately sat down and wrote a list of twenty-five questions for Jackson—questions that he knew were intentionally mundane and easy to answer: What do you think of Tokyo? What have you eaten? What did you buy in the toy stores? What did you think of the people? Are you aware of the craziness around you? What's your favorite thing you've done? Did you like the bullet train? The list went on like that until the very end, when Gold unassumingly slipped in two key questions: Since Frank Dileo's been talking about *you* so much, what do you think of him? Tell me something interesting about him. And, finally, What misperceptions does the public have of you?

That was it. Todd gave the list to Frank. All he could do after that was wait.

Gold and Preston met with the security people about the picture session, and an intricate plan was devised for the shoot, which would take place after dark and before the show that night. Michael would be photographed in the Ginza—the quintessential center of Japanese nightlife, with its bright neon lights and trendy restaurants and fancy stores. If it worked, it would be an incredible shot.

Todd and Neal would be waiting in the preappointed location. Michael would be transported to the location in his van, which would screech up to where the *People* team were waiting. Michael would hop out and the photographer would quickly get off a role of film before anyone realized what was happening. Then Michael would jump right back into the van and be gone. That was the plan.

When it got dark, Neal and Todd arrived at the location. As they had planned, they were there an hour and a half early. Preston had hired a young assistant in Japan to help him, but they still could not believe that Michael Jackson was going to do this. The security people had been concerned, but Michael really wanted a cover in *People*, and he was, after all, the boss.

The *People* team waited for the exact moment to arrive, and during the countdown they took practice shots. They had set everything up precisely. There was a stand for Jackson to hop onto so that he would be positioned exactly right for the photographs to be taken from where Preston would be stationed, ready to shoot. He would only have two minutes for the whole thing. It was not going to be easy.

They were standing on the appointed corner in the Ginza, glued to the walkie-talkies they had been given to communicate with the security people, when the voice of the security chief finally came through: "Okay . . ." The word crackled through the air. "We're leaving the hotel . . ."

From that instant, security continued to chart every foot of their progress via the walkie-talkies, so that Neal and Todd could be ready the exact moment that Jackson arrived. "We're five minutes away . . . We're three minutes away . . . Get ready . . . Two . . . One . . ."

The first van pulled up to check things out. The security man got out, looked around. Traffic was ordinary. Nothing unusual. The van carrying Michael was two blocks away . . . Things looked all right. All systems were . . . go!

The van pulled up and the doors swung open. Three of the behemoth guards—they were more like human walls—got out. That is when the deluge hit. Out of nowhere—no, out of everywhere—came thousands of kids, flooding the street corner, spilling out of the subway station, storefronts, every nook and cranny.

Todd could not believe the sight. "It was just amazing," he says. "Just at the same time Michael's van pulls up, the kids are coming in droves around the van. Motor scooters are screeching up. It was wild, wild! And these bodyguards are huge! They're just like human barricades, but it was wildly out of control."

To Gold's amazement, Michael came anyway. "Michael reluctantly jumps out on the corner," he recalls. "He gets on the little stand we had set up so he would be positioned just right. The photographer was kneeling down. Michael jumps up, surrounded by bodyguards." The reflector Gold was holding for the photographs went flying, knocked out of his hands by the frenzied crowd. The bodyguards were flipping people away like flies. With the flex of an arm they knocked them down. Neal managed to get a few camera shots off before he was trampled. Within seconds, Michael Jackson was gone.

There were pictures, but not many to choose from, and they were not very good. Preston had done a remarkable job shooting the disappearing Jackson amid the human swarm under which the photographer himself had nearly been submerged. But Todd Gold knew something important when it was over: Michael Jackson was game—he really wanted that cover.

The nagging feeling persisted, homing in now on that list of questions Dileo had promised he would give to Michael. The next day, when Gold ran into the tour publicist, he brought the issue up with her. "I gave this list of questions to Frank," he said. "Can you find out what's happening with them?"

She promised that she would try. Gold was shocked when she came back quickly. "Frank thinks Michael is going to answer them," she said.

A day went by and Gold heard nothing more about the questions, but every time he saw the tour publicist he asked her about them again. Finally she had an answer. "I think I'm going to get them after the show tonight," she told him. "Michael really wants a cover."

Things were getting down to the wire. Todd's deadline was pressing in on him. He did not know exactly what he was going to get from Michael Jackson, but he was convinced he was going to get something.

When the show ended later that night, he found the tour publicist. "I didn't get them yet," she told him. "I'm gonna get them later. Trust me." It was after two o'clock in the morning and he had to begin writing the story. The magazine was in the process of closing in New York. He called Cutler Durkee to convince him to hold out—there was definitely something from Jackson on the way. Exactly what it was, he did not know. But he had that *feeling* that it is was going to be good.

He was standing in the hallway outside of the elevator when the tour publicist alit, and Gold's eyes quickly glommed on to the flimsy pages she clutched in her hands. "You have it?" he asked. "You have it?" he repeated.

"Yeah, I have it right here," she said, holding up the two scrappy pieces of paper she held in her hands. Without even thinking, Todd grabbed the pages. "Great!" he said. "I'm on deadline. I just have to type them up."

Without waiting for her to answer, he flew to his room, eager to see what he had.

What Todd Gold saw was beyond his wildest expectations. Not only had Michael Jackson answered the two most personal questions at the end of his list, he had answered them honestly and openly and poignantly, in his very own handwriting, which was not very good. Todd was sure that the tour publicist had not even looked at what he had written, although she undoubtedly should have—she would later lose her job because she had not. Most probably, no one but Michael knew at that point what the pages contained. Todd read the words of the letter over again. They would turn out to be an ironic prelude to the problems of alleged child abuse that exploded with such a devastating impact on his career during another world tour six years later. Gold was astounded by the letter's rawness and the childlike scrawl:

> like the old Indian proverb says
> Do not judge a Man until you've walked
> 2 moons in his Moccosins.

Most people don't know me, that is why they write
such things in wich [*sic*] MOST is not TRUE
I cry very very often Because it hurts and I
wory [*sic*] about the children. All my children all over the
world, I live for them.
If a Man could say nothing against a
character but what he can prove, HISTORY COULD
NOT be written.
Animals strike, not from Malice, But because they
want to live, it is the same with those who
CRITISIZE, they desire our Blood, NOT our
pain. But still I MUST achieve I MUST seek
truth in all things. I must endure for the [power]
I was sent forth, for the world for the children
But have mercy, for I've been Bleeding a
                    long time now.
    mJ.

Stunned, Todd Gold picked up the phone and called New York. First he read the letter to Cutler Durkee, then he faxed it on to them so they could see it for themselves. When they did, there was no doubt that it would be the cover. The letter itself was needed in New York so that it could be photographed and printed in Jackson's handwriting. The fax would not reproduce well enough, and it was decided that Neal Preston would get on the next flight from Tokyo to New York with Jackson's letter in his hands. Gold made him promise to bring it back to him when they were finished.

In the layout room in New York, everyone was shocked at the poor handwriting and the misspellings the note contained. From Tokyo, Todd did what he could to protect Michael from being hurt. "In an early draft there was some talk, or a few lines, that made fun of his misspellings and bad handwriting," he recalls, "and I argued about that and remember getting those taken out. You don't make fun of people for that, but they wanted to photocopy the letter, and I let them."

When the headlines for the story were being written, Gold went to bat for Jackson once more. "I remember being up all night arguing with Gaines about headlines," he recalls. "I forget what the early headlines were but they were kind of derogatory." In the end, he managed to convince the managing editor to change them. "Gaines recognized the news value, and any word from Michael was sensational stuff. The fact that he was saying something revealing was important. It showed that he was really hurt," says Gold.

Not only was a side of Jackson's soul apparent—a touchingly sensitive side that had not been glimpsed until then by the public—but there was a clearly expressed messianic side to this boy/man as well. The message from Michael that had resulted from the extraordinary efforts of Todd Gold revealed a great deal about the man behind the makeup.

Michael got the cover he wanted so badly, and *People* got the story:

EXCLUSIVE
From backstage on
his frenzied world tour
comes a strange, pleading
MESSAGE
FROM
MICHAEL
''I was sent forth for the
world, for the children.
But have mercy,
for I've been bleeding
a long time now.''

Gold saw Michael once more after he left Japan. During what had been billed as Jackson's final concert ever, at the Sports Arena in Los Angeles two years later, in 1989, he was backstage, where hundreds of celebrities had been invited to meet Michael and have their pictures taken with him.

Mayor Tom Bradley had proclaimed it Michael Jackson Day, and before the show began, Michael stood in a little room against a colored backdrop as a horde of celebrities waited in line to step up and be photographed with the singer. As it happened, Sylvester Stallone was at the front of the line. Gold, who had come with a friend of his, the comedian Louie Anderson, had been chatting with Frank Dileo, who was a big fan of Anderson's. They were not in line for a picture, but just as Stallone stepped forward to be photographed with Michael, Dileo put his hand out and stopped him. "First Louis and Todd," he said, "and *then* Stallone." They stepped up to Jackson, who indeed remembered Gold from Japan.

When it was over, Todd held on to a secret that only Michael knew. Michael Jackson had answered his other question—the one about Frank Dileo. Todd Gold still had the letter.

1988

1988 COVERS

Bruce Willis
Elizabeth Taylor
Cher
Broadcast News
Margaux Hemingway
Quintuplets
Robin Williams
President John F. Kennedy
    (Inset, Judith Exner)
Jimmy Swaggart
AIDS and the Single Woman
Michael Reagan
Andy Gibb
Brigitte Nielsen & Mark Gastineau
Robert Chambers (Inset, Jennifer Levin)
Suzanne Somers
Princess Diana & Prince Harry
Leona & Harry Helmsley
Barbra Streisand & Don Johnson
Loni Anderson & Burt Reynolds
    Wedding
Nancy & Ronald Reagan
Ryan White
Laurie Dann
Paul Hogan
Bette Midler & Lily Tomlin
Mike Tyson & Robin Givens

Tawana Brawley
Miracle at Sea
Our American Hostages
Michael & Kitty Dukakis
Princess Diana & Prince Charles
Eddie Murphy
John Lennon
John Lennon & Yoko Ono
Duchess of York & Princess Beatrice
Fall Preview
John F. Kennedy, Jr., Sexiest Man Alive
10th Annual Readers' Poll
Mike Tyson & Robin Givens
Celia Goldie (Aging Parents)
Patti Scialfa & Bruce Springsteen
Sally Field & Tom Hanks
Lisa Marie Presley & Tom Keogh
Prince Charles & Princess Diana
Baby Jessica McClure
Kelly McGillis
Barbara Bush
John F. Kennedy
Christina Onassis & Daughter Athena
Best- & Worst-Dressed
Robin Givens

Top Films: *Who Framed Roger Rabbit*
Coming to America
Good Morning, Vietnam
Big
Crocodile Dundee II

Oscar: *Rain Man*

Top TV Shows: *The Cosby Show*
A Different World
Cheers
The Golden Girls
Growing Pains

Emmys: *The Wonder Years*
thirtysomething

Top Songs: "Roll with It"—Steve Winwood
"Look Away"—Chicago
"Sweet Child O' Mine"
—Guns N' Roses
"Anything for You"—Gloria Estefan
& Miami Sound Machine
"Don't Worry Be Happy"
—Bobby McFerrin
"Simply Irresistible"—Robert Palmer

Grammys: "Don't Worry Be Happy" (record)
"Don't Worry Be Happy" (song)

Bestsellers: *Breathing Lessons*—Anne Tyler
Love in the Time of Cholera
—Gabriel García Marquez
*All I Really Need to Know I Learned
in Kindergarten* —Robert Fulghum
The Ragman's Son—Kirk Douglas
Trump—Donald Trump

Tonys: *M. Butterfly*
The Phantom of the Opera

Marriages: Mike Tyson + Robin Givens
Diane Sawyer + Mike Nichols
Burt Reynolds + Loni Anderson
Chris Evert + Andy Mill
Lee Radziwill + Herbert Ross
Peter Bogdanovich + Louise Hookstratten

Divorces: Julianne Phillips & Bruce Springsteen
Elton John & Renate Blauel

Deaths: John Carradine   Billy Carter
Divine   Enzo Ferrari
Andy Gibb   Sheilah Graham
John Houseman   Robert Joffrey
Louise Nevelson   Christina Onassis
Roy Orbison

NEWS

- Singer James Brown convicted of assault charges
- Television evangelist Jimmy Swaggart confesses "sin" from pulpit and begs forgiveness
- Washington, D.C., Mayor Marion Barry arrested in hotel-room sting
- Geraldine Ferraro's son, John Zaccaro, Jr., found guilty of drug charges
- George Bush elected president

CHAPTER TWENTY-THREE

The Never-ending Nanny Nightmare (and Other Marital Intrigues)

"Sure I'm happy about the movie. But right now I'm moving through
my personal life like a hemophiliac in a razor factory."
—ROBIN WILLIAMS
to Brad Darrach in an interview (published in People *February 22, 1988)*
that would create a harmful backlash for the magazine

A S THE "MESSAGE from Michael" had proved, *People* covers were
chosen with painstaking care. At their best, they could work magic for
everyone—both the magazine and the subject involved. Jim Gaines
knew that better than anyone. He was not only a skilled and prescient editor,
he was a good businessman as well. He knew what it took to make a cover
sell. In the ten months that he had been editor, profits had already risen 44
percent.

When Robin Williams's new film, *Good Morning, Vietnam,* was about to
be released in 1988, Gaines was not the least bit convinced that the comic
should be a cover. Williams had done well on the cover once, a decade
earlier, as "Mork" of *Mork and Mindy,* but after that he had not been a big
draw—this was always a factor to be considered. Besides, as he had already
so aptly demonstrated, Gaines was completely convinced that news was the
key to success. Even if it was not hard news, there had to be something new
and compelling to write about the cover subject. As the second Michael
Jackson cover had demonstrated, there had to be a story.

The publicists handling *Good Morning, Vietnam* and Robin Williams
were well aware of the way *People* worked. They knew what it took to get a

cover from Gaines. They also knew how much a *People* cover could help a movie. Shortly before it was released, Peter Travers, a *People* editor, was contacted by a publicist regarding a piece, possibly a cover, about Robin Williams. When Travers brought the matter up with Gaines, he asked, "What's the story?"

Travers bounced the question back to the publicist: "What's the story?"

"Well," the publicist replied, loading his ammunition for the cover pitch, "you know he's having an affair with his son's nanny."

"No!" Travers said. "That's great," and he went back to Gaines with the news.

"You're kidding!" said Gaines. "That's a great story. You know," he told Travers, "a lot of people have nannies, a lot of people have children, and they worry about their nannies and their husbands—a lot of people have affairs. This is great."

Gaines agreed to the cover. It was perfect, he thought. According to what Gaines had been told, the story was not libelous—the affair was very open. It was not exactly a breaking story, but it was almost as good as one.

Gaines called Brad Darrach, a well-known journalist and highly respected writer who did many of *People*'s weightiest stories. Darrach had a unique ability to draw people out, to get things from them that other writers could not get. He was an excellent reporter. He was as well suited to report this particular story as Harry Benson had been to photograph Mark David Chapman.

As it turned out, Robin Williams was caught squarely in the middle. His career had been erratic over the years. He had soared with *Mork*, but when that show had died, his career had deflated with it. He had skidded along at an unimpressive pace, unaided by films like *Popeye*, *The World According to Garp*, and *Moscow on the Hudson*. Now his career was peaking again, but his personal life was in disarray. His marriage had fallen apart, he had a five-year-old son whom he adored, he was legally separated but not yet divorced, and he was madly in love with his son's former nanny.

In spite of this, the publicists were anxious for Williams to cooperate with *People*—it looked like the movie was going to be a big success, and a cover could only help. His reservations notwithstanding, Robin agreed to do the story.

The L.A. photographer Mark Sennet was assigned to shoot the story, as well as a cover, and Brad Darrach, who was based in New York, flew to L.A. to see the actor. By the time he got to Williams, *Good Morning, Vietnam* was a smash hit.

As he always did on stories he wrote, Darrach spent a lot of time with his subject. Besides a long interview he did with Williams in a restaurant in L.A., he attended the photographic sessions, and he and Williams (accompanied at all times by Marsha Garces, the nanny in question) spent hours wandering around town, dropping into places like clothing stores and other familiar haunts. Darrach began to probe the depths of the complicated, talented man who had suddenly become one of the most beloved stars in Hollywood.

Williams made it clear to Darrach that he had concerns about the *People* story, most of which centered around his personal life. Yes, he told the writer, he was happy about the success of the new movie. "But right now I'm moving through my personal life like a hemophiliac in a razor factory."

It was during a costume change for Mark Sennet's cover photo session that Williams made what would prove to be a crucial error. According to Sennet, the session was intended to capture a fun and lively cover picture to go with the story. Sennet had rented a plastic duck for the pictures and a mini-trampoline. He had Williams jumping wildly in midair while holding the duck—a typical *People*-style picture. Williams was cooperative, bouncing into the air, sweating up a storm.

When Sennet asked Williams to change to a new outfit, they took a break. "I remember it like it was yesterday," says Sennet. "It was a late shoot—it was about ten o'clock in the evening. Brad Darrach broke him. He got Robin in the room and Robin started to talk. Brad had been there for four or five days, and he was elated. When this happened I knew we were in deep shit. Once Brad got Robin to spring a leak, Robin just gushed, and unfortunately the PR guy didn't know what had happened. Robin was exhausted and for some reason he talked. You forget sometimes. You put your guard down— you forget they're journalists. You're with them for five days and it feels like you're buddies."

Williams proceeded to tell Brad Darrach everything, without, according to Darrach, putting any restrictions on what he said. He told Brad that he was torn between two strong women, his wife of nine years, Valerie Velardi Williams, and Marsha Garces, the woman who was hired as a live-in nanny for Zachary when the child was less than a year old. Williams and his wife had signed a private, out-of-court separation agreement providing for shared custody of their son more than a year earlier. Garces, who was of Filipino-Finnish descent, became Robin Williams's secretary after she had cared for Zachary for two years. Nobody would say at what point their affair began, but nobody denied that it had. She was, Williams told Darrach, the one who made his heart sing.

Williams talked to Darrach at length about the complicated triangle: his wife and his child and the nanny. He told him they were all in therapy ("Jesus, I should get a discount"); that they were working hard to make the new arrangement (in which he lived with Marsha) work; that he was concerned about the effect it would have on his young son ("I'll do anything to keep my son from harm"); that the relationship with Valerie was still unresolved. She had begun dating David Sheff, the *People* journalist who had done the John Lennon and Blues Brothers stories and had since separated from his wife, Vicki.

Williams discussed the most personal things openly with Darrach: Marsha, as a nanny, had a relationship with Zachary that intensified the problem with Valerie "because Zachary loves Marsha and Marsha loves the child. So for Valerie, along with the feeling that Marsha took *me* away, there's the threat that Marsha might replace *her* in Zach's affections. That won't happen." He said that it was hard to be living in a "gray area"—and that it was necessary for everyone to get on with their lives; that the issue of divorce had not been discussed, that it made both Robin and Valerie nervous; that the question of whether or not he would marry Marsha made him even more nervous. (He married her one year later.)

He even talked to Darrach about his troubled past, which included a battle with alcohol and drugs. "Cocaine for me was a place to hide." He revealed the two things that had made him quit: Valerie had become pregnant with Zachary, and John Belushi had been killed by a speedball only hours after Williams himself had snorted a line of coke with him at the Chateau Marmont.

If Robin Williams had inhibitions about revealing what was happening in his personal life, he suppressed them well, and Brad Darrach did his job as a reporter. "If he had been more sophisticated about journalism," says Darrach, "he might have conducted some of the interviews differently. He showed me indications that he regarded the whole discussion of his personal life as sensitive at this point, but then he went ahead and told me everything. I did not seduce him into this. I was willing to listen and willing to be very honest with him. At the time I was listening and at the time I was writing, I feel that I was."

While Darrach was still in the process of reporting the Williams story in L.A., Jim Gaines received a call in New York from Jeffrey Katzenberg, the chairman of Disney Studios. *Good Morning, Vietnam* was a Disney film, and Katzenberg asked Gaines to have breakfast with him in New York. Over breakfast, Katzenberg did not wait long to broach the subject that was on his mind. He warned Jim Gaines of the danger of running the Robin Williams story. He had been told the kinds of questions Brad Darrach had been asking Robin, and he knew that Williams had answered them candidly—probably too candidly for his own good. He made it clear to Gaines that the effect of the story Katzenberg surmised they were planning to run could turn a lot of people in Hollywood against *People*. He alluded specifically to "the nanny stuff," and Jim Gaines was not amused.

"Of course Brad's asking about that," Gaines told Jeffrey Katzenberg. "How could he not? That's what's going on."

Once again, Katzenberg made the point to Gaines that the story could indeed have a devastating effect, not just on Robin Williams, but on *People* as well. His warnings served only to strengthen Gaines's resolve. He was not doing anything wrong. The reporter was reporting the truth about a story that had been solicited by Williams's own publicists.

Gaines could feel Katzenberg's elbow in his ribs, and he was not about to let him dig it in any deeper. "Jeffrey, this is really inappropriate," he said. "We won't do anything that's immoral, but we'll say what's true. I'm sure Robin Williams has been interviewed enough so he can take care of himself."

Katzenberg let Gaines know at that point that he had spoken to Williams, who was extremely worried about the story, but Gaines was irritated that Katzenberg had even entertained the thought that he could influence any decision he might make. "I'm not going to tell one of my journalists to stop asking questions," he told him.

At the moment, what Gaines was more worried about than what Jeffrey Katzenberg had just said was whether the Robin Williams cover would sell. For some reason, there were certain things that simply did not seem to work on *People* covers. It was an enigma. Certain stars who were big box-office draws—like Sylvester Stallone, for example—just did not do well. Gaines had not been able to figure out why, but he had learned that there were certain celebrities that people just did not want to read about. Most comics fell into that category. And Robin Williams was one of them.

Brad Darrach's story was substantial, though. He had gotten what struck everyone as astounding information from Robin Williams, and Gaines had no qualms whatsoever about running it. Had he known what would happen after he did, he may have perceived the whole matter differently. Had he been thinking tactically and not just in terms of selling the magazine, he would later say, he might possibly have proceeded differently.

When it was time to lay out the story, Mark Sennet was told that his zany, lighthearted pictures with the duck and the trampoline were no longer appropriate to the more serious story that had emerged. But, as it turned out, *People*'s mistake on the Williams story, if there was one, was probably made in the layout room after the story was finished, as the staff members involved—Jim Seymore, Hal Wingo, Jim Gaines, Peter Travers, Cutler Durkee, and Brad Darrach, among others—labored back and forth over the layout for more than an hour to come up with a cover line. Arguably, what they came up with took the story out of context and projected an image that was not really true. Inside, the story was accurate, but the cover line left it open to misinterpretation:

PUBLIC TRIUMPH, PRIVATE ANGUISH
ROBIN WILLIAMS
Good Morning, Vietnam
has made the comic genius
into a movie star at last,
but his life is a minefield.
Having beaten alcohol and drugs,
he's now entangled in
a love affair with his son's nanny
that has left his wife embittered—
and Zachary, 4, in the middle.
It's the emotional challenge of his life.
"I'll do anything," he says,
"to keep my son from harm."

According to Jim Seymore, everyone was totally unprepared for the reaction to the piece. "We really thought everything it said was honest," he says, still perplexed to this day.

Suddenly Jeff Katzenberg's warning became a stark reality. Hollywood was up in arms at what they felt *People* had done to Robin Williams. Jack Kelley, a genteel, reserved man, who had been the head of *People*'s Los Angeles bureau since 1985, bore the brunt of the criticism. "Robin's principal objection to the story was that, in his view, we seemed to lay the blame for the breakup at Marsha's door and Robin felt that it was inaccurate and unfair," says Kelley. "He made it known, publicly, widely. Almost everyone in Hollywood who had been looking for an excuse not to do business with us, to complain to us, to withhold clients, made that their rallying cry. For the next five years at least, we were still hearing 'Robin Williams' from publicists. Often it was simply an excuse and there were people who had no firsthand knowledge of what had gone on."

Indeed the piece spawned a new generic description for the magazine. "You're not going to do a 'Robin Williams' on me, are you?" story subjects and publicists would ask reporters.

"There's still what they call the 'Robin Williams effect' in Los Angeles," says Hal Wingo. "It's been very difficult." But he understands what happened. "Where everyone felt we had gone over the line was in taking the points that we took out of the story and condensing them into the cover billing," he explains. "If you read the story, it might have given you one impression, but to see it on the cover gave another. I'm not sure he ever denied the truth of the story. He just felt that it had been badly handled by the way the cover was done. It was one of the most damaging things the magazine ever did to itself, in many ways. Getting over it has been very difficult."

Brad Darrach has a different interpretation regarding the publicity people, agents, and movie executives who pushed for the story in the first place. "I think we pursued our interest, which was getting a good story, the real story, and selling it," he says. "And they pursued their interests in trying to sell the movie. When their client was upset, they interpreted the events in a way that was unfavorable to us and favorable to them."

The whole brouhaha made it into the *Los Angeles Times*, which proclaimed that the *People* cover story had "stirred a whirlwind of controversy."

". . . as a result," said the newspaper story, "according to writers for the magazine in Los Angeles and New York, potential subjects are refusing to talk to the periodical . . ."

"The cover seemed to invite the reader to a sleazy tale of adultery," the *L.A. Times* story went on, "but the article inside revealed that Williams's apparently deep and loving relationship with his son's former nanny, Marsha Garces, began after the breakup of his nine-year marriage to Valerie Velardi Williams."

The newspaper also reported that Robin was hurt and angered by the experience and that Jim Gaines denied that it had been *People*'s intention to hurt the actor. "We thought the article showed Robin Williams is a great guy," the paper quoted Gaines as saying. "If we had tried to make it smarmy, we would have done a much better job . . . The approach to this story was exactly right. The cover treatment bears looking into."

Not long after the storm had hit, Gaines received a call from Jeffrey Katzenberg. "I told you so," he said.

To add insult to injury, Gaines's worst fear was realized. The issue did not even sell very well, which in his mind is a matter quite separate from the backlash that it caused. He attributes the reaction of Hollywood to Williams's popularity. "I think Robin Williams is really beloved," he says. "He's really well liked and it was a good time for him—the Oscars were happening right about then, and he was going to get one. Hollywood really liked him. They felt that this was kind of trashy."

There was something else that contributed to Williams's reaction that Gaines had not even known about until after the fact. A picture of Zachary had been used by the advertising agency in the television commercial to promote that week's issue of *People*. The minute Gaines learned about it, he made sure that it was pulled.

No one could argue that Katzenberg had been right. The tale of Robin Williams and the nanny had turned out to be a Hollywood horror story for *People*. It was a nightmare that would not be over for a long time to come.

In an interview Robin Williams and Marsha Garces Williams gave to the *L.A. Times* after his movie *Mrs. Doubtfire* (which Marsha coproduced) was released in December 1993, Marsha said, ". . . I was a nanny to Zachary way before Robin and I were involved."

Robin added, "We were never involved when she did that job. Which is why I hate *People* magazine [which ran a cover story implying that nanny Marsha broke up Robin's marriage to Valerie Velardi] and always will. They wrote an article basically saying things that were untrue. The idea of home-wrecking is b.s."

Fortunately for *People*, there were other stories that year: The Reverend Jimmy Swaggart, who had accused his ministerial colleague Jim Bakker of being "a cancer on the body of Christ" took a giant fall from grace himself, after being confronted with photographs of his own visit to a prostitute. The public's view of television ministries began to change after that.

Author Kitty Kelley came to *People* with the story of Judith Campbell Exner, the woman who had had an affair with President John F. Kennedy in the sixties and claimed to have set up meetings between the president and mob boss Sam Giancana. Kelley sold the story to *People* and split the hundred-thousand-dollar fee with Exner, who believed she was dying of cancer and told the story (about which she admitted she had lied to Congress in 1975) because she wanted to be able to die in peace.

It was an election year, and *People*'s readers expressed their opinions in the magazine's tenth annual Readers' Poll: They preferred George Bush to Michael Dukakis, 42 to 35 percent. They also believed that Soviet leader Mikhail Gorbachev was smarter than President Reagan, 45 to 35 percent. And, as *The Washington Post* observed, "To prove that from the mouths of *People* readers comes wisdom, television's Geraldo Rivera finished third to boom boxes and screaming car alarms when readers were asked what they would most like to eliminate from the planet."

Stories of marital intrigue of one kind or another seemed to dominate that year, however. There was fighter Mike Tyson, who won the heavyweight championship, but appeared to have lost the war in his marriage. He became the first cover subject ever to appear on four Time Inc. magazines at once: *Sports Illustrated, Life, Time,* and *People.* Gaines found out that *Life* was doing a Tyson cover just when *People* had started to do theirs, but that did not deter him. He had not been aware of the other two—*Time* and *Sports Illustrated*—but obviously they did not affect the success of the *People* issue. It sold 1,686,000 newsstand copies, which was 220,000 over its guaranteed circulation.

Then there was the royal couple. *People* had not stopped charting the downhill progress of their marriage. The year before, there had been two telling issues:

SAVE THE WALES!
She's coping, he's moping.
After six years of marriage,
Charles and Di have begun
to lead separate lives.

The marriage was clearly heading toward the rocks. Four months later there was another, even stronger cover line:

THE BIG CHILL
Divorce is unlikely,
but after four frosty weeks apart,
Charles and Di confront
a dead-end marriage

Now, in 1988, came the "Seven-Year Hitch," in which *People* took another opportunity to point out that the marriage was on shaky ground, but this time they were not alone:

HAPPY ANNIVERSARY—OR IS IT?
Charles & Di and five U.S. couples
who also got married this week in 1981
face that awful moment when
marriage can feel like a bad dream.

When it came to the marriage of Michael J. Fox and Tracy Pollan that year, the bad dream belonged not to the happy couple, but to Susan Reed, the reporter from *People* who had the bad luck of having to cover it.

Reed (you may recall from Prince Andrew's party in Newport five years earlier) was less than enthused about celebrity stories. By the time Fox and Pollan got married, *People* was employing a new system for "weekend duty," in which one reporter was assigned each weekend to cover whatever stories might fall during that time, thereby removing some of the uncertainty for staff members when it came to trying to make weekend plans. When the news broke one Friday afternoon that it appeared Fox's wedding was going to happen, Susan Reed was the weekend-duty reporter.

"The weekend-duty editor called me up on Friday afternoon and said, 'We think Michael J. Fox is getting married this weekend, and we think—*we think*—it may be in Vermont. Go find the story and do it,' " she recalls.

It was not the blown weekend that bothered Reed as much as the fact that she was stuck with a celebrity wedding, and nobody was even sure where it was. She called Army Archerd, the columnist for the *Hollywood Reporter* in L.A., with whom she was acquainted, and asked him what he knew. Yes, he told her, he thought the wedding was going to be in Vermont—Michael J. Fox had a farm there. Nobody knew any more than that. It seemed to be one of the best-kept secrets around.

Reed immediately flew to Woodstock, Vermont, with Marianne Barcellona, the photographer assigned to the story. When they arrived, they went to the Woodstock Inn, where they hoped they could quickly learn more about the wedding—it was, after all, a very small town. What they learned was how protective of Fox the town was. People were keeping their mouths tightly shut. Nobody would even say where his farmhouse was. When they finally found out, they might as well not have known. They arrived at the place and it was completely abandoned. It was obvious that the wedding was not going to be there. The only constructive thing they had managed to find out was that the wedding was going to take place somewhere the next day. They had no idea where.

This did not bode well for Susan. "The clock was ticking and I was sweating then," she says. "You're looking at the possibility of having this happen and being in the same state and not being able to find it—having to call your editors and tell them."

Worried and slightly despondent, the reporter and photographer were driving through the Vermont countryside when they passed an inviting little bar. It seemed like an excellent idea to go in. They could have a drink and regroup. Feeling better at the mere thought of it, they sat down at the bar and ordered from the bartender, who had no idea who they were or what they were doing there. As he set the drinks before the two women, he could not resist gloating about the monumental bluff he had just pulled. He had, he chortled, just sent some *National Enquirer* and *Star* reporters—who had been in the bar trying to find out where the Michael J. Fox wedding was—off in the wrong direction. "I told them it was in Brattleboro," he laughed, "and it's really in Arlington."

Reed's ears perked up. She paid her bill immediately and left. She and Barcellona got back into their car and headed for Arlington. When they arrived, it was easy to find where the wedding was—there was a trail of reporters in Arlington headed for the small inn near the home of TV producer Gary David Goldberg, where the event was to take place.

As it turned out, having found the location was of little value. "I have never, ever in my life seen more ridiculous security than was there," says Reed.

An elaborate plan, headed by well-known security man Gavin De Becker, had been employed to keep the press at the bottom of the very long road leading up the hill to the inn. A pool of uncontrollably frustrated reporters began to accumulate at the bottom of the hill.

As they watched, the line of celebrities—including Michael J. Fox—began to arrive, camouflaged to the hilt. Susan could not believe the lengths to which they had gone to prevent themselves from being recognized. "They came in limousines behind tinted windows with garbage bags over their heads," says Reed. "Black garbage bags over their heads! It was so ludicrous. He's one of the most famous celebrities in America. All he had to do was send word up, or come out, or have his press person come out and say a few words, and we would all have gone away and left him to his privacy. But they created this incredibly antagonistic environment. It really soured me even more on celebrities, which is why I don't like to cover them."

According to Reed, it was that particularly uncooperative attitude that resulted in the near ruination of the wedding. "Because of zero cooperation, the *National Enquirer* and the *Star* hired choppers that buzzed the inn during the entire wedding ceremony," she says. "The *Enquirer* reporters were scrambling around in the bushes and around the perimeter of the inn. They were paying the waiters and waitresses, shoving little cameras at them and paying them exorbitant amounts of money for the possibility of a picture. The bottom line was that I did find the wedding—we did find him and had no access. We got some pickup pictures afterward. It was one of those stories that was about how I got the story. It turned out to be about the cake for the wedding instead of the actual wedding. In a way it turned out to be a better story that way."

The lead picture in *People* was of a couple clad in wedding gown and tuxedo walking down the aisle, onto which the white-outlined, cut-out heads of Michael J. Fox and Tracy Pollan had been pasted. The headline read:

MICHAEL J. FOX AND TRACY POLLAN
are true to each other,
but this is a fake photo—
and thereby hangs a tale

The wedding of Burt Reynolds and Loni Anderson that same year was another tale entirely. The photos were not fake, but costly. Reynolds was happy to give the press access, but he was not about to give it for free. There were plenty of details for *People* about that wedding, because Burt Reynolds was paid a reported fifty thousand dollars for the picture rights, having made it quite clear that he would not take, a penny less. (It turned out to be one of the bestselling issues of the year, making the investment well worth it for *People*.)

BURT & LONI:
The Wedding Album
Surrounded by family and old friends,
two Hollywood romantics make
their long-running love official

Picture this: The wedding party included Loni's daughter, Deidra, from her first marriage (to the brother of a fellow Miss Minnesota beauty pageant contestant), which she once said "lasted about twenty minutes." In fact the marriage had lasted three months. Also in the wedding party were her sister Andrea, best man Vic Prinzi, and Burt's longtime friend Lamar Jackson.

There were sixty-five guests (including Ann-Margret and Roger Smith, Robby Benson and his wife, Karla DeVito, Jim Nabors, Perry Como, and Bert Convy) at Burt's 160-acre BR Horse Ranch in Jupiter, Florida, to witness the twenty-minute ceremony uniting the couple who had been together for six years. They had met on *The Merv Griffin Show* in 1981.

Loni wore a clinging, strapless, knee-length jersey dress and beaded, white lace top, while Burt donned a navy blue suit with red pinstripes. When he relaxed enough to stop hyperventilating, he told his best man, "I'm at peace with myself. I really feel warm."

Burt presented Loni with a seven-carat, canary yellow diamond ring that was so big, it caused a friend to suggest she get a sling. Still, it was obvious, even then, that both had reservations about marriage. Loni had been married twice (her second marriage had been to actor Ross Bickell) and Reynolds's marriage to Judy Carne had ended in divorce after what he called "about an hour and a half" (really two years). Even their friends noted that they were opposites. ("Loni is more elegant," noted best man Vic Prinzi. "She's a classy lady. Burt's a warm jockstrap. The thing that makes him happiest is sports."

In spite of that, Burt was the one who planned the wedding. "I hate to say I just showed up," Loni told her personal manager, Linda Jensen, "but basically that's what I did." There were "15,000 pounds of ice; 12 tables set up in the ranch's helicopter hangar with centerpieces of white dogwood, lilacs and tulips"; and "plenty of champagne." The menu included (*People* always reports such things in detail): "coconut shrimp; baby beef Wellington; Belgian endive with caviar; a seafood bar with raw oysters, crab claws, shrimp and clams; Brie baked in pastry served with kiwi; salmon mousse cake; ham served with mango chutney; corn muffins and biscuits; vegetables; and fresh strawberries with chocolate fondue for dessert."

And then there was the three-tiered, heart-shaped wedding cake. Robby Benson thought that Burt and Loni looked like they belonged on top of it: "We all cried," he said after the wedding. "It couldn't have been lovelier. They looked like the perfect couple, the kind you see on the top of a wedding cake, only bigger."

When Burt and Loni arrived at the hangar to begin the festivities after the ceremony, they had these things to say about each other:

> BURT: (toasting his bride): "I'm a very lucky man. I'm surrounded by love and dear friends, and I married my best friend today."
> LONI: "I feel like Cinderella. I married Prince Charming."

Jim Nabors sang the Lord's Prayer and "Love Is Here to Stay" during the ceremony, and afterward he encored with "Love Is a Many-Splendored Thing." Bert Convy added "Just the Way You Are," and a group of tear-struck acting students sniffled through "When I Fall in Love."

With all that emotion, who could have guessed that five years later, the groom would have a new best friend and the bride's Prince Charming would have turned into a frog?

1989

1989 COVERS

Special Preview Issue
Drew Barrymore
Peter Bogdanovich
Barbara & George Bush
Hedda Nussbaum
Ronald & Nancy Reagan
Melanie Griffith & Don Johnson
15th Anniversary Issue
Liz Taylor
Sean Young
John Gotti
Kristy McNichol
Connie Chung & Maury Povich
Tai Babilonia & Princess Anne
TV's 50th Anniversary
Abbie Hoffman
Lucille Ball
Family Ties
Night of the Wilding
Children of Divorce
Gilda Radner
Delta Burke & Gerald McRaney Wedding
Lisa Marie Presley & Daughter Danielle
Prince William
Conjoined Twins, Ruthie & Verena Cady
William Hurt
Hugh Hefner & Kimberley Conrad
   Wedding

Laurence Olivier
Rebecca Schaeffer
Clint Eastwood & Sondra Locke
Lucille Ball
Ordeal at Sea
Ringo Starr
Fall Preview
Leona Helmsley
Tammy & Jim Bakker
Saturday Night Live!
Roseanne Barr, Viscount Althorp
   & Victoria Lockwood
Roseanne Barr
Dr. Elizabeth Morgan
Bette Davis
Heroes of the Quake
Burt Reynolds, Loni Anderson & Son
Jane Pauley (Inset, Deborah Norville)
Fergie
Kitty Dukakis
Michael J. Fox
Best- & Worst-Dressed
Sexiest Man Alive: Sean Connery

YEAR-END DOUBLE ISSUE:
Michelle Pfeiffer, John Goodman, Barbara
& George Bush, Jack Nicholson, Madonna,
Billy Crystal

Top Films: *Batman*
Indiana Jones and the Last Crusade
Lethal Weapon 2
Honey, I Shrunk the Kids
Rain Man

Oscar: *Driving Miss Daisy*

Top TV Shows: *The Cosby Show*
Roseanne
A Different World
Cheers
60 Minutes

Emmys: *Cheers*
L.A. Law

Top Songs: "Another Day in Paradise"—Phil Collins
"Miss You Much"—Janet Jackson
"Straight Up"—Paula Abdul
"Like a Prayer"—Madonna
"We Didn't Start the Fire"—Billy Joel
"Blame It on the Rain"—Milli Vanilli

Grammys: "Wind Beneath My Wings" (record)
"Wind Beneath My Wings" (song)

Bestsellers: *Billy Bathgate*—E. L. Doctorow
Foucault's Pendulum—Umberto Eco
The Joy Luck Club—Amy Tan
A Prayer for Owen Meany—John Irving

The Russia House—John le Carré
Blind Faith—Joe McGinniss
A Woman Named Jackie
—C. David Heymann

Tonys: *The Heidi Chronicles*
Jerome Robbins' Broadway
Our Town
Anything Goes

Marriages: Steve Garvey + Candace Thomas
Jon Bon Jovi + Dorothea Hurley
Hugh Hefner + Kimberley Conrad
Bjorn Borg + Loredana Berte
Ivan Lendl + Samantha Frankel

Divorces: Sir Rudolf Bing & Carroll Douglass
Mike Tyson & Robin Givens

Deaths:

Alvin Ailey	Lucille Ball
Jim Backus	Samuel Beckett
Irving Berlin	Mel Blanc
John Cassavetes	Bette Davis
Abbie Hoffman	Herbert von Karajan
Ayatollah Khomeini	Laurence Olivier
Gilda Radner	Irving Stone
Diana Vreeland	

NEWS

- Zsa Zsa Gabor convicted of misdemeanor for slapping a police officer
- Junk-bond king Michael Milken indicted on racketeering and fraud charges
- Nadia Comaneci defects from Romania to the U.S.
- Rob Lowe's sex tapes revealed from a 1988 Atlanta visit to the Democratic National Convention
- Grace Jones arrested for cocaine possession, claims she was framed
- Actress Rebecca Schaeffer killed at L.A. home
- Jim Bakker convicted of fraud and conspiracy
- Leona Helmsley convicted of tax evasion
- Rock Hudson's lover, Marc Christian, awarded $14.5 million for emotional distress over AIDS
- Pepsi drops Madonna ads over charges of "Like a Prayer" video being sacrilegious
- Hundreds of Chinese protesters killed during pro-democracy demonstrations in Tiananmen Square
- The Berlin Wall falls

CHAPTER TWENTY-FOUR

The Far Side

"... after a while I started thinking, Well, this is getting boring now, so let's try something even better. If I can drink, I can smoke pot. There's nothing to it ..."

—DREW BARRYMORE,
age thirteen, to Todd Gold in an interview from a rehabilitation hospital (quoted in People, *January 16, 1989)*

THERE WERE CERTAIN rules at *People* that were rarely broken: Text approval by story subjects was not allowed, nor was approval of pictures; and covers were never guaranteed in advance—which did not keep everyone who wanted one from trying.

After years of working as a correspondent, Todd Gold was used to the whole gamut of attempts made by publicists, agents, and the like, who were desperate to snare a cover. When he received a call from George Freeman, who was Drew Barrymore's publicist, asking for a cover guarantee, it did not faze him a bit—until Freeman relayed to him the unbelievable story.

Like almost everyone else, Todd Gold remembered Drew Barrymore as the irresistible Shirley Temple–like kid who had played little Gertie in the movie *E.T.* The Steven Spielberg blockbuster was the most successful film in history (until it was beaten in 1993 by *Jurassic Park*), and few people who saw it could forget the look on the beautifully innocent Gertie's face when she caught her first glimpse of the extraterrestrial. Seven years had passed, and Drew had made a respectable number of other movies since then: *Firestarter, Cat's Eye,* and *Irreconcilable Differences.* Her latest film, *See You in the Morning,* was only a month away from being released when Gold had received the telephone call about one of the most popular child-stars of the decade.

"I have a really incredible story for you," Freeman, who was a friend of Gold's, told him on the phone, "but it's got to be a cover."

"We don't make any guarantees," Gold replied bluntly. "What's the story?"

"Well," said Freeman, hesitating slightly, "you can't tell anyone."

"I'm your friend," said Gold. "I won't tell anyone. What's the story?"

"Well," said Freeman, taking a breath, "Drew Barrymore's in a rehab hospital."

"What?" said Gold, completely taken aback.

"Yeah," Freeman repeated, "Drew Barrymore's in a rehab hospital."

"For what?" Gold asked, stunned. "How old is she?"

"Well, she's thirteen," George Freeman replied.

Todd Gold struggled to absorb what he was hearing. "For what?" he repeated. "She's thirteen. What's she in rehab for?" He thought of his own three little children and shuddered. "This is just such a sick world," he said.

"She's in for drugs and alcohol, but you can't tell anyone," Freeman said again.

"Of course," Gold replied, taking it in, "why not? This is L.A.—kids are shooting each other, shooting up—why shouldn't she be in rehab?"

That is when George Freeman began to explain what his motives were in offering *People* the story. "The tabloids are about to break the story," said Freeman. "They snuck somebody into the hospital. One of the tabloid people tried to check his daughter in so they could take a tour of the hospital and they found Drew." Freeman proceeded to explain to Gold that he wanted Drew to be able to tell her story herself.

Todd Gold understood why. It was, he believed, a move that also had to do in part with the young actress's career. "They wanted to fend off the tabloids," Gold later explained, "to allow Drew to tell the truth and to basically off-put any fears producers might have that she was [in]capable of working. Once the tabs started rumors about drugs and stuff, well, there it goes that not only is she under age and therefore more expensive to hire because she has to have a tutor and she can only work certain hours, but now she's a drug addict, too. Who's going to want to hire her? They had to put all that behind her."

Gold knew that there would be little chance in this case for what he referred to as "spin control," as had been so transparently attempted by some of the people involved with the first Michael Jackson cover story he had done. With this story it would be difficult, if not impossible, to hide the truth. Still, the people surrounding Drew preferred for *People* to be the forum for the true story, before the tabloids had a chance to distort it.

"Okay," said Gold, pondering the situation. "Let's get down to specifics, and I'll call New York and see if they're interested."

Freeman began to fill him in. "She's been in there for a couple of months," he said, "and she's about to get out. She was in there for cocaine, pot, and alcohol."

"Okay," said Gold, still having a hard time believing what he was hearing about the little blond girl he remembered from *E.T.* "Let me call you right back." He hung up the phone, and called Jim Gaines in New York. Unable to reach Gaines, he spoke with Jim Seymore instead.

"You want to hear a great story?" Gold asked Seymore, laying the ground-work for his next sentence, which included the fact that it involved the promise of a cover.

"It better be good," said Seymore, "because we don't guarantee covers."

"I know," replied Gold, "but tell me what you think of this. Drew Bar-rymore's in rehab."

"Drew Barrymore?" said Seymore. "Little Drew? For what?" He was as stunned as Todd Gold had been.

"Coke, pot, and booze," said Gold.

"Oh my God, now I've heard everything," said Seymore.

"Yeah, well, it's got to be a cover," said Gold. "It will be ours exclusively, but it's got to be a cover and we've got to act fast because the tabloids snuck somebody into the hospital."

"Let me find Gaines," Seymore replied, and he hung up the phone.

Ten minutes later, Todd Gold's phone rang. It was Jim Gaines. "What's this all about?" he asked.

Todd repeated the Drew Barrymore story.

Gaines understood the tragic dimensions of the sad story Gold told him about Drew Barrymore. He also knew only too well that it satisfied the golden combination for success when it came to covers: the potent mixture of ce-lebrity and tragedy. With Drew's story there was an additional element: pure disbelief. She was only a child, she was a fifth-generation addict and alco-holic, and at thirteen, she had not been sober for four whole years. Her grandfather, the great actor John Barrymore, had died from alcoholism at sixty, and her father, actor and poet John Drew Barrymore, had a long history of alcohol and drug arrests and had not been around for most of Drew's life.

Her mother, Ildiko Jaid, had left him when she was pregnant with Drew, and Drew had hardly spoken to him in her life.

Shocked, yet aware of the power of the incredible information that had just been dropped into his lap, Gaines said to Gold, "What an amazing story—incredible!"

"Does that mean, Go ahead?" Todd asked. It was too good for Jim Gaines to pass up, and in that rare exception to the rule, he agreed to a cover before the story was done.

Two days later, Todd Gold arrived at ASAP, the rehabilitation hospital in the San Fernando Valley where Drew Barrymore had been ensconced for the past two months. There, he met with her therapist and her counselor and learned everything he could about the program the hospital offered, along with all he could find out about the whole concept of rehab. They did not offer much about Drew. He would have to get that from her. Gold was certain they had wanted to "check him out." When they were satisfied that he was okay, they set up an appointment for him to return several days later to see Drew.

The first few moments of their meeting were awkward for Gold. The slightly pudgy Drew, so grown-up in certain ways, yet paradoxically still so childlike, had come bouncing into the hospital director's office clad in a T-shirt and jeans. She seemed timid, even slightly meek to the reporter as he sat across the room from her—he did not really know where, or how, to begin. It turned out not to be a problem.

"So," Todd said carefully to the pink-cheeked adolescent facing him, "what happened? What's been going on?" That was all it took. The floodgates opened and Drew Barrymore barely stopped talking for the next two hours. It was clear to Todd that everything inside of her was bubbling at the surface, bursting to come out. All he had needed to do was ask. When he ran out of tape for his tape recorder, he suggested that they resume the next day, which they did. Throughout both sessions, the tears did not stop. They streamed down the smooth pink cheeks of her pretty face, which still retained what seemed to Gold an ironically innocent quality, as Drew poured out the wrenchingly grown-up details of her short, painful life. It was not hard for him to understand why she was crying.

Drew told him that she had been struggling with her addictions for years. She had started smoking cigarettes when she was nine, and not long after that she had begun drinking alcohol. By age ten, she was, in her words, a clubhopper—she would spend the night at a friend's house and they would somehow manage to sneak out unnoticed to make the rounds. Then she had started smoking pot. Shortly after that, she had graduated to cocaine.

She had already been at ASAP once, but she had been released on several occasions to work. It was when she had flown to New York with her mother for an audition after being sober for about eighty-five days, that she had gotten into trouble for a second time. With money left over from the *per diem* allowance paid her while working, and with more money and a credit card stolen from her mother, Drew had managed to buy herself drugs. With a friend, she took a cab to La Guardia Airport and convinced the airline ticket agent that her mother had given her the credit card so she could get to a business meeting in L.A. After landing there and going to her house, she took her mother's car. ("Even though I'm thirteen," she told Gold later, "my driving was pretty good.") She and her friend had a night on the town, and finally, high on cocaine, she called her mother in New York.

Her desperate mother finally hired private agents to pick her up at their Los Angeles home and take her back to the hospital; they had handcuffed her and taken her from her house. As they escorted her to the awaiting car with her hands cuffed behind her, to her horror they started asking her about her movies. "God," she wanted so badly to say to those men, "you just yanked me out of my house with cuffs on, and now you're asking me what it was like to meet E.T. What a bunch of assholes." After they arrived at the hospital's admitting hall, when they unlocked the handcuffs, the agents had the nerve to ask Drew Barrymore for her autograph.

She painfully recounted to Todd Gold every step of the progress she had made at ASAP, which included her struggle to gain some insight into her complex relationship with her mother, who was also her manager, and her father, who had virtually abandoned her.

By the time Drew finished with her story, it was clear that she liked Todd Gold. She was very drawn to the sensitive reporter who had listened riveted to every word she had said. She gave him a T-shirt from ASAP. Then, hugging him tightly, she said to him, "Thank you. Thank you for being so nice to me." Todd understood that what Drew wanted more than anything else in the world at that moment was simply to be loved and accepted.

Predictably, the Drew Barrymore cover was a huge success, selling well over two million newsstand copies to make it one of the top five covers of the year. Unfortunately, her rehab was far less successful than the cover. Her distance from drugs lasted only six months. One year later, she was back at ASAP again, fighting to put the fragile pieces of her young, troubled life back together again.

*   *   *

ABOUT HALFWAY BETWEEN the time Drew Barrymore checked out of ASAP and then checked back in again, forty-eight-year-old Janet Culver set sail from Bermuda with Nicholas Abbot, Jr., the man she had been dating for five months, on their first ocean voyage together. It was to be a test of their love—two people who had met through a personal ad and shared a passion for the sea. If they were compatible on the seven-hundred-mile trip from Bermuda to their destination in Greenport, Long Island, they planned to marry.

The marriage was not to be. By their fourth day at sea, things went terribly awry. Violent storms hit, and Culver got seasick almost the moment she set foot aboard the thirty-seven-foot sailboat. During the storms, the boat's sail became tangled in the propeller, which came loose, punching a two-foot hole in the hull of the stern. It was the beginning of the end of their dream trip. It was also the beginning of the end of Nick Abbot's life.

As they lost the battle for the sailboat and it sank, they abandoned it for the rubber dinghy they had aboard the boat, with limited resources of food and water. On the tenth agonizing day in the life raft, exhausted from fighting the smothering waters and covered with sores from the burning sun, dehydrated and delirious, Nick Abbot, unable to stand it anymore, dove into the ominously inviting waters of the ocean to end his agonizing torment.

Janet Culver refused to give up. Miraculously, she clung to life in the small dinghy, surviving on a fish that had fatefully flipped itself into the boat, forced to drink her own urine when the water ran out. Finally, near death after fourteen days adrift in the sea, she was spotted by a marine research sailing vessel. Her energy was dangerously depleted, but somehow she found the strength to feebly wave her orange life jacket. Her slender arm was barely visible from the rubber dinghy, but it was visible enough to be detected by the research boat. The anemic, severely dehydrated woman had miraculously survived her ordeal, and she was rushed to a hospital in Hamilton, Bermuda.

The minute the news of the incident got out, reporters from all over flocked to King Edward VII Memorial Hospital in Bermuda, ravenous for details of the incredible tale of Janet Culver's ordeal. No one wanted the story more than Ron Arias, a senior writer for *People*. When he heard the news, he knew he had to have the story. It was, quite simply, a "Ron Arias" story. He felt oddly possessive of it, as though it belonged to him. Arias had been a reporter for the Associated Press in Buenos Aires, "covering coups, running the streets," after dropping out of Berkeley in 1961. He had become an English teacher after that. Then, in 1985, he went to *People*, where he had become known for his ability to capture the emotion-filled stories that were, as he put it, beyond "the glitz and the popcorn," the stories that had by then become his trademark.

Not only did Arias cover the poignantly human side of such agonies as wars and famines and disasters, he thrived on stories of survival like Janet Culver's. He had brought stories back from Nicaragua, Somalia, Ethiopia. No danger seemed too great to keep him away. But, although he appeared to be fearless, Arias was more than just a "parachute journalist." The second-generation Mexican American had grown up in the *barrio* in L.A. He understood the profoundly emotional side of the stories he was so powerfully drawn to, and he had the uncanny ability to convey that deeply riveting emotion to the reader.

Ron Arias was not immune to the gut-wrenching feelings that these stories provoked while he was involved with them, but he knew how to separate himself from those feelings the way he had to in order to get his job done. He had proved that time and again, with stories such as the one he had covered in Nicaragua about the children who were innocent victims of the war there.

He had gone to Managua with the photographer Taro Yamasaki at the beginning of 1988. The two of them shared the same kind of passion—and compassion—which made them a perfectly matched team. They had visited a hospital ward there, where they had seen beautiful children who had been shot up, children who were amputees, being treated without anesthesia because there was none. He and Taro had watched them screaming in what Arias describes as "a chorus of pain—kids waving their limbs, brand-new chopped-off legs."

Ron Arias brought that story back home—and the pain that accompanied it, and he told it in the pages of *People.* A vote for aid to the contras came up for the last time in Congress shortly after the story ran in February 1989, and one of the congressmen had passed out copies of it to every member of the House of Representatives. The vote for aid to the contras was defeated. It was an example of the power of *People,* and the power—not just emotional power—possible in the kinds of stories Ron Arias lived for.

But on the July day in 1989 when Ron Arias heard Janet Culver's name for the first time, it was *her* story that he wanted. He was, as he put it, determined to bag it. "Everybody was there," he recalls, "the *Enquirer,* the *Star,* the networks, *The New York Times,* a lot of them with money, checkbooks."

Jim Gaines had wanted the story as much as Ron Arias did. As it happened, one of *People*'s lawyers was vacationing in Bermuda when Culver was found, and she arranged to have a contract drawn up immediately. But Janet Culver was critically ill from her ordeal, barely conscious in her bed in the hospital in which she was cloistered, surrounded by guards so that no one could get to her, unaware of the reporters keeping vigil outside, milling around and waiting for some way to get her incredible story.

Ron Arias could not wait. "I had to figure out how to get word to her," he explains. He was gentle and sensitive to the plight of the woman who lay badly sunburned and waterlogged and dehydrated within the confines of the hospital, but he knew that someone would get to her, and he desperately wanted to be the one. As it turned out, the advantage Ron Arias had was the fact that he was a Chicano and that his naturally dark skin was even darker from the recent days he had spent in the midsummer sun.

It was simple once the idea came to him. Arias went to the downtown section of Saint George in Bermuda, to a store he had tracked down that sold clothing for domestics, hospital wear for janitors, and other kinds of uniforms. There he purchased a pair of institutional-green Bermuda shorts and a top to go with them. He bought himself a broom in a hardware store, and then he headed back to the hospital where Janet Culver slept.

"I just went in the back door of the hospital," he recalls. "I got in with no problem and went right up to her floor, walked right by the nurses. I was just one of the guys. I had a real dark tan—I was darker than I am now and most of the help is dark, so they saw me and I went on by, and I slipped her my *People* magazine calling card, and I said, 'I have a contract. Have your lawyer call me,' because we had heard that she had a lawyer. That's all I said, and I stuck it in her hand and she saw me, and I smiled. That's all I did, and I walked out. Then I went back to my hotel and I sat by the phone waiting. About twenty minutes later the phone rang. It was her lawyer, and he said, 'Let's talk.' And we got the story."

Not long after Ron Arias nailed down the deal for Janet Culver's story—it was to be a story in her words, with her byline, for which she was paid—there was a press conference at the hospital. The doctor appeared in front of the restless and anxious crowd of reporters, who listened intently to what he said. He gave a perfunctory statement about Culver's condition. She would not be talking with anyone, he told them. With one exception. She had, he announced, signed an agreement to do a story with one publication, which he did not name.

According to Arias, the news was greeted with great dismay by everyone, especially the reporter from *The New York Times*. "He just went ballistic," says Arias. "He went crazy, and he gave a whole speech about these scumbags who come down with checkbook journalism, and I'm thinking to myself, I should feel this is unethical, but I don't feel that it's unethical, because whether it's with money or without money, I can write a better story than anyone, and I think I can do the best story because, given *People*'s format, with the pictures and the way we work—we can turn it around and we get out to more people and we can tell it with dignity, and to me it was a triumph."

Arias spent days with Janet Culver after that, talking with her in her hospital room. "I held her hand, I interviewed her for hours," he recalls. "They'd come in and do the intravenous medications and other treatments, they would feed her and change her and I'd just turn my head away. To this day, if I see *The New York Times* guy, I'll tell him again, 'I think you're wrong,' and I'll even argue with my own colleagues who think it's pathetic to buy stories."

When it was done, Janet Culver loved the story, and the once-obscure woman became known to the world for her amazing story of survival, presented in the pages of *People*.

IT WAS THE Drew Barrymore story, however, which ran on January 16, 1989, that was perhaps a harbinger of the future. An avalanche of celebrity traumas resulted in *People* covers that year: TV star Kristy McNichol cracked up; skating champion Tai Babilonia attempted suicide; sixties radical Abbie Hoffman succeeded in killing himself; Kitty Dukakis took a near-lethal drink of cleaning fluid; and Ringo Starr confessed to a twenty-year addiction to alcohol.

Besides major news events—among them, the fall of the Berlin Wall, the Tiananmen Square massacre, the San Francisco earthquake, and the *Exxon Valdez* oil spill—the year was also punctuated with celebrities who graced *People*'s cover in death as they had in life: Lucille Ball, Sir Laurence Olivier, Gilda Radner, and Bette Davis.

These covers proved that nothing was etched in stone, when it came to guessing how covers would do. Lucy did so well on the cover after her death in May that Jim Gaines did a reprise tribute to her three months later in August. Both of those issues were among the ten top-selling covers of the year. The Gilda Radner cover was in the top five. On the other hand, Bette Davis did not do well, Sir Laurence did even worse, and Abbie Hoffman placed at the very bottom, second only to Ringo Starr. Kristy McNichol was in the top ten, but Kitty Dukakis was in the bottom ten, while the Tai Babilonia cover placed somewhere in between.

What was clear was that the equation was not simple—many factors contributed to the success of the cover. Foremost among them, along with the mandatory compelling angle, was the appeal of the celebrity in question to *People*'s readers, the majority of whom were baby boomers, the primary target for the readers' pool from the moment the magazine had been conceived.

It was not, for that reason, surprising when Lanny Jones was named the new editor of *People* magazine during a shuffling of Time Warner's magazine editors near the end of the year. (Warner Communications had merged with Time Inc. that same year.) After his highly successful two-year tenure at *People*, Jim Gaines was named the next editor of *Life*. He would replace Pat Ryan, who would be leaving the company. Lanny Jones would replace Jim Gaines.

The undeniable synergy between *People* and the unique generation that comprised so many of its readers had grown even greater with time. And after all, it was Lanny Jones who, in his book, *Great Expectations*, published ten years earlier, had coined the phrase "baby boomer."

1990

1990 COVERS

Readers' Poll	Donald Trump
Pat Sajak's Wedding	Princess Diana
Stuart Boston Murder	Tom Cruise (Sexiest Man Alive)
Drew Barrymore	Alison Gertz/Women with AIDS
McMartin Trial	Patrick Swayze
Ava Gardner	New Kids on the Block
Kathleen Turner & Michael Douglas	Connie Chung
Ivana & Donald Trump	Lisa Steinberg
Marla Maples	Fall Preview
Paula Abdul	Mom Goes to War
Rob Lowe	Julia Roberts
The Menendez Murder in Beverly Hills	Brian Watkins's Murder
Spring Styles	Barbara Bush & Millie
Mystery Lovers	Cybill Shepherd
Halston, Liz Taylor, Liza Minnelli	Princess Caroline
Fergie & Princess Eugenie	Kimberly Bergalis
Ryan White	Kirstie Alley
Greta Garbo	Teens & Sex
Marla Maples	Demi Moore & Bruce Willis
Children of the Dark	Kevin Costner
John F. Kennedy, Jr.	Naomi & Wynonna Judd
Sammy Davis, Jr.	Best- & Worst-Dressed
Christian Brando	Liz Taylor
Goldie Hawn & Mel Gibson	Rape on Campus
Jim Henson	Miracle Baby Weston
Gloria Estefan	
Madonna & Warren Beatty	

op Films: *Ghost*
Pretty Woman
Home Alone
Teenage Mutant Ninja Turtles
The Hunt for Red October

scar: *Dances with Wolves*

op TV Shows: *The Cosby Show*
Roseanne
Cheers
A Different World
America's Funniest Home Videos

mys: *Murphy Brown*
L.A. Law

p Songs: "Because I Love You"—Steve B
"Nothing Compares 2 U"
—Sinead O'Connor
"Vision of Love"—Mariah Carey
"Vogue"—Madonna
"Step by Step"—New Kids on the Block
"How Am I Supposed to Live Without
You"—Michael Bolton

ummys: "Another Day in Paradise" (record)
"From a Distance" (song)

Bestsellers: *The Burden of Proof*—Scott Turow
The Witching Hour—Anne Rice
Barbarians at the Gate
—Bryan Burrough & John Helyar
Millie's Book—Barbara Bush

Tonys: *The Grapes of Wrath*
City of Angels
Gypsy

Marriages: Tom Cruise + Nicole Kidman
Kerry Kennedy + Andrew Cuomo
Mick Jagger + Jerry Hall

Divorces: Tom Cruise & Mimi Rogers
Donald & Ivana Trump
Jane Fonda & Tom Hayden
John & Patricia Kluge
Joseph & Sheila Kennedy

Deaths:

Eve Arden	Pearl Bailey
Malcolm Forbes	Greta Garbo
Bruno Bettelheim	Aaron Copland
Norman Cousins	Sammy Davis, Jr.
Halston	Jill Ireland
Ava Gardner	Keith Haring
William Paley	Barbara Stanwyck
Stefano Casiraghi	Rex Harrison

NEWS

- Charles Keating indicted in criminal fraud charges in S & L failure
- Christian Brando arrested for killing his sister Cheyenne's boyfriend, Dag Drollet
- Washington, D.C., mayor Marion Barry indicted on drug counts
- Panama strongman General Manuel Noriega surrenders to U.S. officials
- Fraud by the singing group Milli Vanilli revealed; the duo's 1989 Grammy for best
new artist revoked
- Germany reunites after being divided for forty-five years

CHAPTER TWENTY-FIVE

Pretty Woman (and Other Wars)

"We had a showmobile and we'd go into all the black neighborhoods. Julie would be there in her stroller, and I can still see kids coming up and stroking her soft hair."

—*JULIA ROBERTS's*
mother, Betty Motes, in an interview with People
(published September 17, 1990)

LANNY JONES LIVED in Princeton, New Jersey, with his wife and three children. He had been commuting to the Time & Life Building in Manhattan for fifteen years—since he had started working at *People* magazine at the end of 1974—and the one-hour train ride gave him plenty of time to think. He was delighted to be named editor of *People*. He had put in nearly a decade and countless hours at the magazine. In the early red-eye days, he remembers arriving home in Princeton, walking in and handing his wife Sarah the morning paper just as she was making breakfast for their kids. In 1979 he had taken a six-month leave to write his book; not long after he returned, he became an assistant managing editor at *People*. He then spent six months in 1983 as a visiting editor at *Money* magazine before returning to be its editor in January 1984. In the five years he was there, *Money* had the honor of winning three straight National Magazine Awards.

Lanny knew that *Money* was not like *People*. For one thing, it was a monthly, so the whole process was much calmer. The content was also predictable—capable of being planned well in advance. There was plenty of time to get things done. On the other hand, *People* was at the mercy of the news—timeliness had become a premium. It was also at the mercy of many of the subjects it sought to have in its pages.

Jones knew, too, that a lot had changed in the fifteen years of *People*'s existence—and even in the five years of his absence from the magazine. If *People* had not been the sole creator of personality journalism, it had un-equivocally made it an entirely new entity of immense proportions, and it had brought the phenomenon to the forefront of journalism in every form. *People* had also given personality journalism a strong legitimacy with the indelible stamp of Time Inc.

Almost from the moment of its inception, *People* had spawned countless competitors—new forms of personality journalism had sprung up at an as-tonishing rate. Besides the other magazines that had tried—and usually failed—to imitate *People*, there was television: *Entertainment Tonight* and its various clones; tabloid TV (*A Current Affair*, *Hard Copy*, and the rest); and the talk shows (hosted by Donahue and Oprah and Joan Rivers, among others). Even the morning news shows and the network nightly news pro-grams had taken distinct lessons from the appeal of the magazine, and *The New York Times* itself eventually embraced a gossip column. *People*'s influ-ence was everywhere.

Lanny Jones pondered the task before him. He was about to become the editor of one of the most influential magazines in America. It was read by one in ten Americans (the majority of whom were women, 48 percent between eighteen and thirty-four years of age, with a median income of $36,102), and it was considered to be a barometer of middle-American interests. With "pass-along" readership, the nearly thirty million people a week who read the magazine added up to more than the combined population of the nation's ten largest cities. (Vice President Dan Quayle gave his staff a *People*-reading assignment so they would stay in touch with "real people" who live "in the real world.")

The problems that faced Lanny were much different from those that had faced its editors in the past. More and more, one of the most difficult things for the magazine was getting celebrities to cooperate. By the time Jones took over at *People*, there was good news and bad news in that respect.

The good news was that the tabloids—because of the way they got their material and made it public, without an iota of the journalistic quality or the careful fact-checking employed by *People*—made *People* seem like a "safe haven" by comparison. As Drew Barrymore had done, certain people viewed it as the best place to deal with the inevitable: If the news was going to end up out there, better it should be told fairly and carefully and intelligently in *People* than slapped all over the front pages of the tabloids with sensational, often horrifying headlines.

The bad news was that, more and more, partly because of the Robin Williams episode and partly because there were so many more outlets—alternatives like the television talk shows, which afforded celebrities more control over the way they were portrayed since they spoke for themselves in that medium, fewer people were willing to cooperate with the magazine. As a rule, it was much more difficult to get celebrity interviews by the time Lanny Jones took over *People* than it had been earlier in the life of the magazine.

Lanny knew that this reticence on the part of subjects would not keep the desired story from being published in *People*. Furthermore, it was his belief that some of the stories written "around" the subjects, with reporting that was as solid and often even more extensive (and revealing) than when they themselves agreed to be interviewed, could be stellar examples of good journalism. This kind of story was becoming a genre in itself, known generally by the staff as a "write-around."

Still, in the fall of 1990, after Jones had been *People*'s editor for a year, almost everyone was surprised when Julia Roberts refused to talk to *People* after her film *Pretty Woman* became a smash hit. Roberts had soared to megastardom virtually overnight. Her career was just taking off, though. There was no apparent reason why she would not want to take advantage of the publicity. It had been made clear to her (through her publicist) that the magazine was planning to do a cover story on her, but that did not seem to matter at all.

When she was asked to do an interview, the answer had been absolutely not. Attempts to get Roberts in both Los Angeles and New York had failed completely, but the movie was boiling hot, Lanny wanted a Julia Roberts cover, and he knew that there had to be a way to get one. On top of that, Hal Wingo had been bowled over by the movie—he had already seen it several times—and he wanted the Roberts cover at least as badly as Lanny did, so he called the *People* correspondent in Atlanta, Gail Cameron Wescott. He knew that Julia Roberts had grown up in a little town in Georgia called Smyrna, which was not very far from there.

Gail Cameron Wescott was another one of Wingo's experienced reporters. She had been a correspondent for *Life*, and she knew exactly what to do. She picked up the phone and called Julia's mother, a woman by the name of Betty Motes. Gail had managed to find out that Motes worked at the Catholic Archdiocese in Atlanta, and it had not been difficult to track her down. When she spoke with her on the telephone, Gail told Betty that *People* wanted to do a cover story on her daughter. She asked Betty if she would like to have lunch.

As it happened, Julia's mother had no idea that her daughter, who was in Europe at the time, had refused to cooperate with *People* magazine for the story. She asked Gail when she wanted to have lunch. Knowing that she had only a small window of time to get what she wanted before word of her attempted coup got out, Gail replied, "How about today?"

It was a steaming hot, muggy September day, and they agreed to meet at a restaurant that Betty suggested near the Fox Theater in Atlanta, which was next door to the Catholic Archdiocese, where she worked. Gail Cameron Wescott had never met Roberts's mother, so she made sure she arrived at the restaurant early to avoid the risk of missing her. When she got there, to her dismay, she saw that the restaurant was closed. "This is it," she said to herself, "she's learned that Julia doesn't want a story and she's not going to come." As she stood there, her fear grew out of proportion. For a few fleeting moments, as she waited alone in front of the closed restaurant, she began to feel that getting to talk to Julia Roberts's mother was the most important thing in her life.

Within moments, a woman appeared from around the corner, and it was virtually impossible to mistake who she was. True, she was older, she was heavier-set than Julia, but she had the exact same face—she could have been a clone, Gail thought. Even the smile was the same. She smiled at Gail, and it was Julia's smile. Gail could not have missed Julia Roberts's mother if she had tried.

The two women went across the street to a little outdoor restaurant that was open and they got along like two old friends. Gail had been a reporter for years, and she knew the value of personal contact. She had a certain valuable knack—once she could establish contact in the course of doing a story, it was rare that Gail Cameron Wescott did not get what she wanted. She worked her charms on Betty Motes, who was thrilled at the prospect of a *People* cover story—and totally unaware of the fact that her daughter had not been. The look-alike mom proceed to tell Gail everything she could about Julia.

She talked at great length about her daughter's childhood in Smyrna (population: 32,246), "a peach-pit stop" on the highway northwest of Atlanta; how she had grown up surrounded by acting because Betty and her late husband, from whom she had been divorced, ran an acting workshop in Atlanta; how Julia had been captivating audiences since she was a baby and her parents played Shakespeare in Piedmont Park. "We had a showmobile and we'd go into all the black neighborhoods," Betty told Gail. "Julie would be there in her stroller, and I can still see kids coming up and stroking her soft hair." She went on to say that her daughter had always wanted to act and had changed her name to Julia from Julie after she discovered that a Julie Roberts was already registered in the Screen Actors Guild. She described what their family life had been like and explained, "We had no teen horror stories in our family." She discussed how her daughter's fame was affecting *her:* Betty had accepted a new Mustang from Julia but had turned down a house. "I told her I already had one," she explained to Gail. Besides that, they could not even go out in public anymore without being recognized.

Wescott gleaned everything she could. By the end of the lunch, she was surprised to find out that she lived right down the street from Betty Motes.

Taking advantage of that fact, she asked Motes one more favor: Could she drop by the house and pick up some pictures of Julia? Betty had told her that she had family pictures at home—and some of Julia's high school yearbooks and photographs. All of this was a reporter's dream and Motes told Gail Wescott that it would be fine for her to come and collect whatever she wanted. The reporter stopped by the house to get the pictures as quickly as she could.

Two days later, when Wescott found that she needed more information about the actors' workshop that Julia's mother had started with her husband, she called Betty Motes again. She was chagrined to hear the news. "I've talked to Julie and I've learned that she does not want this story done," Motes told Wescott. Julia Roberts had been furious when she had learned that her mother had given *People* an interview about her.

"Oh, God, I'm so sorry, because I think it's a wonderful story," Wescott replied. She was petrified that Motes would want the pictures back, that she would tell her she could not use them, but she did not.

"If I had known this, I wouldn't have given you those pictures," was all that Betty said. Wescott did not volunteer the fact that Motes had the right to withdraw them if she wanted to.

A few days later, Wescott called Motes again. "I'm really sorry if there's been a misunderstanding here," she told her.

The problem had already been ironed out. "I've talked to Julia," her mother said, "and she said it's okay. She just hopes I didn't say anything wrong."

The Roberts story included extensive reporting, from an array of talkative sources besides Julia's mom. Reporters in L.A. and New York interviewed everyone they could find who knew or had worked with the actress: Joel Schumacher, the director of *Flatliners*, in which Roberts played a medical student; Robert Harling, the screenwriter of *Steel Magnolias*, in which she had also starred; Peter Masterson, who directed her brother, Eric, in *Blood Red* and gave Julia one of her first jobs, playing Eric Roberts's sister in the low-budget film; Mark Levinson, the coproducer of *Mystic Pizza*, in which Roberts had played a Portuguese waitress; Adam Storke, who costarred with her in the film; Garry Marshall, who directed her in *Pretty Woman;* and Joseph Ruben, the director of *Sleeping with the Enemy*.

After she interviewed Julia's mother, Wescott talked with many of her friends, acquaintances, and schoolmates in Atlanta. As it turned out, it was a good thing that she got to them when she did. "An awful lot of Julia's high school friends talked to me," she says, "but that was like the last picture show. That was the last Julia Roberts story that they would be a part of. The next time we went back to all those kids, they had all been completely shut down."

In the end, even without Julia, the cover

JULIA ROBERTS
The Hottest Star

was among the bestselling issues of the year.

There were plenty of other pretty—and not so pretty—women in the news that year: Elizabeth Taylor was hospitalized for two months with a serious case of viral pneumonia; Zsa Zsa Gabor was arrested for slapping a Beverly Hills cop; Jane Pauley tried to start a new show of her own at NBC, *Real People*, after being replaced by Deborah Norville on *Today*; Marla Maples became the other woman in Donald Trump's life; Connie Chung announced to the world on the cover of *People* that she was taking time off from her work in an attempt to get pregnant, to try to beat the biological clock; Princess Caroline's husband, Stefano Casiraghi, was killed in a boating accident; Kimberly Bergalis became the first known person to get AIDS from her dentist; and Prime Minister Margaret Thatcher resigned.

And then there were the men: Panamanian dictator Manuel Noriega surrendered; Washington, D.C., Mayor Marion Barry was arrested on drug charges; Nelson Mandela was freed from prison in South Africa after twenty-seven years; Christian Brando, Marlon's son, was arrested for the murder of the boyfriend of his sister, Cheyenne; and Mikhail Gorbachev won the Nobel Prize.

The biggest story of 1990 was not the release of *Pretty Woman* or the ascension to megastardom by Julia Roberts. At almost the same time that Roberts and her film soared to the top of the box-office charts in August, Iraq invaded Kuwait. When American troops were deployed in the Gulf, Lanny Jones did not hesitate to send troops of his own to cover the events as they unraveled for *People*. One of *People*'s best, boldest, and most respected reporters, Ron Arias (who had landed the Janet Culver story the previous year), was the first to go, along with the photographer Ken Regan, who had an equally stellar reputation. When war was actually declared several months later, just after the end of the year, Lanny would send another reporter—this time a pretty woman who was in no way an actress—a Berkeley grad with a hankering for dangerous stories by the name of Maria Wilhelm, to cover it.

Lanny Jones never lost sight of the fact that a big part of *People*'s *raison d'être* was to cover real people in the real world. Although there were some people on the staff of the magazine who maintained that fighting your way through the agents and publicists and personal advisers in Hollywood could be just as lethal, nothing was more real than war.

1991

1991 COVERS

Oprah Winfrey
Cher
Americans Go to War
Elizabeth Glaser
Princess Diana
Lucille Ball & Desi Arnaz
Julia Roberts & Kiefer Sutherland
Richard Dreyfuss & Wife Jeramie
Fergie
Sandra Dee
Diff'rent Strokes
Reba McEntire
Princess Caroline
Madonna & Michael Jackson
Ted Kennedy
Nancy & Ronald Reagan
Michael Landon
Norman & Brenda Schwarzkopf
Michelle Phillips & Chynna Phillips
Jackie Kennedy Onassis
Gilda Radner
Marilyn Van Derbur
Princess Diana, Prince William
   & Prince Harry
Geena Davis
Julia Roberts
Sally Field

Michael Landon
Prince Charles & Princess Diana
Delta Burke
Matthew & Gunnar Nelson
Jeffrey Dahmer
Johnny Carson & Alexis
Patrick Swayze
Fall Preview
Beverly Hills, 90210
Ann Jillian
Texas Cheerleader Plot
Regis Philbin & Kathie Lee Gifford
Roseanne Barr Arnold
Carolyn Sapp
Liz Taylor, Larry Fortensky,
   Michael Jackson
Anita Hill
Luke Perry
Virginia & Clarence Thomas
Fred MacMurray
Chris Evert
Candice Bergen
Naomi & Wynonna Judd
Best- & Worst-Dressed
Dustin Hoffman

Films: *Terminator 2*
Robin Hood: Prince of Thieves
The Silence of the Lambs
Home Alone
Dances with Wolves

car: *The Silence of the Lambs*

TV Shows: *Cheers*
60 Minutes
Roseanne
A Different World
The Cosby Show

mys: *Cheers*
L.A. Law

Songs: "Cream"—Prince
"Everything I Do (I Do It for You)"
—Bryan Adams
"Rush, Rush"—Paula Abdul
"When a Man Loves a Woman"
—Michael Bolton
"You're in Love"—Wilson Phillips
"Black or White"—Michael Jackson

mmys: "Unforgettable" (record)
"Unforgettable" (song)

tsellers: *Damage*—Josephine Hart
The Firm—John Grisham
Scarlett—Alexandra Ripley

Final Exit—Derek Humphry
Iron John—Robert Bly
Woody Allen—Eric Lax
*You'll Never Eat Lunch in This
Town Again*—Julia Phillips

Tonys: *Lost in Yonkers*
The Will Rogers Follies
Fiddler on the Roof

Marriages: Elizabeth Taylor + Larry Fortensky
Jane Fonda + Ted Turner

Divorces (of sorts): Judy Nelson sues Martina
Navratilova for palimony
Merv Griffin is sued for palimony by
Brent Plott

Deaths: Peggy Ashcroft   Klaus Barbie
Joseph Papp   Harry Reasoner
Frank Capra   Colleen Dewhurst
Redd Foxx   Michael Landon
David Lean   Yves Montand
Fred MacMurray   Robert Maxwell
Lee Remick   Dr. Seuss
Danny Thomas   Gene Roddenberry
Miles Davis   Robert Motherwell

NEWS

- War declared on Iraq
- Motorist Rodney King beaten by L.A. police officers; videotape released to media
- Jeffrey Dahmer arrested after body parts are discovered in his Milwaukee apartment
- William Kennedy Smith tried and acquitted on rape charges
- A pregnant Demi Moore's photograph for *Vanity Fair* stirs controversy
- Warren Beatty and Annette Bening announce they are expecting a baby
- Magic Johnson reveals HIV infection; retires from basketball
- Michael Jackson signs record-making deal with Sony, estimated worth $1 billion
- The Soviet Union ceases to exist and is replaced by the Commonwealth of
  Independent States

CHAPTER TWENTY-SIX

When Liz Married Larry:
The Mother of All Weddings

"It will be fun for her. After all, Elizabeth is no snob. Under the
high gloss of her façade, she is really an ordinary woman who has
led an extraordinary life."

—LIZ SMITH,
in People (October 21, 1991), after attending
Elizabeth Taylor's wedding to Larry Fortensky

AS IT TURNED out, the war for the pictures that would wind up in
Liz and Larry's wedding album was not the hardest part of covering
Elizabeth Taylor's eighth wedding, when she married Larry Fortensky
in 1991. The hardest part was getting the story to go with the fabulous
photographs—for a variety of reasons.

It began when Taylor announced her engagement to the thirty-nine-year-
old former construction worker in August. People had understandably been
besotted with the groom-to-be. Not that getting engaged was anything new for
the fifty-nine-year-old actress—she had certainly had plenty of experience,
having already broken off two engagements since she had divorced her
seventh husband, Senator John Warner, in 1982. The interesting factor in the
equation this time was the man to whom she had gotten engaged.

At People, no one knew much more about Larry Fortensky than the fact
that he and his bride-to-be had met at the Betty Ford Center in Rancho
Mirage, California, near Palm Springs, where they had both checked in for
drug and alcohol dependency in 1988. The minute the news of the impending
nuptials got out, however, the full-force quest began: Exactly who was Larry
Fortensky, and from where had this latest love in Liz's life come?

This time the task at hand fell to Nancy Matsumoto, a solid, levelheaded, and experienced reporter, a graduate of Pomona College, who had been at *People* for four years, having worked as a journalist before that in Boston and later in Tokyo. Like Susan Reed (of the Prince Andrew party and Michael J. Fox wedding fame), Nancy Matsumoto was not the least bit partial to stories of the celebrity persuasion; in fact she much preferred more serious subjects. Still, a good reporter is a good reporter, and when she was assigned to the Fortensky case, she embraced it—as she did everything else—with total dedication.

Shortly after Liz and Larry's engagement had been announced in the papers, small pieces of information about the mysterious man (and future husband) who was twenty years her junior began to surface in the news. One of the most surprising tidbits to dribble onto the pages of the ravenous tabloids was that Fortensky had a string of drunk-driving arrests and was scheduled to appear in court momentarily at what would prove to be an especially inopportune time for him. For Nancy Matsumoto, on the other hand, it would prove to be the opposite. She used the impending court appearance to begin delving into the past of Liz's new love, who had suddenly and quite innocently, at the mercy of his own helpless emotions, inadvertently crossed the treacherous and burdensome line from private to public persona.

The only thing that was clear at that moment was that driving drunk was what had led the unassuming Larry Fortensky to the Betty Ford Center and subsequently, as it turned out, straight into Liz's loving arms. Being the thorough reporter that she was, Matsumoto started at the Betty Ford Center, engaging in lengthy conversations with several members of the board of directors to learn as much as she could about how the center worked: Relationships were not encouraged, she was told, but close—not necessarily romantic—friendships often developed from the experience. Everyone at Betty Ford was treated as an equal. Be they billionaires or paupers, all were expected to make their own beds and attend the same support groups. Essentially, Matsumoto learned that, aside from its primary purpose of coping with substance dependency, the Betty Ford Center functioned as a great leveler of those who populated its hallowed hallways, dining rooms, and dorms.

For more specific information on her subject, Larry Fortensky, Matsumoto turned next to the existent court records, which are accessible to the public. What she found out from the available documents was that Liz's intended had a string of arrests made for driving with open containers. More important than that, for her purposes at least, was the fact that Fortensky had grown up in a small town in Orange County, California, called Stanton, which was where his drinking problems had begun.

From calls she made next to places like the chamber of commerce and the local newspaper, Matsumoto learned what she could about Stanton, California: It was a small town, with a population of only thirty thousand, yet Stanton had the highest crime rate of any town in Orange County. It was mostly lower middle class, segregated distinctly between its white and Hispanic populations, and the inherent rivalries were intense. Shooting guns and shooting drugs were commonplace in Stanton. Matsumoto began to piece together the picture of a town that would not be an easy place for anyone to grow up in—certainly not an easy place to escape involvement with violence, alcohol, or drugs.

At that point, on a stifling hot, late-summer day that was inching toward triple-digit temperatures, Nancy Matsumoto climbed into her car and headed south toward Larry Fortensky's hometown. When she got there, she cranked up to full gear as a reporter, visiting his neighborhood, his former friends, the chamber of commerce, and everyone else she could get close to who knew—or knew anything about—Liz's Larry Fortensky.

The word "big" did not even come close to describing the way the folks in Stanton viewed the news that one of their own, Larry Fortensky, was about to marry one of the most famous women in the world. All because of Betty Ford. Because he was an alcoholic. The very thought was so incredible it really knocked their collective socks off. They stood at the ready to help Nancy Matsumoto find out anything she needed to know about their hero, in any way that they could. Nancy Matsumoto, who had until then regarded this particular assignment with a certain amount of disdain, began to think it was starting to get fun.

It had been easy to track down the house where Larry Fortensky and his mother, Dot Lacy (she had divorced Mr. Fortensky and married again), had lived while Larry was growing up. Near his house, the neighbors told her, was a community center, where Nancy went next—a place where a lot of folks in the neighborhood hung out and everyone seemed to know everyone else. "You should talk to so-and-so—she was his next-door neighbor," she was told. "So-and-so is their cousin who lives across the street . . ." "No, *this* is who you should really talk to . . ." "These are the kids he grew up with and played with . . ." "This is where his daughter hangs out." The list got to be a mile long.

From the neighbors, Nancy learned a lot about what growing up in the Fortensky household was like. They talked about Dot, Larry's mother. One of her kids had a paper route; whenever you would spend the night at the Fortensky house, they told Nancy, you would be up at 3:00 A.M., helping Dot fold papers.

Another person Nancy tracked down was one of Fortensky's two former wives, who had already appeared on the tabloid show *Hard Copy*, talking about her ex. Nancy had gotten a transcript of the *Hard Copy* segment, and she had talked with some of the producers at the show, who had given her their assessment of the wife: "She was really trying to capitalize on his fame," they told Nancy, "to make a buck for herself, and in the process she was probably trumping up her story a little bit." With that in mind, Nancy spoke with her, and when the ex-wife told her she would talk only if she were paid, Nancy said, fine, it would not be necessary.

The more she learned, however, the sadder the story got. That is when Nancy turned inward to examine more carefully her own feelings about what she was doing. "It's very odd," she says, looking back at the way she felt at the time. "Something happens if you're a reporter and you're on a story—your reportorial instincts kick in. My natural inclination is not doing these kinds of stories, not liking celebrity stories—to think, Why do we care? Why do we have to care? Why should these stars be such a big deal? Why is this entire very profitable magazine obsessed with making tons of money off this? I'll start to think, I don't want to do this, this is really unpleasant. But then your reporter's instincts kick in, and at some point your desire to get the story and the fact that you're getting stuff—and that it's really interesting to piece the picture together—takes over. You're putting the pieces of a puzzle together and it's fascinating—in this case because of the contrast between where he is now and where he came from."

There was another thing about this particular story that fascinated Nancy Matsumoto. The people she was dealing with here were not your average Hollywood media-savvy types. "It made it more fun than your typical Hollywood story," she says, "where everyone has been warned and primed and trained, where publicists beforehand talk to reporters and don't tell them anything that's true. There were a few relatives who were great sources in this story, and friends of his who were all so obsessed with it, I found it amazing."

The next stop on the puzzle-piecing tour of the life of Larry Fortensky was another California town north of Stanton, called Stockton, where Larry's family had lived before they moved to Stanton. There she talked with aunts and relatives and cousins. The only one who refused to talk with her was one of Larry's grandmothers. An aunt told how Liz had invited Larry's grandmother and his favorite aunt to Bel Air to take them shopping. She had had them fitted with Nolan Miller dresses for the wedding, and then she had taken them to a swanky Beverly Hills boutique where she had bought them each a pair of four-hundred-dollar shoes.

Nancy also learned about the wedding shower that was in the process of being planned. It was to be, she was told, an all-cotton wedding shower. Although Larry's aunt had refused to tell Nancy what she was going to give her nephew for the wedding, she had told her exactly what her sister was giving Liz for the all-cotton shower: "It's going to be," she told Nancy, "a long T-shirt—like a night dress—and they're gonna have a picture printed on it of Larry when he was real young, standing in front of his red convertible."

In the course of the trip to Stockton and Sacramento, Matsumoto did an extraordinary amount of reporting: She drove from Stockton to Modesto to Sacramento, the state capital, where she went to the hall of records to get birth certificates and other documents. Then she set out for a little town called Lodi to visit Larry Fortensky's father, Harold, who happened to be in the hospital there, suffering from a bleeding ulcer. She had already spoken with him once on the phone, earlier in the course of reporting her story.

Nancy Matsumoto had also spoken with the elder Fortensky's wife, asking her if it would be all right to visit her husband in the hospital. When she was told it would be fine, the Lodi Memorial Hospital became Nancy's next stop. She walked in the door of Mr. Harold Fortensky's semiprivate hospital room and announced herself: "Hi, I'm the one you talked to from *People*. I came to visit you. I hope you're feeling okay."

Harold was in bed. His wife was at his bedside. Next to him was his roommate, who nearly fell out of his own hospital bed as he listened to the conversation that ensued. To say that he was shocked would be a gross understatement. No, Harold Fortensky's roommate simply could not believe his ears: The son of the man in the bed next to him was about to marry Elizabeth Taylor.

According to Nancy Matsumoto, Harold himself thoroughly enjoyed the interview. He seemed to have absolutely no objection to being the center of attention for a change. He did not, however, have much to say about his son Larry because he had not spoken to him for the last twenty years. Nor had he received an invitation to the wedding. "He enjoyed being tracked down and talked to as the celebrity's father because no one had really paid any attention to him," says Nancy. Aside from the *People* reporter, no one else had been able to find the father of Larry Fortensky.

To make her story complete, Matsumoto checked out Larry's career by tracking down the teamsters' union to which he had belonged in El Monte, California. She never ceased to be amazed at how much certain people were willing to talk. A chatty secretary from the union unabashedly spewed forth all kinds of information about Fortensky: what his on-the-job fortes were ("driving the heavy machinery," she said); how much money he made (in the range of twenty dollars an hour plus six or seven dollars in fringe benefits); and even, to Nancy Matsumoto's surprise, his social security number, which would allow Nancy to find out how much money he had made in a year.

When the *People* story about Liz's engagement ran in the August 12 issue of the magazine, it was a two-page spread with a lot of pictures—and very little of the information that Nancy Matsumoto had so painstakingly gathered about the groom-to-be. The magazine had, however, decided to be a bit playful with the headline, which read:

Elizabeth Taylor Hilton Wilding Todd Fisher Burton Burton Warner— and soon, Fortensky (whew!) EIGHT IS ENOUGH

When Elizabeth Taylor saw it, she did not think that it was funny at all, and "Eight Is Enough" proved in the end to have a highly detrimental effect. The L.A. bureau had been in the midst of negotiating a substantial interview with Taylor and her fiancé at Taylor's Bel Air home. Jack Kelley, the L.A. bureau chief, had been ironing out the final details with Elizabeth Taylor's publicist, a woman by the name of Chen Sam. They had gotten down to the last couple of points: who the photographer would be and when the story would be shot. Almost instantly after the engagement story appeared, Jack Kelley received a call from Chen Sam: "Madam is not pleased," she said.

"Come on, Chen," Kelley replied, "it's just lighthearted good fun." Elizabeth Taylor did not see it that way, though, and with that, the Taylor-Fortensky interview fell apart.

Kelley still does not understand why. "At the time, the tabloid press was beating up on him pretty badly," he says. "The *Enquirer* was calling him 'Jailbird Larry Fortensky,' identifying him that way every time. You got to wonder if that was his legal name. They were treating him terribly. We were, I thought, pretty gentle and fair, but they didn't see it that way and so the interview fell apart."

Partly because *People* had their own story in the works before it had fallen apart so precipitously and partly because Lanny Jones had pulled back on the policy of paying large sums of money for stories, the magazine had not done much about covering Elizabeth Taylor's wedding. Lanny's attitude was clear: He was not going to get into bidding wars, especially with the tabloids. "It was becoming a free-for-all," he says, "and we were being identified with the tabloids and a lot of people were debasing us. We have to have higher standards. As professionals, our behavior is more important than the needs of the hour." He knew that the pictures were for sale for an exorbitant amount of money. *People* had made a lowball offer when the wedding was announced and had gotten little more than a laughing response, and they had let the matter go at that.

As the wedding got closer, the momentum began to build. Dick Burgheim, who by this time was working on special issues for the magazine, and for whom Jones, among others, had a great deal of respect, pointed out to Lanny that he should really be doing something about the Taylor-Fortensky wedding, that this would certainly be one of the biggest stories of the year. Suddenly, a few days before the event, everyone was starting to get nervous, thinking *People* had lost something they should have had.

Hal Wingo had, by happenstance, been leafing through a magazine about this time when an interview with the photographer Herb Ritts had caught his eye. Ritts was the one who would be photographing Liz's wedding, and the article Wingo had stumbled upon mentioned that the proceeds from the pictures taken of the wedding would go to Liz's new organization for AIDS research. Although Beth Filler, the assistant picture editor who had been filling in for M. C. Marden while she was on vacation, had been on top of the bidding for the pictures, until then nobody at *People* had wanted to spend any significant money. The fact that the money for the pictures would go to a worthy charitable organization, along with Burgheim's warning—to which Lanny paid attention because of his great respect for Burgheim—changed his thinking regarding the wedding pictures.

He quickly told Beth Filler to go back once more and see what she could do to get the pictures, now that he was willing to spend more money for them. For Lanny, spending money for a charitable cause changed the equation completely. At the same time, Hal Wingo warned Beth that he had been told by his good friend the columnist Liz Smith that Elizabeth Taylor was still sufficiently irritated with *People* about the "Eight Is Enough" story that he did not think the magazine could get the pictures anyway.

Heavy negotiations began, with Beth Filler spelling out precisely what it was that *People* would pay and exactly what they expected to get in return, in terms of the pictures they wanted. As it turned out, she managed to work out a deal for $175,000 in spite of the fact that the tabloids had offered much more for the pictures. Taylor was angry with *People*, but the alternative in her mind was even worse.

In the end, everyone got what he wanted. Almost. The hitch was that, although *People* had gotten the pictures for the wedding, Liz refused to cooperate for a story. The magazine would have no access. She would not be interviewed by anyone, which meant that another *People* write-around was imminent.

In typical style, once again everyone fanned out in *People*'s highly effective swarm technique to start gathering whatever they could about the wedding. Since Nancy Matsumoto already had all of the Fortensky contacts, she would be able to talk with the relatives she already knew after the wedding was over. She did a lot more reporting. She also talked to the designer Valentino, whose wedding gift to Liz was her twenty-five-thousand-dollar wedding gown; she talked with several of Liz's ex-husbands, including Eddie Fisher; she tracked down the honeymoon suite, and talked to the bartender at Mallard's restaurant where she had been told by a newspaperman in Larry's hometown that the couple liked to hang out and eat cheeseburgers.

Another reporter, Robin Micheli, was in charge of the actual "wedding team," which headed for the little town of Los Olivos in the Santa Ynez Valley, where Michael Jackson's ranch was, then disbursed to see what they could find. They covered hotels and restaurants to locate guests who might talk; they found everyone from caterers to family members—anyone remotely connected to the wedding or the wedding party in any way. They knew they would have no official access to the wedding, but Liz Smith, who was an invited guest, agreed to provide some information from the inside for *People*.

Robin Micheli managed to get a few words from Marianne Williamson, the minister who performed the ceremony, although she did not say much; she talked to people at the hotel that ran the rehearsal dinner. She grabbed everyone she could get her hands on; Roddy McDowall was one of the friendliest. The *People* reporters got whatever they could. The scene quickly turned into a carnival atmosphere, with decoy limousines circling the area to keep reporters off their guard. "It was like a little game," says Micheli. "Like a carnival—people lined up in their lawn chairs across the street from the hotel."

Still, on that day, October 6, Liz and Larry managed to say "I do" as helicopters buzzed above to spy on the sacred occasion, which was attended by Larry's grandmother, Mary McGill; Liz's hairdresser—and the best man—Jose Eber; Eva Gabor, Merv Griffin, Nancy Reagan; Liz's mom, Sara; Carole Bayer Sager; Barry Diller and Diane Von Furstenberg; Véronique and Gregory Peck; and Liz's grandkids—among the other 160 invited guests—while Moshe Alon, a former Israeli army officer, stood guard over the event, along with a 100-man security force. That did not stop one photographer from parachuting within twenty feet of the gazebo during the ceremony.

Liz gave Larry a plain gold ring. Hers was set with pavé diamonds. They danced the first dance, and Michael Jackson, wearing *two* black gloves for this special occasion, cut in, with his date, Brooke Shields. According to *People*, Michael paid for the wedding and reception, which cost an estimated $1.5 million, including "Dom Pérignon, chardonnay from Fess Parker's nearby winery, platters of rolled salmon and five tiers of chocolate mousse cake."

Everyone seemed to have a good time, although one observer had expected Michael Jackson to do something more spectacular in the way of entertainment. The Fortensky clan had no complaints. They had all eschewed the limos they were offered and came in their own cars. After it was over they told Nancy Matsumoto that they had had a great time. "They thought everyone would be snobby, but in fact everyone was very friendly," Nancy says, "and they loved the rides in Michael's amusement park."

Eventually *People* enjoyed the wedding, too:

HE DOES, SHE DOES—THEY DO!
Never a bridesmaid, always a bride,
Liz Taylor confounds the skeptics
and marries workingman Larry Fortensky

The issue containing the exclusive pictures from Liz and Larry's wedding album quickly became one of the bestselling issues of the year, ironically placing third behind the covers featuring serial killer Jeffrey Dahmer and actor Michael Landon, after his death.

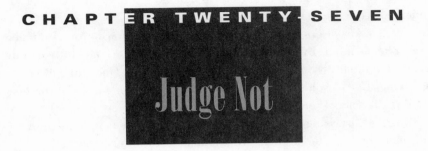

CHAPTER TWENTY-SEVEN

Judge Not

"The Clarence I had married was nowhere to be found. He was just
debilitated beyond anything I had seen in my life."

—*Justice Clarence Thomas's wife, VIRGINIA,*
in People *(November 11, 1991), after the Supreme Court nomination*
hearings and swearing-in ceremony

THE SAME YEAR that Liz married Larry, 1991, *People* had a string
of impressive exclusives: Oprah vowed that she would never diet again;
actor Paul Michael Glaser's wife, Elizabeth, described her family's
ordeal with AIDS; Stormin' Norman Schwarzkopf came back from the Gulf
and invited *People* into his home; Gene Wilder talked publicly for the first
time about the death of his wife, Gilda Radner; and Harriet Nelson talked
about the death of Ricky, her son. But nothing came close—in terms of
stirring controversy both inside and outside the magazine—to the *People*
cover story about the ordeal from which the new Supreme Court justice,
Clarence Thomas, had just emerged, as seen through the eyes of his wife,
Virginia.

It is doubtful there was anyone who was aware of the hearings following
Thomas's nomination who did not have a strong opinion about them one way
or another, after Thomas's former colleague Anita Hill accused him of sexual
harassment while he was her boss at the U.S. Department of Education and
the Equal Employment Opportunity Commission. Regardless of whose side
anyone was on, visions of pubic hairs on Coke cans and other graphic sexual
allusions were permanently etched into the American consciousness during

the three-day proceedings, as the world outside of the Senate hearing room remained riveted to its TV screens.

Thomas was sworn in on October 23, 1991, but the controversy lingered in everyone's mind. Even after the hearings ended, there was little certainty about what the truth was. Only one thing was absolute: One of the two parties was lying. But in spite of intense opinions one way or the other, no one— besides Clarence Thomas and Anita Hill—knew for certain which one.

It is not surprising that *People* wanted to hear from both of them. A story with more news value or compelling human interest—two of the key ingredients of a perfect *People* story—would be almost impossible to imagine. From the moment the bizarre tale began to unravel, the *People* staff started laying the groundwork for their attempt to get both sides of the story. Literally dozens of requests were made on behalf of *People*, asking Anita Hill to talk, but she steadfastly refused to grant any interviews. For the Thomas angle, the *People* editors decided to try a different approach. A reporter in the *People* bureau in Washington by the name of Jane Podesta was assigned to try to get Virginia Thomas, who had been at her husband's side throughout the hearings.

Requests for interviews emanating from the Washington bureau were often done via letter to the desired subject; Jane Podesta wrote to Virginia Thomas, laying out the details of her request. She asked her if she would like to tell her side of the story in *People*—to tell the magazine's readers what she and her husband had gone through during the hearings, what had gone on in their house and in their minds during the harrowing moments of the last few weeks. The letter was delivered to Thomas at the Commerce Department, where she worked as a lawyer. Podesta had a good source there, someone who worked closely with Virginia, who put in a good word for her after the letter was delivered.

Podesta heard from Virginia Thomas almost immediately. She called to say that she was leaning toward the interview, but she was nervous about it and had not yet made a final decision. Podesta herself had mixed feelings about the story. Anita Hill had refused to talk to the magazine, and Virginia was, after all, not a principal in the controversy. "We knew that she had no idea, that she was not even in the picture when Anita Hill was around," she says. "Unless he revealed the truth to her, she would not know whether the charges were correct, so it was just strictly from an historical vantage point that we wanted to find out what was going on. It is your prototype *People* magazine story about what's going on in someone's life, inside somebody's living room, when the world is falling apart. Any journalist has to be objective. There are a lot of stories that would never be done if you had to agree with everything you were doing the story on."

When Podesta heard from Virginia Thomas again, she learned that her subject had decided to go forward with the story; Jane was invited to her home in Kingstowne, Virginia, the next day. Things at the magazine began to percolate instantly. This was a story that could be very sticky—it was certainly fragile—much more so than your run-of-the-mill celebrity story.

In addition, the time made available to the magazine for taking pictures would be limited. M. C. Marden knew immediately that she wanted Harry Benson to photograph this one—among other qualities, he had the ability to get what he needed quickly. "I always choose Harry on the hardest stories that are probably going to allow the least amount of time," she explains. "Some photographers are very slow—they have to do test shots and look at the tests. Harry isn't like that. He can be in and out in half an hour. I had no idea what was going to happen with this story."

THERE WAS ONE minor problem, though. Harry Benson was in California in the midst of shooting a story on actor Kevin Costner. He would have to drop everything and fly to Washington immediately to shoot the Thomas story. Even then, he would have to do it separately from the interview, which was to take place the following day. As far as Harry Benson was concerned, that was better for him. He liked to work quickly, and he also preferred to work alone.

When Lanny Jones received the somewhat surprising news that Virginia Thomas had agreed to the story, he was hoping to make it a cover. That was not going to be easy, however, unless Clarence agreed to pose with his wife. M.C. called Jane Podesta and asked her if she thought there was any possibility that Clarence would pose for a cover shot. Jane forwarded the request to Virginia Thomas, telling her that the magazine would fly the well-known photographer Harry Benson in from the Coast to photograph them. Jane was certain the fact that Harry would come in for that sole purpose helped her cause, and indeed, Virginia had warmed to the idea. She told Jane that she thought that her husband would do it. M.C. had been astounded at the news. "I can't believe they've agreed to do this," she told Lanny. "This is incredible." Lanny was pleased, to say the least.

What happened after that was even more astonishing. Podesta arrived at the Thomas home expecting that she would have only a few minutes to conduct the interview. Virginia answered the door. She struck Jane as "very naïve and very shaken." They sat down at the kitchen table and Virginia

Thomas began to talk. And talk and talk. Jane just sat there and listened, as her tape machine recorded every word that was said. Three hours later, when Virginia had no more to say, Jane asked her again about the pictures. "Do you think we can get both of you together?"

"Yes, I think I can get Clarence."

"Are you sure?"

"Yeah, I think I can."

As she got ready to leave the Thomases' two-story, wood-frame house, Justice Clarence Thomas pulled into the driveway in his black 1989 Corvette and entered the house, shaking his head. "It's been brutal, just brutal," he said. "I don't know if it's over, but we found a way to survive. And we have each other." With that, Jane went home to transcribe the tape of the Virginia Thomas interview. Harry Benson would be there in the morning to take the pictures. By the time she left, Podesta was certain that Clarence Thomas would cooperate.

Still, as she listened to the transcribed tapes, it only helped to reinforce Jane's feeling that doing this particular story was not easy for her. "It was an uncomfortable thing," she recalls. "How could you turn down the interview? But it was sort of like walking into a minefield."

Indeed, Virginia Thomas had poured her heart out to Jane Podesta. The only good day they had had since the announcement of Clarence's nomination, she told Jane, was the first day, July 1, when President Bush had announced it in Kennebunkport, Maine. If they had known then what was about to happen, they never would have gone through it.

Virginia told Jane that she herself had been sexually harassed on one of her jobs; that Anita Hill's charges reminded her of the movie *Fatal Attraction;* that she believed Anita Hill was in love with her husband; that her husband had confided in her one sleepless night, "Virginia, they are trying to destroy me," and then he had asked, "Why are they trying to destroy me?"; that in the end they had gotten through the terrible crisis with the help of God—and friends from their Bible study group—shutting the kitchen blinds and turning on Christian praise music to survive.

Virginia told Podesta how she had called a neighbor who cut hair to come over and give her husband a haircut; how angry both she and Clarence had become; how he had finally decided to do things *his* way, eschewing the advice of the "handlers"; how she had worried that her husband's blood pressure would shoot up and he would have a stroke; and how he had just emerged from the shower when the vote making him the next Supreme Court justice was tallied. "You got fifty-two votes," she had told him. According to

Virginia, "It was the oddest thing. It was like, 'Okay, thanks.' It was as if it didn't matter anymore."

Harry Benson had made it a point to arrange for the Thomas pictures to be taken early in the morning. He had known exactly what he was doing. Although it never appeared that way, almost every single thing that Harry Benson did was entirely calculated for his purposes. "Early morning is usually a very good time to get people," he says, "and that's when I got Clarence Thomas. I got him at nine o'clock in the morning." Besides the fact that their defenses are down, Harry also believes that the less he has to do with his subjects both before and after the pictures are taken, the better. He wants the relationship between himself and his subjects to be confined completely to the taking of pictures, partly to conserve his own energy, and partly to avoid any preconceptions—or any afterthoughts about the pictures that have been taken. "I've made a point in my career of not doing it—I never see people before, during, or after an assignment. I don't want people to have time to think about what I have done.

"My main purpose," says Harry, "is just to come back with pictures and to get away as quickly as I can with it—not to waste time. Time is not everything with me, it's the only thing. Once you say, 'Well, I'll be back, I'll see you tomorrow,' that's usually a fatal error, because now they've got time to think about it. They can call their lawyer. They can discuss it with a friend. I never give people that opportunity."

Harry Benson had not known what to expect that late October morning when he arrived at the Thomas home to shoot the pictures. "My main purpose was to get a cover of him," he says, "and just as many pictures as I could. I thought it was just going to be a little snapshot at the door." But he wasted no time when he arrived at the house. The minute he walked in with Jon Delano, his assistant, Jon quickly began putting up the lights in the living room. Clarence Thomas was outside talking with the neighbors and Harry chatted briefly with Virginia while Delano continued doing everything that needed to be done in order to expedite the shoot. Before the Thomases had a chance to think, Harry turned to them and said, "A nice picture of the two of you together would be good," and he proceeded to shoot them together with their arms around each other, cheek to cheek, for the cover.

Moving swiftly, he continued the picture session exactly as he had planned. "I did it fast," he explains. "After the first shot of them together, I said, 'And I'll do one here, and that, and that, and *boom-boom-boom*.' And it was all over before they knew what the hell had hit them."

It was not at all surprising that Harry Benson's photographs were as controversial as the story that went with them: Harry got Virginia hugging Clarence for the cover. He got them sitting on their living room floor, and standing in their kitchen, sipping coffee. He got them on their living room couch, reading the Bible together. The pictures Harry Benson took of Clarence and Virginia Thomas told as much about the couple as the story itself.

Not everyone agreed with Lanny Jones's decision to run the Virginia Thomas story in *People*, but Jones never doubted his decision for a moment, even after it failed to be a blockbuster on the newsstand. It sold 1.6 million newsstand copies, putting it neither in the top ten bestsellers of the year, nor in the bottom.

Lanny was well aware of the fact that the decision for the cover of *People* was crucial: The swing of revenue from newsstand sales could amount to one million dollars gained or lost depending on what was chosen for the cover. Still, he defends the Clarence Thomas cover, which sold about average, to this day. "The staff was upset," says Lanny. "There was grumbling within the staff and a little bit outside the building. People were upset. Most people believed Anita Hill and were upset that we would publicize a viewpoint that said that Anita Hill was in love with Clarence Thomas. That was the wife's viewpoint. I published the story because it answered a question a lot of people were asking themselves throughout the testimony. They were hearing Clarence Thomas saying, 'This is a lynching,' and then we heard Anita Hill saying he was coming on to her. The question that a lot of people were asking themselves—I heard it again and again—was 'What does his wife think? What does she think when she hears this about her husband?'

"We all wondered what she thought, so we finally found out. We had an exclusive. We were the first people to interview her to find out what she thought. But a lot of people didn't want to hear what she thought. They didn't like what she thought, as it turned out. She thought that Anita Hill was in love with Clarence Thomas. I wasn't making a decision as to who was right or wrong, but I did want to be the person who had the story."

EXCLUSIVE
Virginia Thomas tells her story,
"How We Survived."
The wife of Clarence Thomas
describes the "hell" of the hearings,
her own experience with sexual harassment
and her belief that Anita Hill
"was probably in love with my husband."

Perhaps Washington bureau chief Garry Clifford best summed up the reaction to the Thomas cover—from the viewpoint of the media, at least. "A lot of people in Washington called me up and told me they thought it was the worst thing they had ever seen," she says, "and how sorry they were that they hadn't thought of it."

Regardless of what anybody thought, it was apparent that Lanny Jones was doing something right: 1991 was a very good year. Not only did the magazine's advertising and circulation reach all-time highs, but *People* passed *Time* magazine in advertising revenues for the first time, producing an estimated sixty-nine million dollars in ad revenues in the first quarter of the year alone. *People* had just become the number-one magazine in ad revenues in the entire magazine industry.

1992 COVERS

p Films: *Batman Returns*
Home Alone 2
Lethal Weapon 3
Sister Act
Wayne's World

car: *Unforgiven*

p TV Shows: *60 Minutes*
Roseanne
Murphy Brown
Cheers
Home Improvement

mys: *Murphy Brown*
Northern Exposure

p Songs: "Bohemian Rhapsody"—Queen
"I Will Always Love You"—Whitney
Houston
"Erotica"—Madonna
"November Rain"—Guns N' Roses
"Tears in Heaven"—Eric Clapton
"In the Still of the Nite"—Boyz II Men

ammys: "Tears in Heaven" (record)
"Tears in Heaven" (song)

stsellers: *The Pelican Brief*—John Grisham
Waiting to Exhale—Terry McMillan
Backlash—Susan Faludi

Diana: Her True Story—Andrew Morton
It Doesn't Take a Hero
—H. Norman Schwarzkopf
Sex—Madonna

Tonys: *Dancing at Lughnasa*

Crazy for You

Marriages: Warren Beatty + Annette Bening

Edward Kennedy + Victoria Reggie
Whitney Houston + Bobby Brown
Brigitte Bardot + Bernard d'Ormale
Roxanne Pulitzer + John Haggin
Sting + Trudie Styler
Princess Anne + Timothy Laurence

Divorces: Princess Anne & Marc Phillips
Barbara Walters & Merv Adelson
Tammy Faye & Jim Bakker
Prince Andrew & Fergie (separate)
Prince Charles & Diana (separate)

Deaths: Peter Allen   Isaac Asimov
Marlene Dietrich   Alex Haley
Anthony Perkins   Steven Ross
Eric Sevareid   Lee Salk
José Ferrer   Francis Bacon
Sandy Dennis   Stella Adler
Sam Kinison

NEWS

L.A. riots break out after not-guilty verdict in Rodney King trial

Mob boss John Gotti convicted of racketeering

Mike Tyson convicted of rape

Fighting breaks out in Yugoslavia between the nation's Serbs and Muslims

Indiscreet photos published in tabloid of Fergie and Texan John Bryan

Arthur Ashe reveals AIDS infection

Alistair Cooke retires from *Masterpiece Theatre* after twenty-two years

Jane Fonda announces retirement from acting

Hurricane Andrew devastates southern Florida, leaving sixty-one dead

Jay Leno picked as successor to Johnny Carson on *The Tonight Show*

The AIDS quilt displayed on the Mall in Washington, covering thirteen acres with twenty thousand quilts

Bill Clinton elected president

CHAPTER TWENTY-EIGHT

Capturing Clinton: An Earring Aid

"I had never stopped believing in God. I never stopped feeling better in those big churches in England. But it wasn't anything that guided my life. Religious faith for me now is sort of humbling and provides an incredible amount of protection. But for my faith, I don't know that I'd ever been able to forgive myself for the things I've done wrong in my life . . ."

—BILL CLINTON
in an interview with Lanny Jones in People *(July 20, 1992), shortly before his nomination as the Democratic candidate for president*

O N   A N   E A R L Y summer day in 1992, a few weeks before the Democratic convention that would nominate Bill Clinton as its candidate for president, Lanny Jones boarded a plane for Little Rock, Arkansas, with a tape recorder and a copy of his book, *Great Expectations*, in his briefcase. Being the managing editor of *People* did not allow him much time for this particular indulgence, but the reporter's bug had never left him, and every so often he would allow himself the luxury of reporting a story in which he had a special interest.

The last such story had featured Elizabeth Taylor, who spoke to Jones at her home in Los Angeles in late 1990 following her near-deadly bout with pneumonia. Now Hillary Clinton, whom he had met at a luncheon attended by a variety of magazine editors in New York a few months earlier, had impressed him as being so different from everything he had read about her that he wanted to interview her. "She seemed much more warm and humorous," Lanny recalls. "I really liked her personally and I kind of liked what she had to say. She was a completely different person than I had read about, so I wanted to do the story. I wanted to find out more about the person I *wasn't* reading about in the press."

The road toward the Democratic convention had been a rocky one for Hillary's husband, Arkansas Governor Bill Clinton. The accusation in February by a woman named Gennifer Flowers that she had had an affair with him had nearly toppled his roller-coaster campaign. *People* had covered that story with as much verve and gusto as the rest of the media, and the resulting commotion had helped to bring Hillary Clinton to the forefront—to be even more closely scrutinized by the public. She had stood solidly by her husband, appearing with him on the television show *60 Minutes,* where they had been honest and candid about the ups and downs of their marriage and about their love for each other.

Now, five months later, as the convention loomed dead ahead, it appeared that Bill had weathered that storm, among others. Although Lanny Jones's interest was in Bill Clinton's wife and not the candidate himself, he had not been able to convince the people who were running the Arkansas governor's campaign to agree to a story on Hillary alone. Mandy Grunwald, Clinton's chief media adviser, who also happened to be the daughter of the former longtime editor-in-chief of Time Inc., Henry Grunwald, had been instrumental in that decision.

Mandy certainly understood the power of *People*—she knew very well how much influence the magazine had and what an impact a *People* story could have, but she did not want a story on Hillary without Bill. She did not, she told Lanny, want Bill Clinton to appear to be standing in the shadow of his wife. If there were to be a Clinton story in *People*, it would have to be about both of them.

When Lanny heard this response, he held his ground. He tried very hard—with Kathy Berlin, a media adviser to the Clinton campaign who worked closely with Mandy Grunwald—to come to a compromise and salvage the cover. Through Berlin, he told Mandy Grunwald that he would not agree to a cover with Hillary and Bill Clinton. They came to a momentary impasse, but finally, after much negotiating, a satisfactory compromise was reached: It would be a cover story and it would include Bill Clinton—but it would also include their daughter, Chelsea, who had barely even been seen by the public and had never posed for a magazine cover before.

Lanny Jones arrived at the governor's mansion in Little Rock for the interview at the appointed time. He was greeted by Hillary Clinton and invited into the den, where the interview was to take place. The two of them chatted for about ten minutes, making small talk—saving the substantial conversation for the interview. When Bill Clinton failed to appear after a few more minutes went by, it occurred to Lanny that there might be some kind of problem. On the other hand, Clinton was a busy man, and it was certainly understandable that he might be tied up.

What Lanny did not know was that, at that very moment, Bill Clinton was standing in the kitchen of the governor's mansion, arguing with Mandy Grunwald—about the *People* interview, which he did not want to do. What he was telling her was that he wanted absolutely nothing to do with *People* magazine. She managed to change his mind, nonetheless, and the unhappy governor finally walked into the den for the interview.

From the moment Bill appeared, clad in his faded blue jeans, tennis shoes, and a polo shirt, Lanny knew that something was awry, but he had no idea what it could be. Clinton sauntered over to him glumly and reluctantly put out his hand.

"Hello, Governor," Lanny said, smiling politely. Clinton glowered back at Lanny and shook his hand limply, with an overpowering lack of enthusiasm. There was not even a hint of a smile on his face.

This was perplexing to Lanny Jones. "I had never seen a photograph of him in which he wasn't smiling," says Lanny, "looking up and happy—even when people were saying, 'Tell us about Gennifer Flowers.' He just always smiled when you asked him a question. He looked at me with a look that was sort of Elvis-like—he was looking up at me from under his eyes."

The editor of *People* magazine had no idea what to make of this strange behavior. The interview, after all, had been arranged beforehand with great care, but that seemed to have no bearing on the situation. It was obvious that something was terribly wrong. Clinton slumped unenthusiastically into the cushions of the couch, next to his wife, and Lanny proceeded with the interview, not knowing what else to do. Hillary was talkative and friendly, but regardless of the question, Bill Clinton's answer rarely exceeded one word.

"He was monosyllabic," says Lanny. "She'd give these long interesting answers, and he would say, 'Nope,' 'Nope,' 'Nope.' She and I are having this conversation and he's sitting there with a look on his face that made it obvious he was not pleased." The situation was embarrassingly awkward. Clinton's own people had insisted he be included, and now he was barely willing to utter a word.

Lanny remained confounded by this turn of events, but he forged on with the interview, desperately grasping for something—anything—that might lighten things up. He had already done plenty of homework on the Clintons—he had talked with several of their friends in Little Rock—and somebody had told him that the Clintons had been battling with Chelsea over whether or not she should pierce her ears. Struggling for some new common ground, or even an inch of friendly turf, Lanny decided to try a different tack. "I have a thirteen-year-old daughter," said Lanny (who also has another daughter and a son), "and I probably lost the battle over pierced ears. I wonder how you guys are doing?" There was a millisecond of silence, and then Bill Clinton laughed for the first time since Lanny Jones had laid eyes on him. He had clearly found a soft spot: the change in the governor was dramatic.

"I got one question that humanized things," Lanny said later, "and all of a sudden we were best buddies." The Mr. Hyde side of Bill Clinton disappeared, and he thereafter told Lanny Jones everything he had hoped for and more. What had started out as a nightmare turned into an editor's dream. "They talked about values and what they believed in," says Lanny. "The campaign had been so dominated by media sideshows that the Clintons had never really talked freely about who they were and what was important to them. It was an important interview after he finally warmed up."

Indeed, both of the Clintons were extremely forthcoming. They talked of their role as parents, how difficult it had been during the campaign, spending so much time away from Chelsea, and of course there was the answer to the question about the pierced ears: "We really held out against it," Hillary, laughing, told Lanny. "Well, we've walked back and forth on this. I don't have pierced ears, and her grandmothers don't." Bill corrected her: "One of her grandmothers doesn't." So now, they told Lanny, they had agreed not to talk about it until their daughter's thirteenth birthday. It had to do with more than just Chelsea's ears, they said. They did not want to rush their child into adulthood. "I feel strongly that children deserve to have some childhood and some innocence and time to accommodate to the world of adulthood," her mother told *People* magazine.

Lanny's piece gave a telling portrait of the family that would soon become the nation's First Family, with details that had never been reported before— the kinds of details Dick Stolley knew from the beginning that the magazine would have to deal with: sex, politics, religion, marriage, the intimate details of a person's life. The Clintons talked about their friends, their family, and their faith. They talked in depth about their daughter, who loved volleyball, softball, and ballet. They were vigilant about such things as what movies she saw—her only R-rated film had been *Lethal Weapon 3*. They were careful about television, as well. *Designing Women* and *Evening Shade*, produced by their close friends Linda Bloodworth Thomason and Harry Thomason, were among the few TV shows they allowed her to watch.

It was touching to hear Bill Clinton's reaction to the surprises his young daughter had provided him over the years, how startled he had been at times by the child who, he admitted, had inherited her mother's forthrightness. "One day when she was six I picked her up, and she said, 'Dad, do girls sometimes have babies when they are not married?' I said, 'It's not the right thing to do, but it happens sometimes.' I asked her if she wanted to talk about it, and she said, 'No, I just wanted to know.' "

Hillary explained that she followed the advice a friend had given her long ago: "You should answer every one of her questions, but don't go on like it's now the moment to tell her everything you want her to know for the next 30 years."

The story in *People* also revealed details of both Hillary and Bill's own families. Bill's father, William Blythe, had died in a car accident before he was born and he had taken the name of his first stepfather, Roger Clinton. His mother, Virginia, had been widowed three times, and lived sixty miles from her son, in Hot Springs, Arkansas. Hillary's parents, Dorothy and Hugh Rodham, had moved to Little Rock from the Chicago suburb where they had lived, to be closer to their daughter.

The interview shed light on Bill Clinton's profound interest in music and his proficiency on the saxophone, and the fact that their daughter's name had been suggested by the sixties song "Chelsea Morning," sung by Judy Collins. When Lanny asked which album he would save of his impressive record collection if his house caught fire and he could save only one, Bill said it would probably be Judy Collins's *Colors of the Day*, which contained the songs "My Father," "In My Life," "Both Sides Now," and "Amazing Grace."

Bill Clinton staunchly defended the "cookie controversy" that had recently surrounded Hillary. "It gave a totally false impression of who she was," he told Lanny. "She was defending her right to practice law and be the wife of a governor." Hillary and Bill Clinton talked openly to Lanny Jones about their own relationship, acknowledging the fact that their marriage had had rough spots and expressing gratitude to the friends who had helped get them through the hardest times. They did not avoid discussing the Gennifer Flowers incident, or their appearance on *60 Minutes* to confront the situation publicly. Lanny found out that, when the program aired, they had allowed Chelsea to watch it with them. At the end, Bill Clinton had asked his daughter, "What did you think?" Chelsea had replied, "I think I'm glad that you're my parents."

Clinton also spoke candidly about his renewed faith in the Baptist Church, which he had left when he was younger and had rejoined in 1980. "I had never stopped believing in God," he told Lanny. "I never stopped feeling better in those big churches in England. But it wasn't anything that guided my life. Religious faith for me now is sort of humbling and provides an incredible amount of protection. But for my faith, I don't know that I'd ever been able to forgive myself for the things I've done wrong in my life."

Before the interview was over, Jones gave the Clintons, who were baby boomers themselves, a copy of his book. By the time he was ready to leave, he was pleased with what he had gotten—little had been left unsaid. Still, he could not figure out what had caused Bill Clinton's initial strange behavior. As he walked out the door of the governor's mansion, before he climbed into the cab that was waiting to take him back to the airport, he could not resist the temptation to find out.

"Listen, what was with him?" he asked Richard Mintz, one of the campaign members who had helped set up the interview. "What was all that about at the beginning? Clinton was very unfriendly."

"Yeah, I noticed that," Mintz replied. "I saw that. You know, the governor had spent the last half hour before you got there arguing with Mandy Grunwald, telling her he didn't want to do the interview. She finally talked him into it."

"Oh," Lanny said, curious, "what was the problem?"

It was then that he finally learned what had prompted the puzzling behavior, and after he heard the reason, he understood: During the campaign and right after the Gennifer Flowers episode, a *People* reporter, traveling on an airplane with Hillary, had grilled her about the Flowers incident. Mintz told Lanny that Hillary felt that she had been pestered by the reporter. When she got off the plane, she had called her husband immediately. "What is this?" she had said to him. "*People* magazine just badgered me." Clinton had gotten furious about the episode and had never forgotten it.

"His protective instincts came out," explains Lanny, "and he did not want to talk to the magazine that he felt had upset his wife."

In the end, Bill Clinton emerged a winner in every regard. Harry Benson took the pictures of the family, and Chelsea appeared on her first magazine cover. His photographs revealed a side of the family never seen before: Bill Clinton the father hugging his teenage daughter; Hillary the wife and mother playing baseball in the backyard; the entire family curled up together in a backyard hammock; Bill and Hillary Clinton, kissing each other.

The *People* cover story on the Clintons by Lanny Jones ran the week of the Democratic convention in July 1992—the week that Bill Clinton won the Democratic nomination for president. Not only did the issue sell very well (more than 1,700,000 newsstand copies, which by then accounted for only 54 percent of the magazine's circulation), but during the week that it was on the newsstand, Clinton's public approval rating doubled.

After Clinton won the election in November, Hillary Clinton and Tipper Gore were on *People*'s cover, and that issue sold as well as the cover of the Clinton family had. The week of the inauguration in January 1993, Hillary Clinton finally appeared on the cover alone, and the new first lady was a smash hit—selling nearly two million copies on the newsstand and becoming the bestselling cover in nearly a year. For the moment, at least, the Clintons were on a roll.

1993

1993 COVERS

Famous Models, Dangerous Diets
Real-Life *Home Alone*
Hillary Clinton
Audrey Hepburn: 1929–1993
Whatever Happened to…Julia Roberts
Jane Seymour
Arthur Ashe, His Life, His Love, His Legacy
Elvis's Baby Girl: Lisa Marie Inherits His Estate
Fergie: the Ugly Truth
David Koresh
Eddie Murphy, on the Eve of His Wedding
Roseanne & Tom
Hollywood's Sexy Rebels
Diana on Her Own
Dying Young: Brandon Lee's Death
Teenage Plastic Surgery
50 Most Beautiful People
Hillary Clinton: The First 100 days
Stalked: Obsessed Fanatics Ruin Private Lives
Here's to *Cheers*
Barbra Streisand
Ted & Whoopi in Love
Shannen Doherty

Joan & Melissa Rivers
Burt & Loni's Breakup
Kelsey Grammer's Untold Story
Julia Roberts's Wedding Album
The Battle Over Jessica
Here Come the Brides!
Meg Ryan
Katie Couric
JFK, Jr., and Daryl Hannah
Heidi Fleiss: Beverly Hills Madam
Richest Women in Showbiz
Di vs. Charles: The Battle for the Boys
Loni vs. Burt
Supermodel Kate Moss
Christian Slater
Fabio
Shannen's Secret Wedding
Cindy Crawford & Richard Gere
Best- and Worst-Dressed
The Return of David & Shaun Cassidy
Loni Anderson's New Love
River Phoenix, Dead at 23
At Home with Mariah Carey
Michael Jackson Cracks Up
Diana's Lonely Battle

Top Films: *Jurassic Park*
The Fugitive
The Firm
Sleepless in Seattle
Mrs. Doubtfire

Top TV Shows: *60 Minutes*
Roseanne
Home Improvement
Murphy Brown
Murder, She Wrote

Emmys: *Seinfeld*
Picket Fences

Top Songs: "Dreamlover"—Mariah Carey
"Can't Help Falling in Love"—UB40
"Whoomp!"—Tag Team
"If"—Janet Jackson
"Runaway Train"—Soul Asylum
"Right Here"—SWV

Bestsellers: *The Bridges of Madison County*
—Robert James Waller
The Client—John Grisham
Like Water for Chocolate—Laura Esquivel
The Fifties—David Halberstam
The Way Things Ought to Be
—Rush Limbaugh
Women Who Run with the Wolves
—Clarissa Pinkola Estés

Tonys: *Angels in America: Millennium Approaches*
Kiss of the Spider Woman
Anna Christie

Marriages: Julia Roberts + Lyle Lovett
Japan's Crown Prince Naruhito
+ Masako Owada
Eddie Murphy + Nicole Mitchell
Mary Courtney Kennedy + Paul Hill
Alec Baldwin + Kim Basinger
Shannen Doherty + Ashley Hamilton
Spike Lee + Tanya Lewis
Tammy Faye Bakker + Roe Messner
Geena Davis + Renny Harlin
Michelle Pfeiffer + David Kelley

Divorces: Burt Reynolds & Loni Anderson
Tatum O'Neal & John McEnroe
Ted & Cassandra Danson

Deaths:

Arthur Ashe	Alexis Smith
Cesar Chavez	Audrey Hepburn
Pat Nixon	Richard Diebenkorn
Marian Anderson	Helen Hayes
Lillian Gish	Ray Sharkey
Thurgood Marshall	Brandon Lee
Conway Twitty	Norton Simon
Roy Campanella	Sammy Cahn
Dizzy Gillespie	Rudolf Nureyev
William Golding	

NEWS

- Islamic terrorists bomb New York's World Trade Center, killing six people
- Cult leader David Koresh and followers beseiged in Waco, Texas
- Mia Farrow charges Woody Allen with child molestation in custody battle
- Two of the four defendants in the Rodney King federal civil rights trial found guilty
- After eleven years, the TV hit *Cheers* has its last call
- David Letterman leaves NBC for late night on CBS
- Kim Basinger ordered to pay $7.4 million in damages for failing to appear in *Boxing Helena*
- Summer rains flood the Midwest, killing at least twenty-five people
- Earthquake in India kills thirty thousand people
- Ruth Bader Ginsburg becomes the second woman to sit on the Supreme Court
- Brothers Erik and Lyle Menendez tried for the slaying of their parents in Beverly Hills
- Autumn firestorms ravage hundreds of thousands of acres in southern California
- Joey Buttafuoco admits to having an affair with teenager Amy Fisher and is convicted of
      statutory rape

CHAPTER TWENTY-NINE

When Julia Married Lyle: The Case of the (Potentially) Purloined Pictures

"What women look for in a man he's got in spades. He's sweet, kind and gentle and really a catch. And I bet you he'd do anything to make a woman happy."

—SANDY LOVEJOY,
a longtime acquaintance of Lyle Lovett, about the man who married Julia Roberts (as quoted in People, *July 12, 1993)*

A LOT HAD happened in Julia Roberts's life since Gail Cameron Wescott had lunched with her mother in Atlanta when *Pretty Woman* catapulted her to superstardom in 1990—all of which turned out to be very profitable for *People* magazine. There was her passionate romance with Kiefer Sutherland, to whom she became engaged in 1991, resulting in a "Julia In Love" cover that February; her passionate split from Kiefer in July resulted in a "Julia Roberts: The Big Break-up" cover. After that—and during her subsequent relationship with actor Jason Patric—she avoided the limelight, maintaining a low public profile, but she had sold so well on covers that in February 1993 *People* put her on another cover, asking "Whatever happened to . . . Julia Roberts?"

Not long after that, everyone found out. The rumors began to surface in the middle of July, when Lanny Jones and M. C. Marden both happened to be away on vacation. Beth Filler, who was sitting in for M.C. in the picture department, spotted a small item in a gossip column indicating that Julia Roberts had shown up at one of singing star Lyle Lovett's concerts dressed as a man—purportedly because he was singing the song "Stand by Your Man" from the popular film *The Crying Game* that night.

Being the meticulously thorough and cautious photo editor that she was,

Filler decided that it would behoove the *People* photo department to send a photographer to Lovett's next concert—which would take place in the small town of Noblesville, outside Indianapolis, the following weekend—just in case Roberts decided to show up again. The soundness of Filler's decision to send a photographer was confirmed when the rumor that Julia Roberts and Lyle Lovett were actually dating each other became more persistent over the next few days. Filler conferred with a colleague, assistant photo editor Mindy Viola, and they agreed they had exactly the right person to shoot the concert: His name was Steve Kagan, he was an excellent photographer, experienced and reliable, and he lived in Chicago, which was within driving distance of Indianapolis.

Kagan was out walking his dog that first Friday night in July when his beeper went off. Back at his house, he found out that the call was from Mindy Viola at *People*. It did not sound like a big deal to him. She wanted him to cover a concert that weekend, on Sunday night, by a singer named Lyle Lovett. Rumor had it, Mindy told him, that Lovett was dating Julia Roberts. She had shown up at his last concert but nobody had gotten pictures of them. Even if Julia did not show up at this one, they thought they ought to have some current pictures of Lyle Lovett.

Kagan had never even heard of Lyle Lovett. He wrote down his name on the notepad in front of him and got the spelling of it completely wrong. Yes, he told Mindy, he could cover the concert, but he would have to be back home in Chicago on Monday because he had a doctor's appointment. That did not appear to be a problem, Mindy said. Little did he know then that he would never make it.

Around the same time that Friday night, the vacationing M. C. Marden got a call in the Berkshires in western Massachusetts from Charlie Leerhsen, the senior editor in charge of show business stories at *People*. "We think they're going to get married," Leerhsen told M.C. "Are we under control about getting pictures at the Lovett concert?"

"Let me check," M.C. told Leerhsen. It was eleven o'clock at night by then and she called Mindy Viola. "Are you all set?" she asked Mindy. "Is Steve Kagan going to do it? Because there's this rumor—ha, ha, ha—that they're going to get married."

"Oh, yes," Mindy said. "Steve Kagan's on the case."

"Okay," said M.C. "I'll go to bed and you go to bed and we'll laugh about this on Monday."

The first thing Kagan did after he told Viola that he would cover the concert was to go to the nearest record store, where he bought one of Lovett's tapes. He figured he could listen to it on the drive to Indianapolis. If he was going to photograph the guy, he should be at least a little bit familiar with his music. He arranged to meet the reporter assigned to the story, Janna Wilson, who was a stringer from Indianapolis, the next day at the hotel she suggested in Noblesville. When they met there the following afternoon, they left her car and took Steve's station wagon to the concert.

Janna had already arranged in advance for their credentials to cover the concert: They always carried their general press credentials, but they would need a photo pass for Steve and backstage passes for both of them. It had not been a problem at all—the Lovett concert was not even close to being sold out. When they got stuck in a traffic jam on the way to the concert, Janna was glad she had taken care of everything in advance, because they barely made it to the box office in time. That is when they heard the news: "Sorry," the woman at the box office told them. "All the photo passes have been canceled—they just got married."

Steve Kagan stood there at the window of the box office and thought for a moment. He did not know exactly what to do. What he did know was that the magnitude of this story had just changed drastically. If Julia Roberts had just gotten married, she would probably be there at the concert that night, not far from where he was standing at that very moment; he had better find a way to take some pictures. He asked the woman at the box office about the availability of press tickets. "No, there are no press tickets," she told him. "You can buy a ticket if you want to." Steve and Janna bought two tickets as close to the stage as they could get.

Just as they had finished paying for their tickets, they heard someone paging "Wilson." The voice was calling out "Wilson! Wilson!" and Janna replied, "I'm Janna Wilson from *People*."

"No, no," said the man responsible for the paging, who was from the Chicago office of MCA, Lovett's record company. "I was looking for another Wilson." Janna took advantage of the mix-up to explain the problem of the photo passes. The man from MCA could not fix *that*, but he arranged to get them two complimentary concert tickets, and they got a refund for those they had bought.

At that point, Janna went to a pay phone just outside the gate of the Deer Creek Music Center to try to call the MCA office in New York to see what she could find out. She knew there must be *some* way they could get around this problem of inaccessibility. After all, they were from *People* magazine, the wedding was big news, and Lovett was about to give a concert—the first since he had gotten married to one of the most popular actresses in the world. All Kagan and Wilson wanted to do was to get inside and do their work.

While Janna was on the phone, Steve went inside to use the men's room, where he again ran into the man who worked for MCA in Chicago. He took the opportunity to ask his advice about how he should deal with the photo problem. "Look," the guy from MCA said, pointing at the satchel he held in his hand, "I've got my briefcase here. I've got a camera in my briefcase. Security is really lax here. Just wave your press pass if you have to. Go in and tell them you're official and shoot."

He was telling Kagan to make his own way, to take his own chances—to use his general press pass, which he always had on him as a photographer, to make it appear that he had been sanctioned to shoot pictures. "Once you're inside," the guy from MCA told him, "you're on your own."

The advice sounded plausible to Kagan. He had done this many times before. "That's the way these things are handled sometimes at these concerts," he later explained. "You don't know who's in charge. The guy from Lovett's record company said basically, 'Do what you gotta do.' To me, that's an invitation. I walked in with my camera bag, went back out, got Janna, told her what he said. I took my camera bag on my shoulder. My camera bag is probably nine-by-nine-by-eighteen inches. It's not small and it's got stuff hanging out all over it. It's black. It's obvious what it is. You look at it and you say, 'That's full of camera equipment.' I walked in with it and nobody said anything. I went in and took my seat."

The concert hall was not very crowded. Rosanne Cash opened the show, and Kagan felt that he was one of the only people watching her. No one seemed the least bit interested in Johnny Cash's daughter, but Kagan sat and listened, eyeing the seats in front of him. He pulled out one of his cameras discreetly, and moved forward to an empty seat that would give him a better shot of the stage during intermission. Then he sat and watched Rosanne Cash with his camera on his lap, loaded and ready to shoot.

Julia Roberts appeared on the stage still dressed in her wedding gown to introduce her new husband without any warning at all. When Steve perceived this unexpected vision before him, he automatically raised his camera to his eye and managed to get a few shots of the two of them together. It was as close to a wedding picture as he would get. He was not shooting with a flash of any kind and no one seemed to notice a thing. As the concert went on, Kagan shot some more. Slowly and quietly, he inched his way forward, finding empty seats.

The concert was nearing an end when Julia reappeared. Kagan had been hoping she would come back, and he felt lucky—there she was again, up there on the stage with Lyle. He noticed right away that she had changed her dress. The newlyweds began to sing a duet, and the audience went crazy—they were among the first outsiders to see Julia Roberts with her new spouse.

He shot as fast as he could. Everyone was standing now, including Kagan, shooting his pictures above the crowd. He had taken around six rolls of black-and-white film when he decided to shoot some color. Making his way back to his seat, he reloaded his camera with the color film that he wanted.

He had just shot the first few frames of it when the security guard appeared. "You can't be shooting pictures here," the guard told Kagan, who proceeded to tell the guard that he was from *People* magazine, hoping that he could explain the whole thing away and the guard would just drop it and leave him alone.

"No," the guard said to him, "you got to come with me." Kagan went with him, assuming that he was about to be thrown out of the concert, but that is not exactly what happened. Instead, he was swiftly escorted into a back room of the concert hall. As he sat there, several conservatively dressed men in dark suits appeared and began to grill him. Kagan did not know who the men were, perhaps representatives of Julia Roberts or Lyle Lovett, he thought. "How'd you get in?" they asked. "How did you get your cameras in?" "Why were you taking pictures?" "Who are you?"

Kagan tried to explain the situation. He told the men that he had been advised by someone from MCA to make his own way, that he could take pictures if he could manage to get away with it on his own. He still had the business card the man from MCA in Chicago had given him back in the men's room, which one of the men took from him and never returned. "We don't care," the man told Steve Kagan. "He doesn't have the authority to do that. *We* do and you're going to have to give us your film." As the man spoke, the others with him became more agitated.

Kagan remained calm. He did not budge. He sat on the sofa where he had been sitting for more than an hour by then, and replied, "No, I can't do that."

"Okay," the man in the suit said, "we're going to have to call the sheriff."

Within moments the officer from the Hamilton County Sheriff's Department, Lieutenant Gelhausen, appeared in his uniform, with his badge gleaming blindingly off his chest and a very conspicuous weapon in his holster. He listened while the situation was calmly explained to him. No voices were raised. Steve Kagan sat quietly on the sofa with his arm around his camera bag, which was at his side. He pondered the situation. No one had prohibited him from coming in with his camera bag. They could have asked him to leave if he was disobeying the rules and he would have, but taking his property was a different matter.

The officer from the sheriff's department left for a moment to call the county prosecutor. When he returned, he said, "Well, I'm going to take the film into evidence and we'll let a judge decide it." Kagan's mind was racing as he sat on the sofa, staring into the gun belt of the lieutenant, who was six-feet-two and telling him he had to take his film. The thought of looking down the barrel of the formidable gun dangling so conspicuously from his belt was what finally inspired him to let the officer have the film. Well, it's time to give it up, he thought to himself.

"Could you inventory this?" he asked the officer as politely as he could. The sheriff's officer took the film and began to write down on the envelope everything Steve Kagan had turned over to him. It had occurred to Kagan as he was giving the sheriff his film that he could keep a roll, try to conceal it, but he decided that it was not worth it. He really did not want to spend the night in jail. As the sheriff listed the inventory of Kagan's confiscated possessions on the envelope, Kagan noticed that the men in the suits were poking through his cameras to make sure that nothing was left. "Wait a minute," he said to them. "At this point, this is between me and the officer of the law, not you guys. You don't have any right to look through my things."

After Steve had finally given up his film, the sheriff offered to give him a ride to his car. Everyone else had long since left, and the open-air concert hall was deserted. It was dark and quiet outside, and when they got to the car, Janna Wilson was waiting for him, oblivious to what had just happened or where he had been. Kagan got out, looked at the sheriff, and said, "The lawyers are going to have a good time with this."

M. C. Marden got back to New York from her Berkshire vacation late Sunday night around the time Steve Kagan and the lieutenant from the sheriff's department had parted company. She was sound asleep at two o'clock in the morning when the ringing of her telephone woke her. It was Kagan calling from his hotel in Noblesville, Indiana.

"M.C.," he said, "this is Steve. I was shooting the Lyle Lovett concert and Julia appeared, but the police took my film. Can you get to the lawyers tomorrow? . . . I don't think they should have my film."

M.C. called *People*'s lawyer, Nick Jollymore, as soon as she could reach him the next morning and they discussed what had happened. She also called Carol Wallace, who was filling in for Lanny Jones. They all applauded Steve Kagan's response. "That was the magic of having an experienced *People* photographer there," she explains. "Had it been somebody else, they would have given the film away. Steve is a really ethical guy and he said, 'I'm not going to give you the film.' " Still, *People* was not in possession of those pictures of Julia Roberts and Lyle Lovett and the magazine was more than a little anxious to get them back.

Wallace wanted to meet with M.C. and Jollymore to find out the potential repercussions of any action the magazine might take. "We can do one of two things," Jollymore told them. "We can give up the film, or we can go to court." In nearly twenty years, it was the first time this had happened at *People*. Nick told them what he thought the chances were of winning the case, and what the financial repercussions would be. There was not enough time for Wallace to reach Lanny, with whom she would consult later. As acting managing editor of *People*, she decided that they should go after the film.

That same day, at a departmental lunch in the private dining room on the second floor of the Time & Life Building, Jollymore discussed the matter with his colleagues from the Time Warner legal department. Harry Johnston, the general counsel for Time Warner, encouraged him to go forward with a lawsuit to retrieve the film. Harry Johnston had had a lot of experience with similar cases. He knew which ones were worth pursuing and which ones were not. In 1978, he had been involved in the Ludtke case against the Yankees, in which Yankee Stadium would not allow Melissa Ludtke, a female reporter for *Sports Illustrated,* into the all-male locker room. Time Inc. had won that case, and another one involving a reporter covering the Mike Tyson trial for *Sports Illustrated* in Indiana, in which Time claimed the reporter was being deprived of his First Amendment rights. As it happened, Indiana, where the Lovett case had occurred, was a strong state on First Amendment rights.

Harry Johnston felt this case involving Kagan's confiscated film was a winner. As they sat around the lunch table, he said, "Come on, Nick, sue the bastards! Strike! Come on, Nick, do it!" By that afternoon, *People* went forward full force to recapture the pictures of Julia Roberts and Lyle Lovett that had been taken by—and from—Steve Kagan.

It was Monday afternoon, however, when the decision to go to court was made, which left very little time in terms of *People*'s closing deadline. The pictures of Julia's wedding were as hot as any pictures could be, but only if they made it into the issue that would close on Wednesday; otherwise it would be too late. That meant the case would have to be heard in court and decided in *People*'s favor in the next twenty-four hours if the pictures were going to get into the magazine.

Jollymore hired a lawyer in Indianapolis, Robert Johnstone, an expert on cases dealing with First Amendment issues who had handled cases for Time Warner in Indiana before. As soon as he received the call from Jollymore, Robert Johnstone got in touch with Steve Kagan.

That Monday morning, Kagan had gotten up in Noblesville and driven to Marion, a few miles away, to take some pictures of the church where Lovett and Roberts had gotten married. When he heard from Robert Johnstone, he immediately drove over to the law offices of Barnes & Thornburg in Indianapolis where Johnstone was a partner. They talked at length and Kagan told the lawyer everything he could about what had transpired. He was still wearing the jeans and shirt he had worn to shoot the concert the night before. When he had left for the assignment, he had not planned to stay more than a day, knowing that he had his doctor's appointment on Monday. He would, he told Johnstone, be happy to run down to a clothing store and buy a shirt and tie if they were going to court.

"No, no," Johnstone told him. "It'll be fine. I don't think I'm going to put you on the stand."

Kagan began to get it. "I think he liked the idea that I was looking sort of blue collar and a working guy," he says. Steve Kagan sat there in the law office of Johnstone and signed the necessary documents. He used the telephone while the paperwork was drawn up. Johnstone wanted the case to be heard in federal court. In order for that to happen, he had to establish that the film taken from Kagan was worth more than fifty thousand dollars to the magazine. Although there was no formal way to establish the absolute value of the film, there was little doubt that it was worth at least that much to *People*, given the revenue Julia Roberts covers had consistently brought to the magazine.

Johnstone's biggest problem was time. The pictures in question needed to be returned right away or they would no longer be of value. "Usually in a lawsuit these things take months," he explains, "and our problem was that we had to immediately gain possession. We wanted a court order delivering the property to us."

The case boiled down to the question of who would get the film that Kagan had shot: Lyle Lovett or *People* magazine. After Johnstone got finished with the other two parties, Deer Creek Music Center and the Hamilton County Sheriff's Department, neither one wanted any part of it anymore. "When I first learned of this, I called the sheriff and said, 'I want the film,' and they wouldn't do anything," says Johnstone, "and then I said, 'You took film from somebody, you did it, you have no criminal proceedings against that person, and you have no court order, no civil proceedings. What right in the world do you have to our property? Keep in mind that that film could be worth millions of dollars because of the difference a cover can have in the sales of the magazine.' His reaction was to take that film immediately to Deer Creek and ditch it out the window."

Thanks to Johnstone, the film turned into an equally hot potato for the Deer Creek Music Center. By the time he finished making *People*'s position perfectly clear, they also wanted nothing to do with the film. "Now Deer Creek's lawyers said, 'Okay, here we are with this film, we don't want it but Lyle Lovett wants it and Time wants it and Steve Kagan wants it. What do we do with it?' " explains Johnstone. "Deer Creek's lawyer said to me, 'We have the film, you want it, Lyle Lovett wants it, we don't know who to give it to, we're going to put it in the court tomorrow.' They filed a suit basically saying that they would physically take the film to court."

It was eight o'clock on Monday night before Johnstone learned that the film would be physically placed in the possession of the court on the following day. The clock was perilously ticking away. Between eleven o'clock and noon on Tuesday, *People*'s lawsuit was formally filed in federal court. "We claimed to the court that the film was the property of Steve Kagan—and Time Warner, because it was to be the recipient of the film," say Johnstone. "We asked the court to order that the possession of the film be delivered to us immediately. Lyle Lovett took the position that, because the photographs were of him, he had a right to control the publication of those photographs."

Meanwhile, back at the *People* offices, the tension was building. It was Tuesday afternoon, pressing in close on the deadline for the week's issue, and there were still no Julia Roberts pictures. The case would not be heard until late that afternoon, and nobody could know for sure how it would come out.

It was around that time on Tuesday that Jack Kelley and M. C. Marden, back from vacation, learned that there *were* indeed pictures of Julia Roberts's wedding to Lyle Lovett—beautiful wedding pictures, and plenty of them— Julia's own pictures, in fact, taken by a photographer named Peter Nash. But *People* representatives could not get their hands on them because of Julia Roberts's publicist, Nancy Seltzer. Seltzer was not only in possession of Julia's wedding pictures, she was also in complete control of them. When she had heard about Steve Kagan's pictures, she had wanted to be in control of them too, and that is where the trouble had begun. M.C. was caught in the middle.

"When it became known to Nancy that Steve had taken these pictures," M.C. says, "this was after he had been detained, Nancy Seltzer then started to make this deal: 'If you'll let us have Steve's pictures, let us *see* his pictures, I'd be more than willing to let you have them, but I want to go over them to make sure that, if you use it on the cover, it's a nice picture.' We said to her, 'No way. These are our pictures. We're not going to have an assignment shot by *People*, give you the film, and have you edit our film.' "

What was happening with Julia Roberts's publicist reflected a problem for *People* that had grown to giant proportions over the years: The publicists who handled the biggest stars wanted complete control. They wanted picture approval. They wanted copy approval. They wanted to control every word or image in the media related to their clients, virtually removing the freedom the press had to control its own material. For *People*, this was totally unacceptable.

If Nancy Seltzer could not control which pictures of Julia would be published, she was refusing to allow *People* to publish any pictures at all. Still, Jack Kelley, the L.A. bureau chief, persisted, continuing the dialogue with Seltzer there. *People* was not going to give up on the sanctioned pictures of Julia Roberts's wedding that Peter Nash had taken without a fight.

While Kelley was conversing with Seltzer in L.A., Steve Kagan entered the cavernous marble-and-wood federal courthouse in Indianapolis, where his case would be heard by Judge Sarah Barker to determine if his pictures of Julia Roberts and Lyle Lovett would be returned to him. And while these two dramas were being played out simultaneously, a third factor was added to the equation. M. C. Marden received a call from someone in Houston, Texas, who had attended Julia Roberts's wedding—with an offer to sell photographs from the wedding to *People* for a very hefty price.

"All of a sudden these pictures show up and they wanted a lot of money for them," says M.C. "So Steve's in court, Nancy's on the phone in L.A., and we send a stringer we have in Houston to look at the wedding pictures. The guy in Houston is looking at the pictures and describing them to me. By this time it's seven-thirty in New York. He gives me the description, I go in and talk to Lanny, who is back from vacation by now. There was one good picture, and Lanny and Carol and I were talking about whether or not it was worth it. I have put the guy in Houston on hold. We're in Lanny's office, the phone rings, and it's Jack Kelley. Jack Kelley said, 'Nancy Seltzer has changed her mind, we can have the official wedding pictures.' Lanny said, 'Quick! Leave, M.C.! Go call Nancy Seltzer and make the deal!' " The pictures in Houston had just lost their chance to appear in *People*.

What Lanny, M.C., and Carol Wallace did not know at that moment— and what Nancy Seltzer had just found out—was that only seconds earlier the judge in Indianapolis had ruled in favor of *People* magazine and Steve Kagan, which meant Steve would get his film back. Seltzer's reaction puzzled M.C. somewhat anyway. "I don't know what she thought Steve took," she says, "but I think she thought that he had the world's best pictures of Julia Roberts."

Kagan had appeared in court in front of Judge Barker, clad in his jeans and a short-sleeved shirt, which he still felt slightly embarrassed about, even though Johnstone had wanted him to look precisely the way he looked. Barker was a highly respected judge, a woman who appeared to be in her fifties. As is customary in the courtroom, everyone had risen when the judge had entered, and when they sat down, she started by saying, "First, I want to thank you all for providing me with some good dinner conversation for the Barker household tonight." That had made Kagan feel easier right away. "I knew we were dealing with a human being here," he says, "and also someone who had a little levity about the whole deal who is going to give us a fair hearing."

As Kagan sat there in the witness box he saw his film for the first time since it had been confiscated from him: It was in a big paper grocery bag on another counsel's table, and the bag was covered with signatures and writing, denoting the different places it had been since it had been taken away. "At one point," he says, "we took a recess when the judge went out to decide her ruling and everybody left. The bag of film was sitting there, and I whispered to my lawyer, 'We should grab it and go!' It was tempting."

Kagan did not abscond with the film, however. He spent nearly an hour on the witness stand that day, and after the judge returned from the recess with her decision, he was glad that he had done everything he had done.

The question the judge had to weigh was whether Kagan and *People* had the right to the photographs of Lyle Lovett (and Julia Roberts) that had been taken at his concert: "Under Indiana law, the unauthorized use of photographs of a person for commercial purposes is an invasion of his right to privacy and is actionable," the judge said in her decision. But commercial purposes, the judge explained, meant the use of photographs to make things such as T-shirts or belt buckles.

"In general, when a person's picture is used to illustrate a non-commercial newsworthy article, his interest in the use of his likeness or image must be evaluated in light of constitutional interests found in the First Amendment," she stated. " 'Newsworthiness' is a First Amendment, Freedom of Press, interest and is to be broadly construed ... In this matter the 'newsworthiness' of the images depicted on the films has primacy over any privacy rights which Lovett may have in those images."

The key to the judge's decision was this paragraph:

> Lovett and Roberts are widely known celebrities and in that sense are public figures and, in addition, their appearance on stage before thousands of people on the day of their highly publicized but theretofore unannounced and private wedding ceremony, with Roberts still wearing her wedding dress, was a newsworthy event of widespread public interest ...

Steve Kagan's film was his again. He had no idea at that point that Nancy Seltzer would give Julia's wedding pictures, those taken by Peter Nash, to *People* magazine for that very reason, in spite of the fact that nobody even knew exactly what Kagan's pictures were, because the film had not been developed yet. The saga, however, was not over. While the judge was out of the courtroom making her decision, Kagan had checked on the last possible flight that could get his film to New York if he won. It was at seven-thirty that night. The latest flight out of Indianapolis—the only one that would work—went into Newark airport in New Jersey, and it was already six-thirty when Judge Barker came back with her decision. The minute Kagan knew he had won, he asked if someone could drive his car to the airport or show him how to get there, since he was not familiar with the territory. It was rush hour, and he had only moments if he were going to get the film onto the flight—

certainly not a moment to spare. An associate lawyer at Johnstone's law firm offered to give him a ride to the airport, but when he arrived at the airline ticket counter to ship the film, there was a note from Robert Johnstone awaiting him: "New York called and they want you to take the film, don't ship it."

Kagan did not think twice. He bought a ticket and told the lawyer to put his car in the garage at the airport, he would have to leave it there while he went to New York. Then he boarded the plane to Newark, still wearing his jeans and his short-sleeved shirt, carrying his little but notorious bag of film, rushing toward *People*'s closing deadline.

Not only was the flight to Newark dreadfully late, but when Kagan arrived at the Newark airport at one o'clock in the morning he learned that there was a taxicab strike, which meant he would have to take a bus to New York. It was so late when he arrived at the bus terminal in Manhattan that he called Giovanna Breu, the Chicago bureau chief, to find out if she knew what he should do next. "There's nobody at Time Warner to take the film to, so you're supposed to go find a hotel and bring it in on Wednesday morning," she told him. After a few calls he found that the places he usually stayed were full, so he checked into the first available room he could get, which was at the Waldorf Astoria, only blocks from the Time & Life Building.

In the morning, Steve Kagan put on the same clothes for what he hoped would be the last time, and walked over to the Time & Life Building with his film. When he arrived, M.C. was on the phone with Nancy Seltzer; it was then that Steve Kagan found out about the pictures of Julia's wedding taken by Peter Nash. "My pictures were of value in getting those pried loose," he says, "but all of a sudden their value, in terms of a story, diminished. They were important pictures because they were the only pictures of the two of them together, right after they got married—but they came up with all these wedding pictures of Julia barefoot in the church and all that stuff, which are much better picture-wise and for the story, but didn't help my cause any."

As it turned out, it had not been easy for M.C. to get her hands on the wedding pictures. After she had negotiated the deal with Peter Nash (for a very reasonable amount of money), Nancy Seltzer informed her that the pictures themselves were in Nashville. "Nancy!" M.C. had said to her, "It's nine o'clock Tuesday night!"

"Well," Seltzer had replied, "we must be able to figure out a way." Ken Regan, one of *People*'s best photographers, was shooting the still photography on the film *The Pelican Brief* in Nashville and he graciously came to the rescue, using his expertise to get the pictures rushed to New York. "It really wouldn't have worked if Ken Regan hadn't been there," says M.C. "God was on our side."

In spite of the fact that only one of Steve Kagan's pictures—taken of Julia and Lyle when she had first gotten on the stage in her wedding dress to introduce him—was used in the issue of the magazine about the wedding, he emerged a hero. Even he admits that the outcome was "a little bit" depressing for him, but he was happy for the welcome he got when he showed his face at the *People* offices on Wednesday morning, finally arriving with his film. He was invited to the eleven o'clock staff meeting. "There were probably forty-five to fifty editors sitting around in this room with the speakerphone connecting them to all the bureaus," he says. "I was introduced to this meeting—I'm still in my jeans with my short-sleeved shirt and they asked me to speak!"

After an engaging summary of the events of the last three action-packed days, Steve Kagan left the Time & Life Building for the airport, once more, where he got back on a plane to Indianapolis. When he landed he retrieved his car from where the associate lawyer had left it for him and drove back to his home in Chicago, changing his clothes at last.

The *People* issue with Julia Roberts's wedding pictures instantly became the bestselling issue of the year. *People* was a double winner.

EPILOGUE
Things Change

MIA FARROW began seeing Woody Allen in 1980, six years after she appeared on the first cover of *People*. She has eleven children, two of them adopted by Allen, another, their natural son, Satchel. In 1993, Farrow won a bitter custody fight for the children when she learned that Allen had been having an affair with her adopted Korean daughter, Soon-Yi Previn. The last film Farrow did with Allen was *Husbands and Wives*.

SHEILAH GRAHAM died in 1988 at the age of eighty-four. The last book she wrote, *The Late Lily Shiel*, was an autobiography of her early years, published in 1978.

BURT REYNOLDS and Loni Anderson adopted a son, Quinton. Five years after their wedding, they became enmeshed in one of the fiercest and most publicly vitriolic divorce battles in Hollywood history.

DINAH SHORE lives in Palm Springs, California. The Nabisco–Dinah Shore golf tournament is still played every year at nearby Rancho Mirage. She was seventy-six years old in March 1993.

SHANA ALEXANDER has written eight books since 1975, including the bestselling *Very Much a Lady* about Jean Harris, the convicted murderer of Dr.

Herman Tarnower, and *When She Was Bad*, the story of the Bess Myerson scandal. Her daughter, Kathy, died in 1987.

GRETA GARBO died in 1990 at the age of eighty-four.

BROOKE SHIELDS has appeared on *People*'s cover nine times, among them: for *Pretty Baby*, in 1978; as one of the most intriguing people of 1978; for *The Blue Lagoon*, with Chris Atkins, in 1980; as one of the most intriguing people of 1980; for *Endless Love*, in 1981; with Calvin Klein in 1982. She graduated from Princeton University in 1987 and appeared in *Brenda Starr*, which was filmed in 1989 but not released until 1992.

WARREN BEATTY finally changed his stalwart opposition to marriage when he married actress Annette Bening, who starred with him in the film *Bugsy*, in March 1992. They have a daughter, Kathlyn, who was born two months before their marriage.

MUHAMMAD ALI retired from boxing for the last time in 1981 at the age of thirty-nine. He has been suffering from Parkinson's disease since 1982.

JOE NAMATH retired from football in 1977. He was a pro-football analyst for NBC Sports until he was released prior to the 1993 season, but still serves as a spokesman for the music store Nobody Beats the Wiz and for the pain relief gel Flex-all 454.

JOHN CHANCELLOR retired from his job as commentator on *NBC Nightly News* in 1993. He plans to write books and enjoy his free time.

SONNY BONO became mayor of Palm Springs in 1988, but lost a 1992 bid for the California senate. Mary Whitaker became his fourth wife in 1986. They have two children. He wrote about his life with Cher in *And the Beat Goes On*, a book published in 1991.

CHER's current love is Robert Camilletti, an actor eighteen years her junior, whom she has been dating for seven years. She won an Oscar for her role in *Moonstruck* in 1987. Her last film was *Mermaids*, released in 1990.

TRUMAN CAPOTE never recovered fully from the backlash of *Answered Prayers* and the book was never completed. He died in 1984 of liver disease complicated by phlebitis and drug intoxication.

MARGARET TRUDEAU married a Canadian real estate broker a week after her divorce from Prime Minister Pierre Trudeau was final.

LINDA THOMPSON married Bruce Jenner in 1981. They had two sons and were divorced in 1986. She later married composer David Foster.

TONY ORLANDO reunited with Dawn for a concert in 1988 after an eleven-year separation. They have not sung together since then.

PRISCILLA PRESLEY's acting career succeeded after her television role on *Dallas*, which began in 1983. She appeared in the films *The Naked Gun* (1989) and *The Naked Gun 2½* (1992). She lives in Los Angeles with Marco Garibaldi and their son, Navarone, who was born in 1987. She is grandmother to Danielle, the only child of her daughter Lisa.

ELVIS as a young man has been immortalized on a U.S. postage stamp produced in 1993. In a heated contest, the earlier image won out over what M. C. Marden referred to as "The Fat Elvis."

CLINT EASTWOOD won an Oscar for *Unforgiven* in 1992. His costar in the film, Frances Fisher, gave birth to their daughter, Francesca, in 1993. Eastwood starred in the movie *In the Line of Fire* that same year.

SONDRA LOCKE sued Clint Eastwood for $1.3 million in 1989, charging him with "humiliation and mental anguish" after their thirteen-year relationship broke up in 1989. She directed the film *Impulse*, which was released in 1990.

THE MERV GRIFFIN SHOW went off the air in 1986, but Griffin has been financially successful as the producer of *Wheel of Fortune* and *Jeopardy*. He is the owner of the Beverly Hilton Hotel, as well as resorts in New Jersey and the Bahamas. In 1992, *Forbes* magazine estimated his personal worth at $185 million.

THREE MILE ISLAND remains the worst nuclear accident to occur in the United States. The disaster's cleanup was finally completed in August 1993, at a cost of $1 billion.

YOKO ONO lives in New York. She released a retrospective of her career entitled *Onobox* on six compact discs in 1992.

SLY STONE was arrested in 1986 for failing to pay child support. In 1989 he was jailed on a drug possession charge and has been plagued with problems relating to drugs.

CATHY SMITH was sentenced to three years in prison in 1986 for her role in the death of JOHN BELUSHI.

DAN AYKROYD was nominated for an Academy Award for his performance in the film *Driving Miss Daisy* in 1989.

PRINCE ANDREW was separated from Sarah Ferguson in 1992. He continues to carry out his royal duties as the duke of York.

CAROL ANN, the mother of David, the Bubble Boy, is happily married to *People* reporter Kent Demaret.

PRINCESS DIANA officially separated from Prince Charles in 1992, but continues to carry out her official duties as the princess of Wales, speaking on such topics as AIDS, eating disorders, and child welfare.

SARAH FERGUSON separated from Prince Andrew in 1992 and has moved out of the royal quarters to a home of her own, where she is raising the couple's two daughters, Beatrice and Eugenie. She has publicly apologized for what has been interpreted by the press as "inappropriate behavior" and has claimed publicly that she is still in love with her husband.

MARK DAVID CHAPMAN is serving a sentence of twenty years to life at Attica State Penitentiary for the murder of John Lennon. He will be eligible for parole in the year 2000, when he is forty-five years old.

DONNA RICE is living in Washington, D.C. The effect of the Gary Hart affair has continued to plague her and she feels that the depth of misunderstanding about her regarding the episode persists. In 1993, the *L.A. Times* wrote:

> *People* magazine reportedly paid $150,000 for an interview and pho-
> tos of Donna Rice in the lap of Gary Hart—a leading candidate for
> the 1988 Democratic Presidential nomination until the Rice affair
> surfaced.

The newspaper declined to mention that the money had been paid not to Donna Rice, but to her "friend" Lynn Armandt.

Ryan White's memoirs, *Ryan White: My Own Story*, were published posthumously in 1991. His mother, Jeanne, remarried the following year. The Ryan White Fund raises money for AIDS research and education.

Michael Jackson was accused of child molestation shortly after leaving for his 1993 world tour. Two months after the allegations were made by a young boy who frequently accompanied Jackson, formal charges had not been filed by Los Angeles District Attorney Gil Garcetti. Jackson and his attorneys continue to deny any wrongdoing. In a show of support, the star was visited in Bangkok during his world tour by his close friend Elizabeth Taylor.

Robin Williams lives in northern California with his wife, Marsha, and their two children. In *Mrs. Doubtfire*, his most recent film, Williams played a divorced father who disguises himself as a nanny in order to be near his children. Marsha coproduced the film.

Drew Barrymore wrote *Little Girl Lost*, her autobiography, with *People* editor Todd Gold when she was fourteen. Four years later, in 1993, she played Amy Fisher in the ABC television movie version of the "Long Island Lolita" story.

Julia Roberts ended a two-year hiatus from filmmaking with her role in *The Pelican Brief*, based on the book by John Grisham, which she finished working on after her marriage to Lyle Lovett.

Elizabeth Taylor is still married to Larry Fortensky. She is the national chair for AmFAR, the organization she helped found to raise funds for AIDS research.

Clarence Thomas is a justice on the U.S. Supreme Court. His wife, Virginia, is a policy analyst for the House Republican Conference.

Chelsea Clinton does not yet have pierced ears.

INDEX

About the Author

JUDY KESSLER is the author of *Inside Today: The Battle for the Morning,* and was the co-producer of the movie *Gorillas in the Mist.* She lives in Los Angeles.